PRAISE FOR "THE LOCK ON MY LIPS"

"...Lola's groundbreaking work on gender significantly contributes to Cameroon Literature and theatre. While Gender Studies has been a vibrant and productive area of research in Europe and America for decades, Cameroon dramatists have hardly ventured into gender, sexuality, and gay studies in the scope of *The Lock on My Lips*. Perpetua K. Nkamanyang Lola's work is a seminal blueprint for dramaturgy."
— **Dr. Gerald Niba Nforbin**, *Lecturer of English Literary and Cultural Studies, University of Douala*

"Lola's *The Lock on My Lips* is set against the bedrock of binary oppositions rocking Kibaaka land - the male/female, tradition/modernity, indigenous/foreign, the customary law/judiciary law. These weave into place the modern societies in Cameroon, whose colonial legacies have brought it to the throes of confusion and conflicting ideas. Thus, besides the advocated gender equality, the play raises issues of justice, conflict resolution, law and order, moral decadence, sexual promiscuity, gender-based/or domestic violence, peaceful coexistence, betrayal, and otherness borne in the question of indigeneity, hybridity, and sexuality. Lola seems to posit that aspects of cultural practices that impede human progress should be brought down while those that encourage progress should be upheld and propagated."
— **Geraldine Sinyuy, PhD**, *African Literature*

"Lola's *The Lock on My Lips* is a brilliant meditation on the ambiguity of land ownership in contemporary Cameroon. Lola uses the metaphor of a family misunderstanding over a piece of land to explore the broader and disturbing subject of land tenure, opting for legality as the "woman" gets back her piece of land. The suggestive nature of the allegory carries it beyond the feminist literary posturing evident to those familiar with the history of Cameroon. *The Lock on My Lips* takes prominence in developing national literature in Cameroon."
— **Jesse Moba**, *Associate Professor of African Literature*

"A gripping and mind-blowing feminist play with women battling against an oppressive African tradition that refuses to recognise that women could be equal to, or better than, men in terms of capacity. The play seeks to balance, albeit with little success, tradition and women's (auto) empowerment. The author has succeeded in capturing

the battles of many African women. The lesson from the play is that when tradition oppresses, women can revert to the State judicial system for justice. Lola has shown that women's battles have a future and are worth fighting for."
— **Lilian Lem Atanga**, Associate Professor of African Languages and Linguistics, and Author of *Language, Gender and Power in the Cameroon Parliament*

"*The Lock on My Lips* by Perpetua Lola Nkamanyang stars a woman whose land and rights are seized because she's a woman. The shooting, sometimes mortal wit, on which the story hangs its imagery announces and even celebrates the sustained conflict, suspense and tension born of the stark differences in the couple. The effects of colonisation on a people, the responsibility of the colonialist and their progeny as well as that of the postcolonial subjects for the destruction of the environment and their society, the blowing out, the degeneration and fall into disease and death of families due to sexual promiscuity, the lack of parental care and education… animate the fight for the ownership of a piece of land which only the court can solve fairly. This play is an incredible referent for students of literature at all levels offering courses in Gender/Feminism, Postcolonial Studies, queer studies, and African Literature."
— **Fonyuy Musa Wirtum**, *Editor-in-Chief*, NNAMBS Publishers, Douala

"Lola's *The Lock on My Lips* is a concerto of cultural configurations of power mediated by hollow ideologies. The play picks up with a sprint –women in the streets – and then zaps through evocative discourses, landing on climactic punches, bays, and hoots of legal daggers drawn to an unfinished finale. Hooting traditional taboos face in situ constructs like sex gendering seen through expired forms of fairness. Thus, banned trans and gay indigeneity and hybridity meet fuming hate amidst violent betrayal, while lucre-fixed churchmen replay mere face-value charity…. Action-invested, the play conscripts anarchic themes to the crushing crackles of legal ripostes that refuse to rest even at the close since private and public loyalties gag the stage as unresolved ratatats riddle life with unyielding conflicts. The 'unlocked lips' spew waning fury on rock-hard forms subjected to remodelling at a slug pace. Unsettled motifs unsettle and the world-shaking concerns here rightfully demand many stages and stage hours to evolve this compelling scintillation of wisdom's vision in a turbid world."
— **Ntangnyui Patrick Tata**, *Critic & Editor*, PATAMAE Research and Editing Consultancy

THE LOCK ON MY LIPS

The Lock on My Lips

Revised Edition

Perpetua K. Nkamanyang Lola

SPEARS BOOKS
DENVER, COLORADO

SPEARS BOOKS
AN IMPRINT OF SPEARS MEDIA PRESS LLC
7830 W. Alameda Ave, Suite 103-247
Denver, CO 80226
United States of America

Revised English edition first published in the United States of America in 2023 by Spears Books
www.spearsmedia.com
info@spearsmedia.com
@spearsbooks

Information on this title: www.spearsbooks.org/the-lock-on-my-lips
© 2023 Perpetua K. Nkamanyang Lola
All rights reserved.

No part of this publication may be reproduced, distributed, or transmitted in any form or by any means, including photocopying, recording, or other electronic or mechanical methods, without the prior written permission of the publisher, except in the case of brief quotations embodied in critical reviews and certain other noncommercial uses permitted by copyright law. For permission requests, write to the publisher, addressed "Attention: Permissions Coordinator," at the address above.

ISBN: 9781957296142 (Paperback)
ISBN: 9781957296159 (eBook)
Also available in Kindle format

Cover art by Toh Bright
Cover designed by Doh Kambem
Designed and typeset by Spears Media Press LLC

Distributed globally by African Books Collective (ABC)
www.africanbookscollective.com

DEDICATION

For Prof. Dr Ansgar Nunning (my doctoral dissertation mentor and supervisor) for deepening my insight into the art of storytelling and creative writing. His mentoring, supervision, as well as gifts of books on a wide range of subjects in Literary and Cultural Studies, notably, creative writing, narratology, postcolonial studies, literary genres, and memory and identity cultures which I was privileged to receive from his generous hands have largely broadened my understanding of generic features of drama and other literary genres.
&
For my dear Mother, Mary Kfekfe, and all women.

PROLOGUE

Life swarms beyond the restrictions of sight,
And sails beyond cultural borders,
Wherein lurks tradition
To ambush and sting.
Why then remains a slave to sight
When with toil and sweat,
It has been proven that
Where the eyes cannot reach also exists.

Contents

Foreword   *xi*
Preface   *xiii*
Cast of Characters   *xvii*

Act 1	1
Scene I	1
Scene II	25
Scene III	43
Scene IV	49
Scene V	66
Act 2	71
Scene I	71
Scene II	74
Scene III	87
Scene IV	92
Scene V	95
Act 3	97
Scene I	97
Scene II	107
Scene III	118
Scene IV	127
Scene V	131
Act 4	135
Scene I	135
Scene II	136
Scene III	156
Scene IV	159
Scene V	179

Act 5	**183**
Scene I	183
Scene II	205
Scene III	245
Scene IV	255
Scene V	259
About the author	283

FOREWORD

From the original Edition

The fight for women's rights continues to be a major issue amongst feminist scholars, writers, and activists since Mary Wollstonecraft. While it must be admitted that major grounds have been covered over the decades and women are seen to be more and more efficient partners in development and not just subordinates or people who provide existential whims for men, women in most parts of the world are still yoked to some resistant cultural practices which prevent them from some privileges and from exercising their full human rights.

Feminism today has developed in a number of ways, representing different political, social, religious, moral, educational, and cultural aspirations. The arguments and controversies have also taken varied dimensions, including Marxist, psychoanalytical, Eco-critical, postmodernist, and cultural critical perspectives. The different dimensions and controversies, of course, indicate the fact that the fight for women's rights is important and affects humanity, having become the concern of not just women, but of men too. What seems to create the rift in a compromising stand, however, is perhaps the fact that theoretical considerations and criticism infringe on the cultural norms of the different peoples of the world. This is the hallmark of the controversy in feminism when some cultures claim some versions of cognitive and ethical absolutism.

In the early reception of feminism in Africa, most African feminist scholars and writers thought that equal rights for men and women meant the implantation of radical Western models on African societies and cultures. The result was, of course, the gradual and visible wreckage of African families, African culture, and social order. With time, positions began to change. African feminist scholars and critics began to realise the danger of embracing foreign ideologies without checks and balances. Today, African feminism seeks to institute women's rights without necessarily dismantling the cultural framework of which the woman is an important stakeholder. Today's challenge seems to be the need to eradicate fossilised cultural practices that hold women back from effectively performing their roles.

This is the position that Perpetua Nkamanyang Lola takes in her scintillating play, *The Lock on My Lips,* in which she refuses to take the extremist positions that flaw most feminist writers. She attempts to reconcile conflicting ideas and opinions between husband and wife, tradition and modernity, men's rights and women's rights, darkness and light, etc., masterminded by her main character, a powerful model of a woman, whose immutable respect for her husband and the culture of the people does not mitigate her intransigent fight for her rights for which she employs the power of humility, politeness, and subtle rationalisation.

The serious didactic value of the play cannot be overemphasised. It is a play in which conflicting opinions and ideas are put on the table and debated upon; an important contribution to the age-long controversy, an insurmountable crusade for women's rights, and a good instrument for raising awareness about the right modes of living with one another.

Professor John Nkemngong Nkengasong,
Writer & Critic

PREFACE

I want to convey immense thanks to the Cameroon Ministry of Higher Education and the University of Douala for partially financing the production of the first edition of *The Lock on My Lips,* on which this edition is based. My undying gratitude goes to an intellectual baobab - Prof. Dr. Ansgar Nunning, University of Giessen, Germany, who has continued to prove that the role of a teacher encompasses more than the classroom. The books on specific subjects in Literary and Cultural Studies, including *Introduction to the Study of English and American Literature* which he sent to me, have been instrumental in broadening my choice and scope of contexts, subjects, genres, cultures, cultural discourses and dramatics found in this drama text.

The first edition of *The Lock on My Lips* received constructive criticisms, corrections and suggestions for improvement from resourceful scholars, proofreaders and editors, including Professor John Nkemngong Nkengasong, Dr Nforbin Gerald, Professor J. K. Bannavti, Lola Vitalis, and Musa Wirtum. The suggestions were carefully integrated into the work. Bannavti's theatrically informed suggestions taught me that writing a play goes beyond words in the mouths of characters; it also means using appropriate settings, stage directions, and a range of dramatics. Peter Jaibee Lola's incredible input on the legal perspectives has been fully incorporated into the text, and Orlando Lola's wealth of indigenous proverbs, wise sayings, and cultural myths have been gladly used in the play.

This revised edition of *The Lock on My Lips* takes the illuminating exchanges with Dr Nforbin Gerald Niba into minute consideration. Not least, he suggested the further development of issues of gender, ecological literature, ethnicity, and the postcolonial experience: "Ma, you need to develop this gender thing further, and also the postcolonial dimensions; let the issue of environmental destruction and also the postcolonial voices come out strongly through the church and Wirkitum. Your portrayal of the coloniser is one-dimensional. That could be the result of your German experience, though, but do something...." The suggested broadening of gender and its related issues, which resulted in the greater focus on ethnicity, group-based power, gay culture, body grafting and consequences, sexuality, identity crisis and the politics of belonging, colonial legacies, the fight for the rights of women, women's empowerment, conflict resolution, environmental destruction and conservation as well as discourses of feminism, patriarchy and colonial ideology was thus essentially the result of exchanges with Dr Nforbin. I owe Dr Nforbin immense gratitude for his discerning recommendations, proofreading, and encouragement, reminding me that the writer can still conceive and hatch even when mental menopause threatens.

The PATAMAE Research and Editing Consultancy of Patrick Tata provided the most needed editorial expertise, meticulous corrections, and illuminating advice on structuring, which I greatly appreciated. Dr Sinyuy Geraldine did a marvellous job of editing the work and identifying linguistic infelicities that strayed into it.

My children, Fombu Junior Grodjinovski Nkamanyang and Ngambam Mac Nkamanyang, deserve special recognition for their love and ceaseless questions and arguments, which equally contributed to broadening the explored scope of gender issues. Despite his tender age (10), Ngambam said to me: "You should give your money to Daddy to keep because he is your husband and the head of the house." He never stopped asking questions about the rights of men and women. My mother, Kfekfe Mary, who suffered all sorts of prejudices in the 'colony within' but who, with my siblings, never stopped farming and hustling to finance my studies, remains my treasure.

This work attempts to respond to my husband's question, "What can a woman do?" which arose from a heated debate on the importance of the International Women's Day. Like others, he tended to circumscribe it to mere competition with men and festivities. This generates misconceptions about gender equality, feminism, women's rights, and emancipation. In the hope that the work does highlight the issues and appeals to readers of all ages, I would like to thank my soulmate, Clement Achiri Nkamanyang, for painstakingly going through various versions of the manuscript and locating flaws for my attention, for cooking, supervising our kids and ensuring that the house was in order whenever I took time off to focus on the work, and for tolerating my inconveniences and absence from the bedroom during moments of inspiration. Most importantly, he is the reason why the laps of my mind gave birth to *The Lock on My Lips*.

On March 8th, 2009, I woke up early and cooked *fufu corn and Ka'ti Ka'ti* to add to some of the frozen dishes in the freezer to ensure that my soulmate would have his three meals that day (as I usually did/do to ensure the uninterrupted flow of my kitchen allowance). Then, I dressed up, ready to attend the International Women's Day March past scheduled for 9 a.m. prompt. My

International Women's Day heavy gown (*Kaba*) looked on me like a jacket of suckers clustering on a plantain trunk as I stood seeking attention and compliments from my husband, who uttered no word. I communicated my plans for the day to my husband while he ate breakfast: "I am going for March Past and to attend the feast organised by Bongkisheri Douala Women's Cultural Association before returning home." His response was a stern and disarming "no". After a brief intimidating visual encounter, an angry voice descended on me: "You are going nowhere! What is even the essence of this Women's Day? My children are still too young to be abandoned for Women's Day! What can you bring back from Women's Day apart from drinking corn beer, eating, dancing, and making claims that what a man can do, a woman can do and even better? By the way, what can a woman do?"

I was aware that my kitchen allowance could suffer a severe reduction just when I was expecting an increment if I failed to heed my husband's prohibiting order regarding my participation at the March 8th official march past ceremony and festivities. Before that day, it was rumoured that the Government was planning to increase the salaries of civil servants. So, no woman in her right senses could do something stupid at such a moment that a salary increase was anticipated. Jokes aside, I felt devastated, especially as my Bongkisheri Douala Women's Group was highly anticipating my participation at the event as one of its coordinators and EXCO members. My eyes welled up with tears, but I knew it wasn't my husband speaking. I knew that what he said was an unconscious replication of the 'Graffi' cultural thought that tends to exclude and, at times, deny women their natural rights. It became evident that the fight for women's rights, one of the reasons for commemorating the International Women's Day, was still grossly misunderstood and needed greater clarification. I reluctantly returned to my room and pulled off my gown, whose caption seemed to have lighted the flames of the cultural anger that corroborated the impression that the International Women's Day was only a platform for women to be contaminated/infected with stubbornness by 'toxic feminists' clamouring for the rights of women and the equality of the sexes. Downcast and seated on the bed, I wondered, "How do I respond to what my husband just said?" That is how I immediately decided to use the power of the pen to address the issue of women's rights and the equality of the sexes. I spent that day writing on tear-soaked sheets of paper. By the close of the day, I had written some fifteen pages, the nascent pages of *The Lock on My Lips*.

I wrote from the victim's standpoint to tell my story in my own words. From my African cultural perspective, I felt the need to clarify the idea of women's rights and the equality of the sexes. I was writing my own history in my own words hoping that humanity would bury the biased and unhealthy values, norms, beliefs, and practices that limit women's aspirations, that humanity would clamour for a society where men and women would be given the same opportunities, access and training to get empowered, and put their talents to productive use for the home, the community, and the nation at large. I wanted to give the woman a voice and confidence through empowerment, I wanted women who have experienced any form of abuse, marginalisation and injustice to know that there are better ways to address such challenges; that there is someone somewhere who is willing to listen to them; that there are coping or redress strategies, and that they can seek justice in the legal system when traditional or cultural structures deny them justice.

I am solely responsible for any shortcomings in the work, however.

Perpetua K. Nkamanyang Lola

CAST OF CHARACTERS

Ghamogha:	Paramount ruler of Kibaaka, variously known as Your Highness, Nginyam, Bvereéh, or simply the Fon.
Manka:	Wife of Fon Ghamogha, also known as Mrs Ghamogha, Mother of Children.
Fomu:	Son of Your Highness and Manka.
Bame:	Son of Your Highness and Manka.
Kila:	Daughter of Your Highness and Manka.
Bush Faller:	Manka's cousin, living in Dubai.
Yulem:	Oldest wife of the Fon, inherited from the late Fon.
Jaidzeka:	Daughter of Yulem and late Fon Ghamogha V.
Ndzebarah:	Son of late Fon Ghamogha IV and Yulem.
Shufai Laika:	Traditional Prime Minister of the Kibaaka clan, Adviser to the Fon and member of Nwerong/ the Council of Elders.
Ability Mvem:	Military Officer, discharged from service on moral grounds, Member of Nwerong/Council of Elders, and leader of Kibaaka Vigilante Group, also known as Mvem.
Biiywong:	Ability's wife.
Ntumfon:	Son of Ability and Biiywong.
Shufai Wirkitum:	Honourable Member of Parliament, member of the Council of Elders.
Barrister Johnson:	Wife of Honourable Wirkitum; Lawyer and Human Rights Activist.
Gheeh:	Member of Nwerong and the Council of Elders.
Foka:	Wife of Taa Gheeh.
Verdzekov:	Retired Civil Servant.
Binla:	Member of Bongkisheri.
Fola:	Primary School Teacher; One-time Coordinator of the Information Gathering Department of the Council of Elders.
Beri:	Wife of Fola.
Father Anthony Morgan:	(Fada Anton)
Regular:	Sister of Manka.
Aladji Musa:	Leader of the Hausa/Bororo community in Kibaaka and

	member of the Council of Elders.
Abiba:	Wife of Alhadji Musa, (also known as Habiba).
Pa Jacov:	Catechist and Member of the Council of Elders.
Ndzewiyi:	Member of the Council of Elders.
Medzefen:	Member of the Council of Elders.
Biy Wiiba:	Wife of Medzefen.
Chicha Kisito:	Teacher and member of Nwerong and the Council of Elders.
Dzekewong:	Domestic Servant to Wirkitum and leader of Vigilante Group.
Barrister Simon:	Lawyer.

Judges
Court registrar
Savage
Katika & Livinus
Dzekem (Aginir)
Venkika/Dinka/ Mbiame: Messengers.
Members of the Bongkisheri Women's Association, Secretary, members of Vigilante group, Judges, Town Crier, Police Officers, Elders, Villagers, Doctor, Nurse, students on scholarship abroad (*Jaika, Betty, Yuri* and others).

ACT 1

Scene I

KIBAAKA PALACE CULTURAL HALL

(*In the centre stage of the hall is an imposing high-back carved stool for the Fon and short ones at the rear for the others. Fon Ghamogha, a huge and dark-skinned man with tiny ridges and furrows across his forehead, seems to be the only person in the palace. He leans back on his high-back stool, and holds his thick lips squashed as he stares absent-mindedly at the wall. He has on a zebra-coloured gown and an interwoven beaded cap made from raffia fibre. On the walls are carvings of leopard skins, a beaded calabash, gun-wielding men, cowries, a peace plant, and a woman holding a hoe, with two babies strapped to her back).*

YOUR HIGHNESS

(*Thinking aloud*). Who sold land to a woman? How do I get my wife to see the danger and humiliation that await me if the Land Title remains in her name? What would be the reaction of the Traditional Council when they hear that my wife has bought land in her name? Somebody has to pay the price for allowing such an abomination to happen in Kibaaka land. My red feather, the cowries around my neck and the leopard-skin cap on my head would be removed and given to the next in line of succession on the Royal family tree. Authority follows titles; it dies when power changes hands. I would be evicted from the palace… Where will I carry my shame and family to? This palace is my home so long as I am the Fon. I don't have another house. I don't have land. (*Gets up and begins to walk back and forth*). What do I do to have my name on the land title before news leaks into the ears of the Elders that a woman has bought land in her name? She has refused to cede ownership of the land to me. What do I do now…? Well, I married Manka and paid her bride price. Either I am the man and her husband or not! Where's she? (*He turns and faces Manka's apartment, calling*) Manka! Manka! She hasn't yet gone to work…; her car is still parked in the yard. Where could she be? (*Nearby rising and falling voices suddenly begin to waft towards him from the palace entrance down the path. He sticks out his neck and wiggles his stare through the scattered trees and the imposing buildings with overhead electric poles and cables that stretch down the path).* What is happening in my backyard? Another motorcyclist has certainly knocked down a school child trying to cross the road. *(Looks around).* Why is there nobody in the palace? *(Kila, Bame, Fomu and Jaidzeka suddenly run up the path and stagger to a stop in front of Your Highness).*

BAME
Y-y-Your Highness *(pointing toward the Palace Entrance)*, t-t-the women! *(Fomu, Kila and Jaidzeka nod in approval).* T-t-t-the women… *(gasping)* hah, hah, hah, hah, hah…

YOUR HIGHNESS
What's happening to the women? *(Heavy footsteps distract Your Highness and his children and they turn to the direction of the footsteps. The Elders surge up the path, stride across the courtyard and stop before the Fon who stares at them open-mouthed).*

GHEEH
(A frail man in his 70s steps forward. The middle of his head looks like a tarred road with a hedge of grey grass along its fringes. The tiny ridges and furrows across his forehead give his face the look of someone about to sneeze. A dirty brown moustache separates his upper lip from the nostrils while a shaggy beard hangs below his chin. He wears a threadbare leopard-coloured jumper over trousers sparingly butchered at the knees. His chest is rising and falling with his voice). Y-y-Your Highness, Your Highness. *(Points towards the direction of the noises, panting).*

VERDZEKOV
Your Highness, what we are about to tell you will break your heart *(shrugs).*

ABILITY
(Shoves Gheeh aside and steps forward while Gheeh crouches to the ground. He wears an unbuttoned shirt inside out, leaving exposed what looks like tiny ants scattered across his chest. On his head is a flat hat with a half-rounded part at the front, shaped like a bicycle seat). Your Highness, I hate to be the one to inform you that we have not brought good news.

GHEEH
Fon Ghamogha Shindzev saw it coming, and it has happened!

YOUR HIGHNESS
Can someone just tell me what is happening?

GHEEH
Rats are dancing in the presence of cats.

YOUR HIGHNESS
What?

ABILITY
Organised chaos is germinating in the land!

YOUR HIGHNESS
I don't still understand.

ABILITY
Your Highness, as we are talking to you now, there is a gathering of stubborn hens at the entrance to the palace. *(The Elders nod their heads).*

YOUR HIGHNESS
What are you talking about?

FOLA
I saw mine sitting there with only a wrapper tied below her breasts.

ABILITY
I don't even know whether what I saw was the tapper's calabashes dangling from the chest of a palm tree or the thing we hide from children *(Your Highness opens his mouth wide).* It actually looked like the lifeless body of a man that has committed suicide by hanging from a tree *(The Elders nod).*

YOUR HIGHNESS
Sons of the soil, I am not a fan of comedy… *(Pa Jacov, Dzekewong and other villagers scamper across the yard, panting).*

SHUFAI LAIKA
Ability, Taa Gheeh, Fola, if you teach somebody, that person will never pass an exam even if the question was set by Dzekewong.

GHEEH
Your Highness, the women are marching bare body.

YOUR HIGHNESS
Bare what!

GHEEH
Body. (*Dzekewong plasters his eyes with his fingers*).

YOUR HIGHNESS
Ngiri! (*Native Lamnso expression of surprise*).

GHEEH
It has happened.

SHUFAI LAIKA
They look like jujus with wood ash smeared on their bodies.

YOUR HIGHNESS
Gheeh, what do you mean by the women are marching bare body?

ABILITY
Your Highness, had it not been for the calabashes nodding from the walls of their chests, I would have thought I was watching the naked statues which Fola always stops to watch and to take pictures with at the Arts and Crafts Centre. (*Your Highness opens his mouth leaving teeth sticking out like the teeth of a roasted goat*).

GHEEH
Your Highness, they are bare-bodied. They gathered at the place where the road bends its buttocks three times (*twists his buttocks from the left to right and then, back as he narrates*) and opens its legs like a woman who opens her legs to deliver a baby, and started marching to the palace... They started marching immediately the cock started crowing to announce the beginning of a new day.

They were already marching up to the palace courtyard when Shufai Laika stopped them and reminded them that the Lion and Sun *(Points to the Fon)* of Kibaaka land will disappear if he sees the thing down there *(touches his groin).*

VERDZEKOV
All the exit and entry roads into Kibaaka town are blocked by the naked women. They were pouring into the streets from side roads and marching to the palace, but we managed to stop them. As I talk to you now, they have blocked all major entrances to the Palace.

YOUR HIGHNESS
How is that possible in the palace yard?

ABILITY
They have even mounted a large ridge of trees and raffia branches across the street below the palace to block the movement of cars. The Police Officers are standing there, monitoring the protesters. They begged the women to return home and cover their bodies, and to maintain peace while carrying out their protest. The protest has paralyzed activities in town. Passengers are leaving the vehicles that are conveying them to their offices and to other places and carrying their luggage on their heads. Some are trekking. People travelling to Kibaaka International Airport are dropping from cars and trekking down the road to climb the overhead bridge to join the exit road that goes round Abakwa and connects with the Airport Road at the Kimbo neighbourhood. *(The Fon widens his stare and shakes his head).* Yes. Air travellers are trekking to Kibaaka Airport, carrying big bags on their heads to avoid missing their flights. Some travellers are riding on commercial motorcycles. Motorcyclists are charging 3000frs to Central Area, 2000frs to Government High School, Kibaaka, and 5000frs to the Airport… *(The Fon leans back, open-mouthed, wide-eyed).* Yes. Cars and loaded trucks are parked just everywhere in the streets, and passengers are dropping from cars to watch the embarrassment. Even the school children missed the way to their schools this morning. It is bad! It is bad! I would have suggested that the Fon go down there and see it for himself; unfortunately, the Fon does not see the bare body of another woman in public.

YOUR HIGHNESS
Taa Gheeh, when you say the women are sitting at the entrance to the palace

bare-bodied, does it mean your eyes actually saw this (*touches the breasts positions of his chests*), this (*touches his buttocks*), and this (*touching the place where the legs meet*)?

GHEEH

Your Highness, do you know how many seasons I have shaved this thing? (*Touches the beards under his chin*).

ABILITY

This is not roadside talk.

VERDZEKOV

I covered my eyes with cassava leaves to avoid an abomination befalling me.

ABILITY

I turned my head when my eyes fell on the full high chest of Mother of Children…

YOUR HIGHNESS

Ability, did you see clearly? Mother of Children will not take off her dress until the lights are turned off and the room is dark; not to talk of taking them off for the public to feast their eyes on what is mine.

ABILITY

I have not tasted palm wine since I woke up from bed. What even shocked me most was not just that Mother of Children was naked. Photographers, Journalists and bachelors took the best positions to catch a glimpse of the thatched surfaces. (*Fola nods in approval*). Honourable Wirkitum and Fada Anton were also there, taking pictures of the naked women. (*Your Highness tightens his lips*). Honourable Wirkitum closed his eyes partially and smiling to himself as he took pictures of the two pumpkins on Manka's chest.

YOUR HIGHNESS

How could Mother of Children expose what is mine to public eyes? How could she? Did our fathers not say only the landowner knows the boundaries of the land? (*Ability throws his hands up and open*). I must put some order in this madness!

ELDERS
Rengreng. (With goading nods, the Elders chorus in native Lamnso expression of approval, and incitement).

VERDZEKOV
Your Highness, the women that we just saw are not the women we knew. They did not even try to spread their fingers over this and that *(touches his chest and the area below his navel)* when Honourable Wirkitum, Fada Anton and Journalists started taking pictures of their bare bodies and recording interviews with some of them.

ABILITY
They are turning into something else. They were singing a song *(sings).*: "The woman's voice is born. No longer in the shadows forced to sit at home. There shall be no peace without land rights. This is the woman's turn. Power to the woman. Give back our land." *(The Fon's chin drops).*

YOUR HIGHNESS
Is that what they said?

ABILITY
(Cups his hands to his chin in the typical customary manner when affirming to the Fon or Royal Majesty). Mbeeh.

YOUR HIGHNESS
Wait, wait. Are we actually talking about the women of Kibaaka?

GHEEH
Government has put teeth in the mouth of hens.

YOUR HIGHNESS
Our people say that no matter how hard a log of wood is, it finally gives way to the axe. The man in the woman must be crushed.

ELDERS
Rengreng!

ABILITY
This thing appears contagious. Bororo Fulani women and other Come-no-Gos came out in their numbers and joined the women.

YOUR HIGHNESS
Ability, are you saying that the guests in the house are also marching?

ABILITY
You haven't even heard anything yet. The white-haired daughters of Eve with ginger-like fingers and toes were the ones leading the bare-bodied march. The human riders that climb on their kind from behind like pumpkin plants clambering over the buttocks of ridges to channel their creeping stems into furrows are also there. *(The elders nod).*

YOUR HIGHNESS
Ngiri! (Your Highness shrugs).

ABILITY
They are ready to commit suicide. I saw our women with my two eyes mixing with Livinus, Savage, and Katika. The tall muscular woman with large eyes that Verdzekov lifted from the streets and transformed into a housewife just for one year was there. Right in the presence of school children, she stood in front with the clenched fist of her right hand lifted, exposing her manly chest that she has transformed into a drawing board with a tattoo of a key. *(Gheeh nods).* Even when Biy Wiiba leaned on her trying to hide what looked like matted ants at the place where the legs meet, she shoved her aside and stood erect like a lamp post. She wore two chains on her ankle, two rings on her nose, and four rings on the many holes she had made on her left ear. I am talking about this lady that Fola keeps telling me she is a tigress in bed *(Ability taps his head repeatedly, trying hard to remember, attracting more attention).* What's that her name again? *(Fola tries to close Ability's mouth with his palm but Ability shoves his hand).* Regular. *(Verdzekov leans back, open-mouthed, wide-eyed).* Yes. Fola has always told me that Regular is a tigress in bed and refuses to lie below. *(The Elders lean back, baffled and wide-eyed. They lift up their arms and cross their hands over their heads, looking at Verdzekov with disbelief and shifting their stares to Fola who has suddenly dropped his eyes to his feet).*

ABILITY
Regular has also carried her 'tigritude' outdoors, metamorphosing this morning into one of the kitchen rebels.

VERDZEKOV
(*Suddenly begins to rain slaps on Fola*). *Pah! Pah! Pah! Pah!* So, this is how my own goods became communal property! So, it is you that destroyed my marriage! *(Pointing at Fola)*.
Gheeh and a few others sway from side to side, trying hard to tear Fola from the grip of Verdzekov who has clutched Fola's shirt.

SHUFAI LAIKA
Verdzekov, this is the heart of the land. Please, calm down...

YOUR HIGHNESS
If Regular has been lying on Verdzekov instead of beneath him and thinks she can also lie on us, it will not work! *(The Elders nod)*. It will not work! She must learn that this is Kibaaka and a woman's position is below, not above! Husbands must be husbands; and wives must be wives. If she has been running Verdzekov's affairs in bed and thinks she can together with other women dictate to us how to run the affairs of Kibaaka, then she will soon know that we are not Verdzekov or Fola. *(The Elders nod consent)*.

VERDZEKOV
Fola, how did you know about my wife's bedroom skills?

SHUFAI LAIKA
Ability, it is not everything we see that we say.

VERDZEKOV
So, it was Fola that broke my home?

ABILITY
Verdzekov, I warned you that you should not abandon your wife for a woman whose skills in love tourism is unparalleled, but you did not listen.

VERDZEKOV
(Roars). Was it my fault? What did you expect me to do? How could a woman

whose bride price I duly paid delight in giving me just girls for children? And you expected me to fold my hands and do nothing about it! Lawan gave me only girls, seven in number. I became a laughingstock in the village. Each time she got pregnant, Gheeh and Ability simply said, 'it's a girl!', and whenever one of her daughters returned from the hospital to report that she just gave birth, I got the same response, 'it's a girl.' Ability, did you expect me to fold my hands and watch Lawan bury my name and my family lineage? No! I only wanted to avert the shame and also the pain of being surrounded by girls with no boy to bury me when I finally join my ancestors. That is why I married Regular. My hope was that Regular will make me a real man by giving me a son; one that will not only take my place in the Council of Elders but will also marry many wives and make my name to stretch like a river. But see what I got! This thing *(Points to Fola)* broke my home! *(Suddenly thrusts his right hand at Fola but the Elders stop him).* Fola, you will not always have this fence around you! *(Points to the Elders who have built a fence with their arms between him and Fola).*

SHUFAI LAIKA
Verdzekov, calm down. I know how you feel. Be the man that you are. We cannot handle this matter now.

VERDZEKOV
Shufai Laika, this matter is not ending anytime soon.
   (Shufai Laika beckons Fola and a few Elders and they drift behind. Shufai lifts a Finger to Fola's face as he speaks to him in a hushed voice while Fola keeps a fixed stare at his feet).

(Twenty minutes later)

AT THE ENTRANCE TO THE PALACE

The main access road leading to the palace is swarming with women, villagers, school children, stranded travellers, and onlookers including Honourable Wirkitum and Fada Anton who are taking pictures of the protesters.

BUSH FALLER
Good morning, Fada Anton…

FADA ANTON

(A huge man with full-blown jaws and a tanker-size stomach. He is wearing a lose-fitting foot-length high-neck white gown and a rosary around his neck with a cross dangling from the front. He pushes back his head slightly and his long wavy white hair falls over his neck). Hello, what can I do for you?

BUSH FALLER

I am the cousin of Mrs Ghamogha Manka … *(pauses and stares at Fada Anton).* I am the one she used to send to transport readymade Bongkisheri *toghu* to your house…

FADA ANTON

Euh! Euh! You've changed! You've grown bigger! You now keep beards! I'm happy to meet you. Where have you been?

BUSH FALLER

I live in Dubai…

FADA ANTON

Really! *(Bush Faller nods).* Your sister didn't tell me you were around.

BUSH FALLER

I just arrived, Fada. I haven't reached home yet. Our car is blocked somewhere down the street.

FADA ANTON

Yeah, the protesters have blocked the streets. You are welcome. You did well to come and see your people. Many of the young people who travel abroad hardly come back home. They don't even pay church contributions. They come around just to celebrate weddings and Xmas. You did well.

BUSH FALLER

Yeah. I want to invest in Kibaaka. Life is too hard in Dubai. We work like ants and donkeys and earn very little. Living abroad is very expensive and I need to think about my future. I really want to start a business with the little I've saved. My sister encouraged me to invest in Kibaaka.

FADA ANTON
That sounds great. You need to invest at home because you will need your savings some day when you are old and perhaps *euh* not physically strong to work, and not financially viable any longer to cope with the challenges of living abroad. What kind of investment do you have in mind?

BUSH FALLER
My sister suggested that I try toghu business. I need the readymade toghu and other African wears that Bongkisheri sells in the UK and America through you. I have come to buy and take the products to Dubai. Every time I wear my toghu to an event, Africans, Asians, black Americans and other races alike would be asking me: "where can I get mine? I love this dress so much. How much does it cost? I want to buy for myself and for my wife and kids as well."

FADA ANTON
It's good to know.

BUSH FALLER
I even sold mine and made an interest of 90%. *(Fada Anton hangs his mouth open, wide-eyed).* Yeah. I already have a command for two hundred pieces of toghu from a company that sells African costumes.

FADA ANTON
Really!

BUSH FALLER
Yeah, everybody likes toghu and wants to buy it.

FADA ANTON
I'm glad to know toghu has put Kibaaka and Africa on the map of the world. I would like to be your supplier.

BUSH FALLER
I prefer to buy directly from Bongkisheri women.

FADA ANTON
I have a copyright contract with Bongkisheri women to market their toghu. You can only buy through me. *(Bush Faller screams in shock, wide-eyed,*

open-mouthed). Yeuh. I bought the industrial sewing machine which the women are using in exchange for the copyright. The women are entitled to royalties. But I can sell the copyright to you, though. Meet me in my office tomorrow let's discuss the deal. I receive from 11 am to 3 pm, on weekdays. What time do I expect you?... What time do I expect you?

BUSH FALLER
(Visibly disappointed). Let me have your telephone number, Fada. I will call to fix an appointment with you.

FADA ANTON
Sounds good. *(They exchange numbers)*. I'm expecting your call. If you come early, we can have lunch together. You won't regret doing business with me.

(A huge, fair-skin man with a sharp pointed nose and a wobbling stomach leaking over his laps, approaches Fada Anton and stops. His bulging eyes peer at the crowd from behind his gold-coloured eyeglasses as he takes pictures of the bare body women sitting across the path that leads to the palace. He wears a designer long-sleeve white shirt over an oversized combat jeans short butchered on the thighs, a big chain around his neck with a big cross dangling from the front, small rounded-clingy earrings, and a light stretchy scarf with the colours of American flag tied around his head to form a tail behind. As he bounces back and forth, bending forward and leaning back, taking pictures, his scarf drops off to the ground, revealing his cornrow-plaited hair with tiny tails on his neck.

Dzekewong, his bodyguard, picks up the scarf from the ground, dusts it, and returns it to Honourable Shufai Wirkitum who ties the scarf around his head, steps forward and taps Fada Anton on the shoulder).

WIRKITUM
Hi, Reverend *Entoni*, aren't you tired of taking pictures? Let's join the Elders in the palace now...

FADA ANTON
I don't go to places where they worship calabashes and carvings. Their ways are different. They do things differently.

WIRKITUM
I don't do that either. We're actually going there for a different reason. It's good to see what they are doing to calm the women. We should be part of the solution. We can't tame them if we don't mix with them.

FADA ANTON
You're right. Let's go. *(They exchange smiles and turn to go).*

(Ten minutes later).

Kibaaka Palace Courtyard

SHUFAI LAIKA
Verdzekov, we are sorry about what happened, but we have to focus on what brought us here.

FOLA
(His stomach begins to grumble like a moving vehicle, attracting all eyes to him). I feel like a sharp knife is tearing through my lower stomach. *(He groans, rushing out).*
   (The sound of a car is heard off the yard and distracts all attention. Dzekewong - the driver, steps out and opens the door for Honourable Wirkitum and Fada Anton who walk across the yard and join the Elders).

FADA ANTON
(Lifts his hand, touches his forehead, breasts, the shoulders, and then, says). May the peace of the Lord be with you all…

ELDERS
(In a chorus). And with your spirit, Fada Anton.

WIRKITUM
(Waves to the Elders). Hi folks! Glad to join you, guys.
   (Wirkitum's manner of greeting incurs the wrath of Ability who pushes his squashed lips forward as the Elders respond simultaneously).

YOUR HIGHNESS
Shufai Wirkitum, have you come?

GHEEH
Honourable, is it daybreak?

SHUFAI LAIKA
Let us continue where we ended. We were talking about the bare-bodied protest by the women. But there is another big problem. Kibaaka women are mixing with the converts of "man marry man" and "woman marry woman" religion that strangers have smuggled into our land.

YOUR HIGHNESS
Nwerong had banned those bad seeds from Kibaaka land.

ABILITY
Nothing has changed. Kibaaka is fast becoming the heart of a new breed of kitchen rebels and cultural rebels. Our sons now parade the streets with grafted chests and buttocks. Dzekewong, Medzefen, Gheeh, grafting means to cut a part of your body and plant in another part of your body… *(Your Highness maintains a purposeless stare while still holding his face and eyes in the stiff squeeze of someone sneezing).*

VERDZEKOV
Women and climbers have brought shame upon the land.

GHEEH
The ways of our land are just one finger away from the grave.

ABILITY
From the day the cross-dressers and the men who sheathe their swords in the wrong place were detained for riding each other and Barrister Johnson released them claiming that *(mimics)*: "due process was not followed; they have the right to become who they want to become," they have carried their 'man-turn-woman' and 'woman-turn-man' religion to the streets. Livinus, Savage, and Katika now enter the house through the backdoor. They wear shoes with long tiny soles; they wear skirts, earrings, and nose-rings. They are winning souls each passing day. Women want to be men. Men have become women. Young boys and girls enjoy seeing their skins cut and sewn like dresses. *(The Elders shake their heads, their lips tightened).*

GHEEH
It was not like this before. Who will plant the seeds so that our names will continue to germinate and stretch like a river when we are no more? *(The Elders throw their hands up and open)*. Who will bury us when we join our ancestors?

YOUR HIGHNESS
Are we confirming that the boys who have lifted their chests and their buttocks to stick out like pumpkins were mixing with our wives? Abomination! Are they women? Do they think they can be women because they cut and sew their skins like dresses and wear skirts and gowns? Do they have the same medical needs? Men must be men! Women must be women!

ABILITY
My father used to say that when the pricking grass begins to grow in the farm and you do not remove it immediately, it will spread its roots, overgrow, and choke out the good plants. I have always said that when something begins to happen and you keep quiet about it, excesses will follow, this is exactly what is happening now. Elders of Kibaaka, if we must stop cancer from spreading to other parts of the body, we must weed it out from the roots.

ELDERS
Rengreng!

WIRKITUM
We cannot condemn somebody simply because of their sexual orientation. *(Fada Anton nods; the Elders lean back and stare at Wirkitum and Fada).*

GHEEH
Fada Anton, Wirkitum, our ways are different from your ways. When a boy child is born, everybody is happy because the family name will stretch like a river when the head of the house is covered in earth. If we allow our boys to become women, what will happen to our names when we join our ancestors? Our names will die. *(The Elders make various approval signs).*

SHUFAI LAIKA
Ability and Gheeh have spoken our minds. We cannot continue to keep people like Savage, Katika, and Livinus in this land. We need to protect our children and our women. My father used to say when a viper has hatched, eliminate

the viper with all its young ones because they can grow up and sting.

VILLAGERS
Rengreng!

ABILITY
If we don't act now, we will wake up one day and find the streets of Kibaaka swarming with climbers and human grafts.

WIRKITUM
This is wickedness and ignorance, *mehn!*

ABILITY
(Stares briefly at Wirkitum and speaks). This is the price we must pay for opening the doors of Kibaaka to strangers just because they claimed that blood test showed that their great-grandfather was from here. Their roots might not even be Kibaaka. It might be somewhere else. Who knows? There are many people who have come back like that, claiming that their great-grandfathers were from here. And before you know, they have started insulting our ways just like Wirkitum is doing now.

WIRKITUM
DNA does not lie. Stop exposing your ignorance in public.

ABILITY
Who was there and saw the blood test conducted on you? Liar! *(Fada Anton glares at Ability).*

SHUFAI LAIKA
That is not what brought us here! The women, the Come-no-Go, and the 'men-turn-women' are now the ones telling us what to do! Fon Ghamogha, is this how Kibaaka was when it was handed over to you?

NDZEBARAH
This is the consequence of putting the Red Feather on the wrong head. *(The Elders turn towards Ndzebarah).*

YOUR HIGHNESS
(Your Highness stares at Ndzebarah, face twisted, and then turns his face away). Elders of our land, were you able to find out why the women are protesting?

SHUFAI LAIKA
Your Highness, I copied some of the captions *(reads from the sheet of paper)* #Women Rights Matter#; *(Your Highness shrugs),* #The woman's turn#; #Power to the Woman#; #Beijing has Spoken#; #The Lock on our lips is removed#; #Collective strength is victory#; #The woman's voice is Born#; "Give back our Land Rights"; "Solidarity without Compromise"; "A people united can never be defeated". Livinus, Savage' and Katika held up another banner with the caption: "I have the right to be who I want to become."

YOUR HIGHNESS
(His facial expression saddens). Shufai Laika, did you just say the women are asking for land ownership rights?

SHUFAI LAIKA
Mbeeh! The only song they are singing is *(sings):* 'Give back our land rights, give back our land rights.' *(The Fon leans back, an air of frustration in his posture).*

FADA ANTON
What sin or crime is committed if a woman decides to get her own land? *(The Elders shift forward in shock).*

YOUR HIGHNESS
This is Kibaaka! Land belongs to the man! Crops belong to the woman. *(Fada Anton shakes his head disapprovingly).*

FADA ANTON
There are only two laws: the law of God and the law of Government and none of these two denies woman land *(Wirkitum smiles).* I do not remember anywhere in the holy Bible where God decreed that Eden belonged to Adam alone. And if I might add, which of the ten commandments states that a woman cannot own land?... That belief is not merely primitive and superstitious; this grossly discriminatory belief is immoral and sinful before God. *(The Elders shrug).* Your Highness, why do you think God took flesh from Adam's side to mould Eve with? The answer is obvious: if he took the flesh from Adam's head, Eve would

trample on him; but if he also took from Adam's feet, Adam would trample on Eve. He deliberately took from Adam's rib to teach us that Adam and Eve are equal soul mates. Why do you and your men want to bring disorder to God's work on earth? Besides, Government has made it clear that there is nothing illegal in women buying land. Even if it hasn't happened before, it doesn't break any law or any of the ten commandments. Even if it hasn't happened before, it doesn't mean it cannot happen.

ABILITY

Until we stop using the invader's currency, language, markets, goods, and praying to their gods, they will always think they can impose their ways on us!

ELDERS

Rengreng!

FADA ANTON

Why is the taming mission always the black man's excuse for performing poorly? *(The elders shrug).*

YOUR HIGHNESS

Fada Anton, you came from where people respect even animals, but I don't feel that respect in you when you talk about the ways of our land.

GHEEH

Fada Anton is not the threat. Women are asking for land rights! They were not like this before. Where are they taking this power from?

ABILITY

(Cuts in). Bongkisheri.

YOUR HIGHNESS

I am beginning to think that the biggest problem we have in this land is Bongkisheri.

GHEEH

Our people say that the weevil that lives in the trunk of the raffia tree is the thing that will destroy the raffia tree. Fon Ghamogha Shindzev, the lion with eight eyes! He saw it coming when he was still breathing and warned that the evil that will destroy Kibaaka will pass through Bongkisheri *(Fada Anton and Wirkitum express embarrassment)* but nobody listened to him. See what is happening now! Bongkisheri has put teeth in the mouths of the hens!

YOUR HIGHNESS
What do we do now?

GHEEH
Our people say that until the rotten potato is pulled out of the bag, the disease will spread to the rest.

ELDERS
Rengreng.

ABILITY
Our people say that when a disease invades the body, we kill it from the roots. Bongkisheri must be banned to save our ways! *(Fada Anton squints painfully and then shrugs).*

ELDERS
Rengreng.

WIRKITUM
Hi men. Bongkisheri and the women are like the trunk of the tree and its branches. If you cut down the tree, you kill the branches that suck on the trunk of the tree to survive. Dudes, the teeth and the tongue must learn to live together.

YOUR HIGHNESS
If the teeth cut off the tongue to render it useless, how would they live together?

ELDERS
Ohorrrh!

FADA ANTON
Honourable is right. How can you ban a group that has done a lot and is still doing more for your women? *(Wirkitum throws his hands apart in a questioning gesture).* Huh! Barrister Hallen Johnson is in charge of the education

and welfare of the girl child in Bongkisheri and she is helping orphan female children, your own children, to travel abroad for education… *(Wirkitum repeatedly nods in approval)*. She is the one finding scholarships for them. She is the one doing the legal papers. She does that through me. As we speak, Bongkisheri has sponsored four orphans to study in Motherland to come back and open your eyes, and also tame and teach other women how to become more useful. Jaika, Betty, and two other orphan girls are now studying abroad on scholarship. Bongkisheri has paid their fees already with the royalties they earn from their *toghu* and African Wears business. *(Shufai Laika smiles and Fada nods)*. The only intelligent orphan girl we didn't find a scholarship for is Binla and that's because she is physically challenged and would always need extra assistance which we cannot afford. You know her legs are looking inwards. Besides, Bongkisheri has trained the women, including Binla to mark *toghu* and other African wears which they sell to sponsor orphans in school and to help themselves. Those that go out of the country are channelled through me. Children of God, we need to appreciate the women's group for the training and empowering programmes they and the girl child are benefitting from….

YOUR HIGHNESS
Fada Anton, are you so blind that you can't see the damage that the so-called women 'empowerment' programmes have caused us? *(The Elders gesticulate in a questioning manner)*. Huh! Is it not this same doctrine of empowerment that has caused our women to start disrespecting their husbands and asking for rights to land ownership? Fada Anton, if you still wish to extend your stay in Kibaaka, you have to watch your tongue! *(The Elders nod)*. Who even invited you to this gathering? *(The Elders throw up their hands open)*. Elders of our land, what do we do to stop this madness from the women and the 'man-marry-man' before things get out of hand?

ABILITY
The thing you carry between your legs is a disciplinarian. That weapon can bend the most stubborn woman. Any woman who is participating in the land rights' protests should miss her turn whenever she returns….

SHUFAI LAIKA
You might be the one missing your turn and thinking your woman is missing her turn. Ability, what do you think Manka actually meant when she openly declared that the lock on the lips of the woman is removed and as part of their

strike action it will be transferred below...? *(Fada Anton looks away while Your Highness scowls).* I bet you, your strategy is way too late. You might be surprised when you get back home to find that your wife is already implementing it.

YOUR HIGHNESS
Shufai Laika, did you just say it was my own wife that said the lock on the lips of the woman is removed and transferred?

SHUFAI LAIKA
(Cups hands to his mouth) Mbeeh. *(Your Highness shrugs).*

NDZEBARA
I saw it coming and started implementing it in my house.

ABILITY
I repeat, any woman who was seen mixing with Livinus, Katika and Savage, and who participated in the bare-bodied protest must miss her turn for four months... *(This second condition attracts different reactions from the men, some nod their heads in consent; some look hesitant).*

FOLA
How can a man whose urine can hit a banana trunk five meters across the yard starve himself for four months? *(Alhaji Musa shifts his buttocks uncomfortably).* Ability, can you tame the contents of your loins for four months?

ALHADJI MUSA
I *wanda*!

ABILITY
No member of the Traditional Council should be tempted by hunger of the loins to break the oath of boycott...

SOME ELDERS
Rengreng! (A few Elders nod).

ABILITY
Dzekewong, boycott means you will not eat from the second dish for four good months.

GHEEH

Bility, is your cutlass still sharp? If your anthill is still stiff, you would not tell a man with balls to starve for four full *moons (Fola grins).*

ABILITY

Taa Gheeh, I am talking to men. I am not talking to people whose male members have a history of relapsing into shyness and unresponsive wakefulness. By the way, is there a rope tying anybody down to the waist of his wife? If you feel hungry during the hunger strike period, just go out there and lift one side-hen from the street as we always do.

FADA ANTON

God forbid! Ability, the Bible forbids adultery! *(Pa Jacov nods).* My mission in Kibaaka is to tame you, to bring light, and to rescue you from darkness. I will not fold my arms, sit quiet, and watch you prepare my Christians for hell fire! No, no. You cannot abandon the clean toilet at home to excrete in the bush. A snake can sting your buttocks. *(Pa Jacov nods and others try to suppress a laugh).*

SHUFAI LAIKA

Fada Anton is right. I cannot eat good food from a filthy dish *(Pa Jacov nods in approval).*

ABILITY

Shufai Laika, hens are fighting the ways of the land right in the presence of cocks. As if they have not sufficiently insulted our authority, they have ganged up with Barrister Johnson, the Come-no-Gos and the converts of 'man-marry-man and 'woman-marry-woman' religion whom we should be afraid may germinate and bear fruits in Kibaaka. Take note that in their bare-bodied protest on our soils, the accursed daughters of Eve and the climbers committed two crimes in one. They violated the sacredness of the land and betrayed the trust of the owners of their thighs *(the Elders nod).* And people with cassava between their legs are here, talking like women, listening to Fada Anton *(Fada frowns at Ability and then turns his face away).*

SHUFAI LAIKA

In that case, I suggest we go by vote counts. Those who want the four-month hunger strike strategy, move to my right hand; those who are against the boycott and prefer another form of punishment, move to my left. *(His Royal*

Highness, Ability, Medzefen, Aladji Musa, Pa Jacov, Verdzekov, and Ndzewiyi take two steps to the right while Dzekewong takes a step to join Shufai Laika, Gheeh, Ndzebarah, and Fola on the left-hand side but confusedly swerves to join Ability). Ability, the majority have voted against the boycott strategy.

ABILITY
The kitchen rebels and the climbers should be dragged before *Nwerong* to taste the sting of our tradition…

ELDERS
Rengreng! Suiru! Dzebei! (Chorusing approval in native Lamnso).

GHEEH
Our people say if you don't weed out the pricking grass together with its taproots, the roots will spread across the farm and kill the plants… *(The Elders nod).*

SHUFAI LAIKA
The presence of Barrister Johnson in the protest means Nwerong will face a stiff resistance. She can open doors that Nwerong is afraid to knock at.

ABILITY
Who owns the land? Nwerong or someone else? Huh! Your Highness, if you still value the cowries around your neck; if you still want to extend your days on the throne of Kibaaka, do not listen to Shufai Laika.
Kila begins to cough persistently attracting attention.

YOUR HIGHNESS
My children have not gone to school yet! Kila, Bame, Fomu, Jaidzeka! Go inside now, collect your school bags and start running to school, immediately! *(The children withdraw. Beckons Ability, Shufai Laika, Honourable, Gheeh, and Verdzekov to his side. They speak in hushed voices.*

ACT 1

Scene II

AT THE PALACE CULTURAL HALL

(The Elders are seated in the cultural hall about to start a meeting. Ba Kimfoi, the great seer suddenly storms the hall, his face and lips twitching. He steps forward, shrugs, looks around, shakes his head and grumbles).

YOUR HIGHNESS

Our people say that when an owl hoots from the rooftop during the daytime, it means that something bad has happened. Our people say that when the double-headed mother earthworm which we revere appears on the floor of the house, it is because it has a message, or that the gods of the land are angry. Mother earthworm has appeared on the floor of the house. *(Stares at the Seer).* Eyes and ears of the gods, the one who sees in darkness, what is the message from the gods?

BA KIMFOI

The insect that eats the leaf, lives within it. The beetle that destroys the raffia tree lives in the heart of the raffia tree. *(Groans).* A fish bone is stuck in the throat of Kibaaka. Remove it now or face the fury of the gods. *(The Elders sit back from each other, silently look on, lips tightened, their open palms held apart. Baa Kimfoi dances around and storms out through the door).*

FADA ANTON

(Pointing grudgingly at Baa Kimfoi as he tears away across the yard). There's only one God! He lives in Heaven. There's no other God in Kibaaka! *(The Elders shrug).* That character is misleading you.

YOUR HIGHNESS

Fada Anton, we did not hear of god for the first time from you! Watch your tongue! *(The Elders nod consent).* Fathers of fathers, we heard what the great seer has just said. An abomination has been committed before our eyes. We need to find out what has happened…

Heavy footsteps are heard approaching. Chicha Kisito tears across the courtyard and storms into the hall, churning up different emotions from the Elders expressed in different facial and body gestures.

CHICHA KISITO
Y-y-Your Highness, a woman h-h-has bought land in Kibaaka! *(The bombshell revelation invites shocking reactions across the hall and reignites the ethnic crisis of belonging).*

ELDERS
What! *(The Fon's chin drops; the elders are aghast, and Fada Anton's eyes shift from one elder to the other, confused).*

GHEEH
Bought land?

ABILITY
From who?

SHUFAI LAIKA
How?

FOLA
Abomination!

VERDZEKOV
Not in Kibaaka, I guess!

CHICHA KISITO
It has happened!

ABILITY
Who is the woman we are talking about?

CHICHA KISITO
Manka!

ELDERS
Ngiri! (The Elders lean back, stare at Your Highness open-mouthed, look at each other, and then turn their faces away. Each then lifts and crosses their hands over their heads, breathing restlessly).

ABILITY
Tradition has been brought to its knees.

GHEEH
I thought I had heard and seen everything, but now, my eyes have seen my ears.

ABILITY
(Spits in the air to express aversion, then pouts and starts to walk out of the hall; Gheeh follows, grabs him from behind and drags him back to his seat).

GHEEH
Ability, that is not the right thing to do. You cannot go away when your house is on fire. *(Shrugs).* Fon Ghamogha brought us ant-infested wood and must now entertain lizards as guests. *(Your Highness drops his head as the visibly shocked elders stare at him with their mouths hanging open).*

ABILITY
This is a serious allegation! Chicha Kisito, are you sure of what you just said of our queen?

CHICHA KISITO
I can swear with my blood.

SHUFAI LAIKA
Chicha Kisito, where did you get the information that Manka has bought land?

CHICHA KISITO
Shufai Laika, I am just coming from the Lands and Surveys Office. A land dealer wanted to sell the land that shares its boundary with the land that we all thought Manka was renting for Bongkisheri activities. The buyer was advised to confirm the owner of the land with the neighbours to avoid future problems. The man contacted me with the understanding that Lukong was my brother and I would definitely know something about the boundaries of his

land. I took him to the Lands and Surveys Office today. The head of that office is called Mr. Essomba. He is the one that informed us that the land advertised for sale shares its boundary with Mrs Ghamogha Manka.

ABILITY

Your Highness, is it true that Manka has bought land in Kibaaka?

YOUR HIGHNESS

I also stumbled on the land title.

ELDERS

Heeeei! Ngiri! (The Elders openly express shock variously).

VERDZEKOV

So, our Fon knew that a woman has desecrated tradition and kept quiet? *Hei!*

ABILITY

Your Highness, for how long have you held this information hostage? *(Ndzebarah nods).* For how long have you obstructed justice? Can anybody deny that Your Highness is an accomplice in the abomination Manka has committed? *(The Elders throw their hands open).*

YOUR HIGHNESS

Elders of *Kibaaka* land, my silence should not be taken to mean involvement or collaboration. I have struggled to get answers to the same questions you are asking now. I thought I could repair the damage my own way.

VERDZEKOV

Is Your Highness confirming that the land that hosts Bongkisheri activities is owned by a woman?

YOUR HIGHNESS

I have been living in shock since the day I discovered the Land Title carrying my wife's name because she had once told me she was renting the land for capacity-building activities of the women's group.

GHEEH
And what did Your Highness do upon finding the Land Title carrying the name of a woman? *(The Elders nod).*

YOUR HIGHNESS
I loved and trusted my wife. I had total confidence in her and thought that with time, she would cede to my demand and tell me how she got the land as well as transfer its ownership to me. For the past three or four days, I have been putting pressure on her to transfer ownership of the land to me, but she refused.

ABILITY
Your Highness, you speak like someone under the influence of wine obeying a beardless youth. What is worse in your case is that you are our Fon and no member of the family is spared the shame of their father's madness. *(The Fon drops his head).* Now that the disease is diagnosed, how do we cure it before it spreads to the other parts of the body? *(The Elders nod).*

FADA ANTON
Why is it taboo for a woman to buy land?

YOUR HIGHNESS
The people whose presence almost led to the extinction of our ways were led to Kibaaka by a woman.

SHUFAI LAIKA
Fathers of Fathers, I believe that this abomination is committed because our women and beardless youths do not know why it is taboo for a woman to buy land. Your Highness, tell us that story so that we can spread it to them.

YOUR HIGHNESS
It was through a woman that trouble came to Kibaaka and turned things upside down. My father told me the story. Her name was Tantan Ngonso. She was the Princess of Kibaaka and the first child in her family. Unfortunately, she was a woman and naturally disqualified for the throne. Following the ways of the land, the first male child from her womb was to be the heir to the throne of Kibaaka. She was a good woman and the gods of our land rewarded her by giving her a male child. The clan was happy that the future Fon of Kibaaka was born. The brothers of Tantan Ngonso became jealous and planned to eliminate

her son to inherit the throne. Ngonso was informed by a palace maid of the conspiracy to eliminate her son due to rivalry over succession. She escaped with her son to the Catholic Mission and informed the white-skinned man who brought the church to Kibaaka about the plans to kill her son. His name was Fada Goodluck. Tantan begged Fada Goodluck to give his son baptism and to also train him as the catechist or priest of the God of the skies, hoping that the almighty power of baptism would wash away his sins and protect him from harm and death as Fada had taught them to believe. Fada Goodluck took pity on Tantan Ngonso and decided to save the life of her son. He baptised them, gave them new names, Lisaber and Friday, and sent them to the land of the rising sun where Tantan was to serve as a domestic servant for his brother, and Friday was to be trained as a Roman Catholic priest. Tantan was tall and very beautiful and had a good character. After serving the brother of Fada Goodluck for many seasons, and also allowing her son, Friday, to go and preach the word of God in the lands where there was war, where people's heads were empty, he compensated her by marrying her. He had two children with Tantan, the mother of the mother of Wirkitum and Savage, and another one whose name I cannot remember.

While in the land where the sun never set, Tantan Ngonso told the father of her children many stories about Kibaaka; how we had large forests with big trees; how we did not know God and did not know book; how men killed each other to inherit land and titles; how we had shining stones. The white-skinned man heard that our heads were empty and barren and concluded that we needed help. He decided to come and help the people of Kibaaka and to also tame us. When he came, he gave our Fon a hat, a torch lamp, a pair of khaki trousers, a jacket, a pair of socks, a pair of rain boots, a raincoat, a mirror to confuse thieves, a bottle of whisky, a pair of scissors, and a packet of bonbon in exchange for land to build a church and a school. Papers were signed between Fada Goodluck and the Fon conferring ownership of a parcel of land in Shisong to the white-skinned man. When he had built the church and a school, Fada Goodluck invited his brothers to join him to spread the word of God to the people of Kibaaka. Like the man who carried an elephant on his head and still dug the soil for a cricket, invaders began to flow in from the land of the rising sun like bees in search of honey. They came like locusts following the smell of fresh maize. The excitement with which many Kibaaka people received Fada Goodluck and his people soon died following their activities in the land. They cut down all the trees in Hunting Forest and carried all the big timber to their land. They cut down our palm fronds to build schools and churches. Fada

Goodluck and his Christians destroyed all the young raffia trees in the name of celebrating Palm Sunday. He even took more land than what was stated on the papers he signed with our Fon. Hunters lost their jobs. Many people were displaced from their family lands with little compensation in the form of free education or training for their children. Whenever someone fell sick, the women cut raffia trees and leaves and took to Fada who in turn poured holy water on the leaves. The leaves carried Jesus Christ and could drive away diseases and evil spirits from the compound and from the body of the sick person. Our forests and raffia trees soon disappeared. Rivers and streams dried off leaving only bony banks. Roasting heat visited our land, killing people, fowls, plants, and crops. Rains came late and women planted late. Crops did not do well. For many seasons, hunger visited the land, killing many people. An alarm was raised blaming Ngonso for bringing strangers to Kibaaka.

The Fon and *Nwerong* were not happy with the activities of the strangers and took measures to stop similar unwanted acts from happening in the land. *Nwerong* immediately declared that women and strangers would never own land in Kibaaka. Nwerong also created a group to teach all the Come-no-Gos of Kibaaka the ways of the land, and to also restore order in the land. That is how the Traditional Council was born. Things went on well until the season of locusts came with diseases. People were dying every day. The white-skinned man built a hospital and invited his wife to Kibaaka. She has learned the white man's magic and book and did not use our herbs to treat the sick as Baa Kimfoi was doing. She brought white seeds which she gave to the sick to heal them. She stopped us from using herbs to cure diseases and directed the sick to her hospital for treatment.

Like the other Come-no-Gos to Kibaaka, the woman-healer or white man magician joined our group to learn our ways. There, she started talking to women about the new ways. She introduced adult schooling and encouraged women to join and be drugged with the new ways. Soon, the women she trained began to ask for rights. The group soon went out of hand and Elders withdrew from it to cause its collapse. But things did not happen the way our people wanted.

As time went on, Wirkitum traced his roots and returned to Kibaaka. He came with his brother, Savage, and his wife, Barrister Johnson. Some of us can still remember when Wirkitum came and told our late Fon that blood tests traced his roots to Kibaaka. He said his parents went swimming and drowned and our people believed him because he mentioned Tantan Ngonso as the mother of the mother of his mother.

The woman healer soon fell sick and returned to their land and Barrister Johnson took over from her. It was in this group that Johnson met Manka. Johnson and Manka picked up the pieces of the group and transformed it into an NGO. They wanted to promote the education of the girl child and to empower the women, they claimed. That was how Bongkisheri started and became what it is today. It was believed that trouble came to Kibaaka through a woman and that is the reason a woman cannot buy land in Kibaaka. (*The Elders nod in approval*).

FADA ANTON
Your Highness, your reason for denying the woman the right to land ownership is purely the result of ignorance. It is not founded on any legal or religious basis.
(The Elders lean back wide-eyed, surprised at Fada Anton, look at each other, and then all turn their faces away).

YOUR HIGHNESS
Fada Anton, you have overstayed your welcome (*shows Fada the door with his finger. Honourable beckons Fada to follow him out of the hall*).

ABILITY
Now that we know why the woman cannot own land in Kibaaka, for those who did not know, let us go back to where we ended. As we were saying before we were rudely interrupted by Fada Anton, a woman has bought land in Kibaaka. As if that wasn't enough, she has a land title in her name. Your Highness, what did you do when you found the land title carrying the name of a woman (*The Elders nod their heads in approval*).

YOUR HIGHNESS
I threatened to report Manka to Nwerong. I am sure their protest is the result of the pressure I have been putting on her to transfer ownership of that land to me.

ABILITY
Is Your Highness saying that Manka heard the word *Nwerong* and still decided to organise the protest against the ways of Kibaaka land in order to remain the landowner?

YOUR HIGHNESS
She even walked out of my bedroom and has since refused to perform her domestic duties even when the timetable says it is her turn *(The Elders shake their heads).*

ABILITY:
There you go again Your Highness! For how long have we been living in this shame? How could our ancestors have abandoned us like this? Where did we go wrong?

SHUFAI LAIKA
My people, what did I tell you? You might be the one missing your turn and thinking your woman is missing her turn. See now! Did you know the Fon was already forced into your boycott scheme? I was wondering why the Fon quickly agreed with this boycott strategy.

ABILITY
How can a man be starved of his bed right in his own house? What is this land turning to? When a woman refuses to be a woman, must a man also refuse to be the man? No! A man must be a man. And a man must have some pride. Your Highness, when a man ceases to be the man, he develops a hunch back. *(The Elders take up their heads and smile wryly).* We are going to tell our wives that we are men!

ELDERS
Rengreng.

YOUR HIGHNESS
You will not understand. My wife has changed since Bongkisheri took her to Beijing. She organises her activities and only informs me, and when she informs me, it is not because she needs my opinion. She attends endless meetings with big groups in and out of the country. Right in the middle of the night, she glides out of my arms to answer telephone calls from Barrister Johnson about meetings here and there. Is that the person you want me to bend in just one day?

ABILITY
Your Highness, so, this is what you have become, letting a woman make decisions for you? *(Ability looks a little contemptuously at the Fon who simply drops*

his head). Hei! Our people say that when a man ceases to be a man, he pays homage to a woman. But the man in question is the Fon himself. Tell me, how can someone carry the clan on his shoulders and not know what to do to a woman who wants to become a man right under his roof?

ELDERS
Ohhorrr!

YOUR HIGHNESS
Ability, what would you do if you were in my shoes?

ABILITY
I cannot be in the shoes of a coward.

YOUR HIGHNESS
What?

ABILITY
(Springs up fuming). Yes, I can't be in the shoes of a woman!

YOUR HIGHNESS
Ability, I can take anything but not an insult!

SHUFAI LAIKA
How do we go forward from here?

ABILITY
The Fon has failed us. The Vigilante Group has failed us. We agreed in this same hall that Fola and Dzekewong were the most qualified members of the Traditional Council to coordinate the Information Gathering Department of the Vigilante Group and to be our eyes and ears everywhere because they know all the bars in town. In Kibaaka land, a man is levied 1000frs CFA every month for security; a woman is charged 500frs. The Council of Elders pays the Vigilante Guards salaries every month. Fola, Dzekewong, do you think we struggle to raise this money for your beer and palm wine? How did Manka buy land under our nose and got the land title established in her name without you knowing? How did that happen? *(The Elders make questioning gestures)*. Dzekewong, when Fola raised an alarm during the last Council of Elders' gathering

that you had started abandoning your duty post and driving Barrister Johnson to Bongkisheri meetings, even spending working hours washing her dishes, cars and her underpants, what did I say? Do you still remember what I said in reaction to that accusation? Have you forgotten that I said your closeness to Bongkisheri and Barrister Johnson was a blessing in disguise because you would be our eyes and ears everywhere? Did I not say so? *(Dzekewong nods sheepishly)*. Shufai Laika also said that the work of the Vigilante boys was not only to stop thieves and armed gangs from stealing fowls and goats, or from rustling cattle and breaking into homes… (*the Elders nod in approval*). Kewong, Fola, how comes you did not know that a woman had bought land in Kibaaka? Kewong, you drive Barrister Johnson and Manka around. Don't you know you can sit close to the dining table after serving them tea, close your eyes, hang your head over your shoulder as if you are sleeping and even sway back and forth like nodding trees just to listen to their conversation and inform us? Don't you understand English?

DZEKEWONG
I de hear one one. I de hear English well, well, but when Barista Jonsin bends her tongue inside mouth and speaks through her nose, *dat time I go de hear na one one word.*

FOLA
Elders of our land, we have heard you. I promise to double my efforts (*All hands roof the nostrils as Fola's annal track grumbles and belches garrulously, leaving a reeking stench wafting across the hall*). I am sorry…. (*Fola quickly holds his trousers from behind and runs into the visitors' toilet*).

ABILITY
If you ask my opinion, we have more serious people who can better coordinate the Vigilante Department than Fola and Dzekewong.

SHUFAI LAIKA
The Council will see what to do.

VERDZEKOV
A woman has bought land in her name. As if that is not enough, they are asking for land rights. Who is behind this?

ABILITY
What we are seeing today results from opening our door to strangers, including the Bongkisheri NGO that we allowed to be planted in our soil.

GHEEH
Our fathers say, a bird claims to have a home and to belong when you allow it to build its nest on the rooftop of your house.

ABILITY
From the day Johnson fought for the release of Savage, Katika, and Livinus from jail, claiming that their human rights were abused, the liberty the Court granted them has been interpreted by the women and the human riders to mean any individual or group of persons can hide under the umbrella of human rights and do whatever they want in Kibaaka.

YOUR HIGHNESS
Ability is right. I am beginning to think that Bongkisheri is the cause of what is happening in our land today.

GHEEH
People of Kibaaka, you do not allow the thief to break into your house before you raise an alarm. That is where we went wrong. It did not start today. Two market days ago, the mother of my children did not cook because she spent the whole day at their so-called Bongkisheri Women Centre marking *toghu*. I did not eat in my own house. It is not the first time I have gone to bed on an empty stomach just because my wife was busy attending meetings and marking Bongkisheri *toghu*. I told the father of my wife that each time Bongkisheri has an order to supply *toghu* to Fada Anton, there will be no food in my house on that day. Her father told me to be the man.

FOLA
I threatened to withdraw my wife from Bongkisheri so that she would learn how to be a good housewife, but she said Fada Anton placed orders for 500 pieces of *toghu* and Bongkisheri women had to produce and supply on time to avoid owing monthly tithes and other church contributions that Fada subtracts directly from their joint business. I don't even complain again because when I do, she asks me to pay her tithes. I simply go to the next bar, buy palm wine and drink.

SHUFAI LAIKA
I thought I was the only one that does not have food when there is Bongkisheri *toghu*-marking day.

MEDZEFEN
I don't *compilain* at all. I beat.

ABILITY
Now that Bongkisheri has taught women that they have the right to become landowners, and now that we already know that each time the women attend Bongkisheri meetings, no husband eats in Kibaaka, we need to stop the activities of that group…

ELDERS
Rengreng (The Elders signal assent).

YOUR HIGHNESS
How will that be done? I have been asking this question.

ABILITY
Elders of our land, if we must restore Kibaaka to what it was before, then, *Nwerong* should place the ban plant on the land Manka bought. *(The Elders nod).* Should our Vigilante Boys find any woman on that land after banning Bongkisheri and Manka from stepping her feet on that land, they should flog and leave them with broken and bleeding limbs!

ELDERS
(Some Elders scream approval). Rengreng.

ABILITY
Bongkisheri has succeeded in challenging tradition with impunity! Their protest and worst still, direct links with the human riders and cross-dressers is tantamount to deliberate disregard for the ways of our land and a slap on the face of tradition! If we allow them to get away with this shame that they have brought upon the land, people will call us women! *(The Elders nod vigorously).* We must fight protest with protest! *(The Elders nod).* Our people say that when a storm refuses to abate, we need another storm to calm it down!

ELDERS
Rengreng!

SHUFAI LAIKA
We will not beat anybody. There are better ways to calm the storm. Let us challenge the protest in court. Let us take Manka and Bongkisheri to court.

YOUR HIGHNESS
Did Government not say it has given powers to the local chiefs? What is the role of the Local Traditional Council if a local issue like a land dispute must be settled by Government? What is our own role if we cannot handle chieftaincy and land matters? Does one sell the goat and hold the rope? *(The Elders throw up their hands apart, groaning).* Can you give out your daughter in marriage, collect her bride price and still remain the owner?

ELDERS
Ngang! (No)

SHUFAI LAIKA
Elders of our land, in as much as I am worried about the bare-bodied protest by the Bongkisheri women and the activities of human riders, I do not think we should involve Nwerong, or even use brute force. Remember the raging 90s. We still remember what happened when Nwerong dispatched the Vigilante guards to Yer-Bukang village to destroy the small palace and the water tank because we felt we owned the land and its water sources and should not pay any Water Bills to the Government Local Council. Let us avoid doing something that will attract the anger of Government again. The question we should ask ourselves is, who sold land to a woman?

VERDZEKOV
I think Shufai Laika is right. Our first step should be to find out who sold land to a woman. *(The Elders nod in approval).*

ABILITY
Is it not obvious from our performance in the last elections that anyone who hurts us will always have Government on his or her side? Is it not also obvious that if you join Government against us, all your sins are forgiven?

SHUFAI LAIKA
Ability, how does Government come into this matter?

ABILITY
Who else apart from Government issues land titles, talk more of issuing it to a woman or to come-no-Gos?

SHUFAI LAIKA
(Bites his lower lip, closes his eyes and opens them). Something keeps coming to my mind. Verdzekov, Chicha Kisito, your late brother was the owner of the land that now belongs to Manka. When he was alive, he rented out the land to her as I was told. How did she suddenly become the owner after Lukong's death? Do you have any idea? *(The elders stick out their chests).*

VERDZEKOV
It is true that the land we are talking about was the property of Lukong, my older brother. But there is another story to it that people do not know.

SHUFAI LAIKA
Tell us.

VERDZEKOV
When Honourable Wirkitum traced his roots and came back to Kibaaka, he discovered that the father of the father of his mother had a lot of land. He requested all the lands his people had left behind. Pa Kintang was the oldest man in the land. He showed Wirkitum the stump of a kola nut tree, the stump of a grave, and the base of a building where their great-grandfathers had settled. The stumps were found on one of Lukong's farmland. Pa Kintang explained that the farmland was given to Lukong as compensation by Wirkitum's grandfather. The day he brought Wirkitum to recover their family land, my brother invited me to witness the handing over. *(Closes his eyes briefly trying hard to remember the conversation).*

WIRKITUM
This farmland was the property of my granddaddy; it was his heritage from his father. I have come to take back what is mine. The land is now my heritage from my grandfather.

LUKONG

I will cut what is yours and give it to you. The part of the land you see in front belongs to me. I joined the two lands when I became the owner but I know the boundary line. Your land begins where you find the stump of the tree. Wirkitum, you need to know how your family land became mine. When the father of the mother of your mother was sick, all his children abandoned him. They were all in the city working; some were married, but we sent word to them. Kpuyuv sent a letter stating that he requested permission to come home and take care of his sick father but his Master refused to grant him leave of absence. Rebeka also sent word that her husband refused to release her because there was no other person to cook for the family. I could not abandon the father of your mother to die in shame. He was my friend. I asked the mother of my children to take good care of my friend. She fetched water for him, cooked food for him, and changed his clothes when they were wet. She fetched firewood and made his fire to keep the house warm. When he felt that death was at his doorstep, he invited me to his farm. We stood right there. He picked up a stone, threw it across the land, and then took me where it landed and said: "Lukong, this parcel of land now belongs to you. My father gave it to me. I kept it for my children but they turned their back on me when I needed them. Your wife gave me water and food, and also made my fire every morning. Nobody should take the land away from you. This is the only way I can thank your wife for the help she gave me when my children turned their backs on me." Wirkitum, the boundary line passes here. The part of the land in front is mine. I only merged it with the land that was given to me.

VERDZEKOV

(Opens his eyes slowly). That is exactly what happened. But that's not all. When my brother drew the boundary line and returned what was given to him to Wirkitum, Wirkitum begged him to sell his own land to him because he needed a road to his land situated directly behind my brother's own. My brother was angry and refused. One season after that meeting, my brother fell sick and needed money for surgery. He had no money and decided to sell his land. Wirkitum rushed back to him again to buy the land, pleading that there was no way he could create an access road to his own land without tearing through my brother's land. But my brother once more refused to sell his land to Wirkitum. When Wirkitum left, a dealer came and bought the land. His name was Mutumba. When my brother asked me to sign the hand-written agreement on the sale of land because his own hands were shaking due to ill-health, it

was the name of the land dealer that was written on the agreement. None of the papers I signed on behalf of my brother carried Manka's name. What I can also add is that the land we are talking about was rented to Manka before the dealer bought it and continued the contract.

ABILITY
(Rolls a disbelieving eye). If the land was rented out to Manka, how come her name is written on the land title?

ELDERS
(Throw their hands open). Ohorrr!

ABILITY
I don't trust Wirkitum. Don't you think he might have sent the dealer to buy the land for him and then resold it to Manka? There is a strong solidarity among these Come-no-Gos and, as my people say, birds of the same feather....

SHUFAI LAIKA
Wirkitum is a member of the Traditional Council. He cannot sell land to a woman.

ABILITY
Who else did it? *(Shakes his head).*

VERDZEKOV
The land dealer who bought the land from Lukong had the habit of leasing land to farmers for seasonal crops. I suspect Mutumba was the one that sold the land to Manka. He was not from here.

YOUR HIGHNESS
My wife equally told me she rented the land for Bongkisheri projects.

ABILITY
A tenant suddenly becomes landlord, and we still trust her! *(Rolls his eyes).* I don't know who to trust anymore if I cannot trust Lukong and our Queen...

SHUFAI LAIKA
Verdzekov, do you have any idea where we can find Mutumba?

VERDZEKOV
He was arrested and jailed for selling a parcel of land that did not belong to him to five people. He later escaped from prison.

SHUFAI LAIKA
That makes matters more complicated now. *(Twists his face).*

ABILITY
We need further investigation into this matter. I don't trust Wirkitum.

VERDZEKOV
My own suspect is Mutumba. Ability, leave Honourable Shufai Wirkitum out of this.

SHUFAI LAIKA
Your Highness, Elders of our land, since Mutumba is no longer around to tell us what he knows about the land, or why he sold land to a woman, let us look for the way forward. Our women are still at the entrance to the palace, bare-bodied. That is not good for the image of the palace, and particularly, the owners of their thighs. *(The elders nod).* We need to bring them back home before anything. The boycott strategy has been rejected by many; the bullying strategy of the Vigilante boys once landed us in trouble; and as I see it, if the land matter is taken to Court, the Law of Government, not the law of our traditional customs would decide on the rightful owner. As it stands, I suggest that we try dialogue first *(The Elders nod in approval).* Our people say that you must throw grains of corn on the ground if you want to catch a fowl. This is a cultural battle. It is also a domestic battle. Many of the women protesting in the streets know little or nothing about the ways of our land. We can win this battle with pillow diplomacy. If that doesn't work, we will look for another strategy. Verdzekov, Ndzewiyi, and I will go and beg our wives to return home. Let us go home now. Let us meet here again tomorrow at the sound of the gong.
(The Elders walk out through the door led by Shufai Laika).

ACT 1

Scene III

(Your Highness is sitting on his throne, staring fixedly and absentmindedly across the room. Bame, Fomu, Jaidzeka, and Kila enter, returning from school).

KILA
(Bends her knees forward as a sign of respect, sniffs the air twice and asks). Your Highness, is something smelling in the room? Your Highness, has smoke entered your eyes…? *(Steps forward and stares at her father's twisted face as she asks questions).*

BAME
(Stares at the ridges and furrows across his father's forehead and asks). Your Highness, why is your face as if you are sneezing? *(The others nod in acceptance).*

YOUR HIGHNESS
(Silently points to short wooden stools at the rear). Bame, your mother is the reason my face looks as if I am sneezing.

BAME
Your Highness, what has Mami done?

YOUR HIGHNESS
She is becoming a man.

KILA
There is no beard on her chin.

BAME
Your Highness, is it because they were marching bare-bodied?

YOUR HIGHNESS
Kila, Jaidzeka, go and get something to eat. After eating, go and fetch water. I

want to talk to Bame and Fomu. *(Jaidzeka and Kila withdraw).*

YOUR HIGHNESS

Bame, Fomu, I woke up in the morning to an empty bed. Your mother left the house without my knowledge, but that is not all. You need to know what is happening because you will also take over the responsibility of your own households when you become husbands and fathers. Your mother has bought land.

BAME/FOMU

Weeeeeeeeeh!

YOUR HIGHNESS

(Barks). Will you shut up! *(The children shrug).* Shut up!

BAME

Your Highness, you just told us that Mami has bought land…

YOUR HIGHNESS

My throne will pay the price. I am a husband and a father, but not a man. This Palace is not my compound. I live here because I am the Fon of Kibaaka. The palace belongs to the Fon. If Nwerong rips off the beads around my neck and puts them around the neck of Ndzebarah, your uncle, because your mother bought land in her name, I will lose the throne.

FOMU

Your Highness, is it Nwerong's money that Mami used in buying the land? *(Bame nods).*

YOUR HIGHNESS

Land belongs to the man. Crops belong to the woman. Land is power. If you give land to a woman, you have given her power. If she gets married to another family, she would carry the land to that family. A woman belongs to her father when she is young and unmarried. She belongs to her husband and his family when her bride-price is paid. She belongs to any surviving male member of her husband's family after her husband's death. The woman is like land and the man the owner. A man worthy of the name is expected to own a piece of land. I sold all the cattle I had to raise money for my campaign project, hoping I would buy a piece of land when I become Parliamentarian. Before I knew it, the Come-no-Go called Wirkitum walked into my plantation and harvested all my supporters leaving me with nothing. That is how I found myself where I am today. I am a husband and a father, but not a man. I don't have land. I don't have a house. I own this palace and the entitlements of Royalty as long as I stay in power as the Fon of Kibaaka. The palace belongs to the lineage and not to an individual. Fons come and go, but the palace remains. If I join my ancestors while still on the throne, there is the possibility of my son becoming the Fon. But, if the beads around my neck are removed and passed on to another household, the new Fon will automatically take overpower and everything I worked hard to achieve, including even your mother and you, my children.

FOMU
Your Highness, we cannot allow that to happen *(Bame nods)*.

YOUR HIGHNESS
It has happened. Your mother has bought land and the Elders have been informed. My red feather is shaky on my cap. I am accused of allowing her to buy land in her name. The throne can be taken away from me because of your mother's atrocity. She must transfer ownership of the land she bought to me. That is the only way to save my throne…

KILA
(Crying off the courtyard) Weeeei, weeei, weeeei…
(Your Highness and his sons immediately rush outside).

JAIDZEKA
(Descends on Kila). Pah, pah, pah… *(Bame and Fomu dart forward to confront Jaidzeka but Your Highness stops them).*

YOUR HIGHNESS
Stop it now! Stop it! Bame, Fomu, stop, there! Jaidzeka, you have started again! Why are you beating your sister? What did she do to you that you couldn't forgive her, or inform me? Did I not warn you to stop beating her? What is wrong with you and your mother? Why are you beating her, even tearing her dress?

JAIDZEKA
She said she saw my mother's *bum bum* and also calabashes on her chest *(touches her chest, and then, her buttocks to indicate what she meant).*

KILA

(Wipes tears trailing down her cheeks with the back of her hand) it was Jaidzeka that started it. She said that my Mum is a Come-no-Go…

YOUR HIGHNESS

(Shakes his head). Jaidzeka, so, you have decided to join your mothers in transforming my palace into a battleground? *Huh*? If it is not your mothers quarrelling, bickering, and refusing to greet each other, it is you, the children. When will there ever be peace in this palace? Is it my own bad luck or what? This madness has to stop! Jaidzeka, Kila, what you said to each other was wrong. I do not want to hear that you insulted an elder and this is the last time I should hear that the two of you were fighting. Report any offence to me. Am I understood? *(They nod their heads).* Apologise to each other now! Jaidzeka, start the apology because you started the insults… Is there another Jaidzeka standing here?

JAIDZEKA

(Reluctantly unfolds her squashed lips). Sorry.

YOUR HIGHNESS

Will you do that properly? You are as stubborn as your mother.

JAIDZEKA

(Grimacing) I said I am sorry *naa*!

YOUR HIGHNESS

Ngiri! *(Shakes his head).* Jaidzeka, kneel down now! *(She kneels).* *(Your Highness rains insults at Jaidzeka). Nyamfuka!* You will be kneeling there for one hour. That's the punishment for rudeness and insubordination. Like mother, like daughter. The baby cobra is never free of venom.

YOUR HIGHNESS

Kila, apologise to your elder sister!

KILA

Jaidzeka, I am sorry for insulting Big Mama. I will not do it again.

YOUR HIGHNESS
Jaidzeka, this is how you apologise to somebody you have offended.

FOMU
Your Highness, why do people call my mother a Come-no-Go?

YOUR HIGHNESS
Your mother's mother was not from here, but her father's father had a bit of our blood flowing in his veins. A long time ago, a son of Kibaaka was trained and sent by the first Missionaries to teach the white man's language in Catholic School, Pinyin. His name was Verdzengai Nso Pasika. Pasika stayed long in Pinyin and married a woman from that village. She gave him a son and his father named him Mungwa Verdzengai. Mungwa Verdzengai later traced his roots to Kibaaka. He came along with his wife, Miyanyui Manka. Mungwa Verdzengai and Miyanyui Manka gave birth to your mother, Manka, and her sister, Regular, as well as to Pa Ngwan.

BAME
Why are people like Anti Lawyer, Honourable Wirkitum, Uncle Savage, and others called Come-no-Gos?

YOUR HIGHNESS
Come-no-Go means stranger. They are different. Some have white skin. Some have only a bit of our blood. Some came here to teach our people the language and the ways of the white man and never returned to their land after their work. Some came here to look for jobs in the cocoa, rubber, and banana plantations. A long time ago, people used to leave distant lands to travel to Kibaaka in search of jobs. We have many of such people working in the palm oil, banana, cocoa, and rubber plantations. The White Missionaries were not alone.

BAME
Why do people hate Come-no-Gos?

YOUR HIGHNESS
They are not from here. Almost all the big positions in our plantations are controlled by the Come-no-Gos. They represent us. Almost all the big schools and houses and hotels belong to them. Sons of the soil are now beggars in their own land. Almost half of our land is owned by strangers. They do not respect

the ways of our land. They occupy all the top jobs in Kibaaka. For example, Honourable Wirkitum is not from here, but Government has made him a big man with two big positions and Kibaaka people are under him.

BAME
Your Highness, why is Honourable Wirkitum called Shufai if he is a Come-no-Go? Are there Shufais in the land of the white man?

YOUR HIGHNESS
His father's people gave us a language. I am talking about the language you use in school, church and business, the language you find in books. It was brought to Kibaaka by Wirkitum's people.

BAME
Why is our own language not taught in our schools? *(Fomu nods).* How can somebody come to our land and force us to abandon our language and use his own language?

YOUR HIGHNESS
Before the first White Missionaries came to our land to teach our people the new ways, we had no schools. We had a language but we did not know how to read and write. That does not mean that our heads were like an empty calabash. We sang, danced, and told fireside stories. That is how we spoke to the world. When Fada came, he built a school and taught our people how to read and write. The books he taught our people were written in his language. That is how the white man forced the English language into our throats.

FOMU
Chicha Kisito beats us when we speak Lamnso in school.

YOUR HIGHNESS
My father told me that Fada Goodluck used to flog them for speaking Lamnso during doctrine classes *(The children grin).* When you are in school, speak the white man's language. You need to learn it because you will need it when you travel to other lands. You also need it in the office. If you can't speak and write in English, you cannot have a job. Go back to your mother's apartment now. *(The children withdraw).*

ACT 1

Scene IV

AT THE ROAD JUNCTION

(Enters the Town Crier Hitting the Gong)

TOWN CRIER
(*Nkung! Nkung! Nkung!* Nkung! People of Kibaaka land, People of Kibaaka land, all roads lead to the Palace now! All roads lead to the Palace now! The Council of Elders has spoken!)

(A few minutes later)

AT THE PALACE CULTURAL HALL
(The Fon is seated on his high-back Royal seat, (Kava'a), on a raised area facing the audience whose seats are arranged in shelving rungs, beginning with titled elders. The Elders file in solemnly across the floor, heads bowed. One after the other, an Elder would clap his hands three times, cup them to his mouth, and hum before sitting down).

SHUFAI LAIKA
(Hands cupped and held beneath his chin, he bends forward before the Fon). Mbeeh! Nchang-nchang! Bvereéh!

YOUR HIGHNESS
Elders of our land, have you come?

ELDERS
Mbeeh!

YOUR HIGHNESS
Honourable and Fola are not here? Are they in Kibaaka?

ABILITY

Your Highness, must that Come-no-Go be present in a meeting of sons of the soil? As for Fola, he had a runny stomach and went to get his drugs. He will join us soon.

(The sound of a car is heard off the yard. All eyes turn toward the yard. Verdzekov opens the door of the car and Honourable steps out and walks across the yard).

WIRKITUM

Hi folks!

ELDERS

Mmmm.

YOUR HIGHNESS

Honourable Shufai Wirkitum, have you come well? What held you back for so long?

WIRKITUM

Official duties and the women's protest kept me doing a few things in my office. We shall be having a meeting with the women's leaders in the afternoon. I needed to give directives to my secretary to get the hall ready. I needed to also forward a brief report to the President of the National Assembly on the state of micro-projects in my community....

ABILITY

Honourable, I hope you remembered to tell the President of the National Assembly that the only micro-projects you have realised are *(counting his fingers)*: the small bridge linking Kibaaka Central Area to the Yerr-Bukang Fulani community; the borehole and a single toilet in the Bukang Market, and the twenty benches you donated to Government Technical High School, Kibaaka. Hopefully, you have not added the five Hilux vehicles, ten Prado cars and four Mercedes Benz you and your wife, Barrister Johnson, drive around town to your list of projects.

WIRKITUM

Ebilidy, I won't take such baseless allegations lightly next time…

SHUFAI LAIKA

Ability, that is not what brought us here. Your Highness, now that a majority of members of the Council of Elders are here, we may proceed. Ndzewiyi, make sure you take down the minutes *(Ndzewiyi nods, holding a paper and a pen). Enters Fola, cups his hands to his mouth facing the Fon, hums, and sits down.*

YOUR HIGHNESS

Fola, have you come? Shufai Laika, you led the Elders to talk with the women yesterday. What news have you brought for us?

SHUFAI LAIKA

Elders of our land, we told the women that we were sent by the Council of Elders to beg them to return to their homes. We also assured them of our readiness to listen to them and to seek solutions to their grievances.

YOUR HIGHNESS

And what did they say?

SHUFAI LAIKA

They lifted sheets of papers with messages to my face. I copied everything on my own sheet of paper as they sang *(Reads from the sheet of paper).* "#The Woman's Turn#; #Give Back our Land Rights#; #Power to the Woman#; #End-Culture-Promoted Human Rights Abuses#. Manka said they will only call off the land rights protest when *Nwerong* has signed an agreement granting land ownership rights to women.

ELDERS

Ngiri!

YOUR HIGHNESS

So, we are now reduced to children to be taking decisions from those we are supposed to decide for? Women truly want to take over the world. They want to put on the thinking cap too. Well, they will all grow bald-headed too.

DZEKEWONG

Dat is the reason why I will niva get marit to a woman who knows book and has big sense. Dem go climb sit for your body. Dem no get respect, at all.

SHUFAI LAIKA
Elders of our land, you have not heard anything yet. *(Reads from a sheet of paper Mother of Children distributed at the demonstration arena).* "Fellow women do not be afraid anymore. Beijing has freed us from chains. The lock on our lips is removed. The rope with which the woman was tied to the kitchen is now untethered. Women can no longer sit quiet and tolerate culture-promoted human rights abuses against them. Bongkisheri is ready to seek social justice for women. We call on Government, Non-Governmental Organisations, traditional and community leaders, Nwerong, and the larger community to be key partners in educating and creating awareness on the need to respect the rights of the woman and the girl child."

GHEEH
Our people say that a squirrel dances on the road in bright daylight because its drummers are in the nearby bush.

FOLA
And who are their drummers?

ABILITY
Beijing has clad women in strange garments. The taproots of Beijing are deeply planted in the soils of Kibaaka land. Toxic doctrine is spreading across the land like ravaging storms. Kibaaka is fast becoming a fertile ground for testing the fruitfulness of the so-called emancipation of the woman.

YOUR HIGHNESS
If it is the madness she contracted from her travels to Beijing that has misled them, then, the man in the woman must be crushed! *(The Elders nod consent).*

ABILITY
Bongkisheri masterminded the plot to give land rights to the women and is behind their protest.

GHEEH
We allowed locusts to settle on our farmlands and now they are preying on our crops.

ABILITY

The threat has been there for long and we were blind to it. From ceding our land to a stranger *(stares at Wirkitum)* on mere allegations that he traced his roots to Kibaaka to admitting him in the Council of Elders and giving him the highest title in the land! From buying land in her name to public protests demanding for land rights for women, it is evident that a pattern is emerging from which we should expect the escalation of domestic rebellion if we sit quiet and watch Bongkisheri and the Come-no-Gos destroy our women and the youths.

YOUR HIGHNESS

What do we do now?

ABILITY

Our people say the ticks that eat the cow hide in which it sleeps must be boiled in hot water with the hide.

ELDERS

(Approving). Rengreng, Feyi, Jisi.

ABILITY

If Manka said they will not stop the protest until Nwerong grants land rights to women, I think the *Nwerong* way is the only language Bongkisheri and kitchen rebels can understand.

ELDERS

Réngréng!

ABILITY

We will reply rebellion with rebellion and protest with protest! *(The Elders nod vigorously).*

SHUFAI LAIKA

How can we fight women without provoking legal instruments that protect their rights? *Huh!* Women are becoming a road one needs to trek with care. There are better ways of expressing our dissatisfaction. Let us protest in court, not in the streets. Elders of our land, take note that our wife, Manka, did not only say Bongkisheri is ready to fight for women. She also said the lock on their lips is removed. She also said the rope with which the woman was chained to the kitchen is now untethered. What that means is that Government has given them rights.

ABILITY
When the storm refuses to abate, we need another storm to stop it.

ELDERS
Réngréng.

ABILITY
Bongkisheri is dangerous and toxic and must be banned…!

ELDERS
Réngréng.

WIRKITUM
Ebilidy, you can't insult and condemn a group that has done so much for your land. Bongkisheri NGO is teaching Kibaaka women the new ways; their activities are just about empowering the women.

ABILITY
(Cuts in). Honourable, respect your definition of new ways and empowerment but also respect how we understand the words! What do you mean by Bongkisheri is empowering women, and teaching them the new ways? Where is my wife? Didn't she walk out of my life through the influence of Manka whom the same Bongkisheri sent to Beijing to learn the new ways? Didn't Manka tell my wife that polygamy is unholy and a killer disease, the same strategy Fada Anton has used to turn our wives against us? Is it not the same Bongkisheri that has pushed the women and Come-no-Gos to ask for land ownership rights in Kibaaka? Huh! Is it not because of the so-called women's rights that Fola gained access to Regular and started celebrating her unparalleled bedroom skills in public? *(As the Elders convulse with laughter, Verdezekov stares at Fola with a frown while Fola drops his head).* Elders of our land, shall we wait until Fola has written a novel about the bedroom potentials of all our wives before we see the havoc the so-called empowerment and 'new ways' have caused in our homes?

ELDERS

Ngang! (Answer in the negative).

ABILITY

Bongkisheri NGO must be banned!

ELDERS

Réngréng.

VERDZEKOV

Elders of our land, the activities of Bongkisheri are affecting almost every home, I must say. Even before Fola ruined my marriage, what used to pour from Regular's mouth when we had a tiny misunderstanding was *(mimicking)* 'I don't depend on anybody, I can take care of myself; nobody tells me how to spend the money I make from my bar and *toghu* businesses. It is my money.' *(the Elders hang their mouths open).*

ABILITY

Verdzekov, is it not because you kept quiet for so long that she also eventually thought nobody should tell her how to spend her energies in bed? *(Shakes his head).* I thought I was the only man whose marriage Bongkisheri destroyed. Biiywong could not give me a male child and had even proposed to look for a young woman from her village for me. The story changed immediately she joined Bongkisheri and started questioning my movements: *(mimics)*: "Where are you going to? Where are you coming from? I am not ready to welcome another woman in my house."

GHEEH

Ngiri!

ABILITY

Yes! A tenant calling my home her home! She even told me the marital home belongs to husband and wife in equal proportions. When I told her that I am a man and can marry as many women as I want, she said Manka, Fada Anton, and Barrister Johnson have taught them that polygamy is unholy and also a cooking pot for diseases.

ELDERS
Ngiri! (Stare at Ability with eyes rolling and mouths wide).

ABILITY
She even poured hot water on the girl I wanted to marry. When I gave her a corrective slap, she screamed insults at me… *(the Elders scream in surprise)*, describing the corrective beating as gender violence.

VERDZEKOV
That word has become a weapon in the mouth of women.

ABILITY
She even took pictures of her broken nose and bloody face and gave to Manka and to Barrister Johnson who is always there to pour fuel on fire in all homes. Johnson immediately took the pictures to another wicked woman who works with the Social Welfare *(the Elders roll their eyes, mouths opened in surprise)*. That same week, I received a summons from the Social Welfare to come with my wife. I took the summons and tore it. The so-called Social Welfare is still behind me. Manka and the Social Welfare advised my wife to leave my house. My wife is no longer with me. The girl I wanted to marry does not want to see me again because she is afraid of my wife. When I was growing up, my mother would load a mountain of *fufu* and *njama-njama* in my father's dish, accompanying it with a calabash of palm wine or corn beer, as a way of apologising for the corrective slap my father landed on her face. Bongkisheri and strangers have changed our ways. A new name is now invented for a corrective slap. The common corrective slap our fathers used to calm down our wives with is now called domestic violence. Polygamy has suddenly become unholy, and a pot of diseases that should be cured with separation. Elders of our land, Bongkisheri and Come-no-Gos like Fada Anton and Johnson are accomplices. They teach things contrary to our ways. The group should be banned…

ELDERS
Rengreng! Dzebei! Ru'u! Feyi! (The Elders scream their support for the ban in various Lamnso native expressions of approval).

WIRKITUM
Hi folks, Bongkisheri and the same people you call Come-no-Gos have done a lot for you. They opened your blind eyes to see. *(The Elders shrug,*

open-mouthed, wide-eyed). I will explain. Bongkisheri provides skill training for women in *toghu* marking, for free. They sell their *toghu* through Reverend Entoni. They are also trained to produce domestic goods like soap and omo and sell them. Does that not lighten the kitchen loads on your shoulders? Is your domestic cost not reduced? Guys, since its inception, Bongkisheri has been organising Adult Education classes to teach your women and those who didn't go to school the English Language. With the help of Reverend Entoni, my wife and Mrs Ghamogha introduced Evening Classes for School dropouts. Binla attended only evening classes and passed the Advanced level examination with excellent grades. You are all aware of that. Bongkisheri has a scholarship project which you all know. At the moment, the group is sponsoring four Kibaakan young girls in technical education and one of them is the daughter of Pa Jacov *(Pa Jacov nods in approval).* As we speak, Bongkisheri has sent two girls abroad on scholarship through Reverend Entoni. Dzekewong, Medzefen, and many others have been attending Adult Education classes co-organised by Bongkisheri and Reverend Entoni. Your people now speak English and pidgin English. Your homegrown goods are sold in *Britn*. Guys, how many of the Elders sitting here would have been able to speak English language if you spoke only Kibaaka Lamnso language? Is it not thanks to the same people you call Come-no-Gos that many of you can now read and write? The Come-no-Gos taught you how to pray. We gave you education. We gave you a language. We opened your eyes, we tamed you. We sell your *toghu* abroad. We put you on the map of the world. What was once a land of thick shadows with unfriendly forests and less-known rugged pathways is now an emerging city on the map of the world with highways and train routes. You are better than we met you. Before I forget, I used my personal funds to create roads for the suffering people of Yerr-Bukang *(Ability opens his mouth and eyes wide).* Dudes, how can you insult the very strangers and the NGO that rescued Kibaaka from the fangs of darkness?

ABILITY

(Cuts in). Hold it there! *(Stares at Wirkitum briefly, shakes his head and yells).* What a powerful sermon, and again, well dressed in colonial religious wraps! Wirkitum, I have a question for you. Was there no language in Kibaaka before Bongkisheri and the Come-no-Gos came? *(The Elders opening their palms in questioning corroborating gestures).* How did we speak to the world if we had no language? Was there anything that did not have a name and needed strangers to come and give it one? Is it not said in books that we sang, danced, and told

fireside stories to pass ancestral wisdom to our young ones? Honourable, let me tell you that the same old wolf has returned in a sheep's clothing. There is no NGO involved; the invader from the other side of the river can no longer return directly. They now disguise as NGOs to create the same old havoc: break up homes, condemn polygamy but encourage 'man-marry-man' and 'woman-marry-woman' religion, teach men to enter the house through the backdoor, turn children against their parents and divide us in various ways. Let me tell you that your supposed NGO is the same old heavy log on the shoulders of Kibaaka. Honourable, don't you realize that the NGO beats the same drum as the initial invaders? Does the NGO not claim our culture is dangerously bad; that polygamy is unholy and a cooking pot for diseases; do they not break homes as Fada Goodluck did? *(Spreads out his left palm in a questioning gesture)* Can you deny that the Royal family is heading for the rocks? Where is my own wife? Has the NGO not intoxicated her against polygamy as their forebears did? Do I still have a family? Have you assessed how many broken homes Kibaaka now has? Do you know the number of climbers or human riders freely parading our streets? Is that the education and empowerment or new ways the NGO talks about? Elders of our land, let's be careful. The branches suck from the same trunk. The fact that the new actors now have the colour of our own skin should not blind you to their true agenda; judge them from the effects of their actions and not from their faces *(the Elders nod in agreement)*. By their deeds we shall know them *(Ability stares at Honourable for a while, then continues)*. Honourable, I laughed when you mentioned scholarship and free training. Do you think all the supposed assistance to that gathering of hens called Bongkisheri is free? Fada Anton collected a parcel of land from Medzefen in return for training his son as catechist, that is free training. My people, open your eyes. They suck on the breasts of our soils. They feed on the marrow of our land. They take away our best gold. They take away our timber. No ripe tree stays for one week in our forest without attracting the claws of raging machines. You can't even find a forest in Kibaaka, let alone a virgin forest. Where is River Mairin? Has it not become bony banks? Of course, it dried off with its umbilical cord, leaving only lengthened bony chests to mock us. Do we still find fish, crayfish, and tadpoles in our markets? Have our fishermen and fisherwomen not become jobless during the day and homeless during the night? Besides rendering our forests barren and our soils thirsty, their so-called Fada Anton Morgan, the one that Jacov is enslaved to, connives with his supposed Christians every year to destroy all palms in the village under the pretext of celebrating Palm Sunday.

They cut big and young branches from raffia trees to plant at all entrances and pathways to the Catholic Church. They use some to decorate the walls of the church on Sundays; Fada pours holy water on the ones they take home to drive away evil spirits. They take away our coffee and cocoa for free. If you ask my opinion, Bongkisheri is an enabler, a middleman in a juicy trade that our women know little about. That's the truth. In Bongkisheri, I see our past with the white man re-emerging to haunt us in a more dangerous manner. As we will all agree, these new but more dangerous enemies of our land require draconian measures. That is why I am still asking the right-thinking men of Kibaaka this question. Shall we fold our arms while this leopard in new clothing devours all that holds the clan together, or shall we like men and descendants of Kibaaka warriors break its neck before it lifts up its head?

(Hand claps intermingled with beating of drums tear across the hall in approval of Ability's speech).

WIRKITUM

Call me whatever name, my people brought development to Yerr-Bukang village. I created the new village. Yerr-Bukang was a land of trees with no demarcated boundaries. The land of trees and hills is now a village with a map, settlements, houses, boundary lines, roads, and pillars. I prepared allocation letters which the City Mayor and the Senior Divisional Officer signed. Many people now have parels of land in that village. I used my personal funds to create roads for the suffering people of Yerr-Bukang.

ABILITY

What do you take us for? Why are you only interested in helping where land is concerned? Do you want to tell me that you love Kibaaka people more than the people of the land you came from? Tell me. I hear that in your country, children carry guns to school. Is that not a problem that needs a solution? You suddenly realized that the people of Bukang needed roads and development when the State surrendered fertile land to them. *(Shakes his head).* Why did you choose to become chief only in the community where land was returned to the people?

ELDERS

(They throw their hands apart in questioning gestures). Orhooor.

ABILITY

Things are happening and nobody is talking. I am surprised to see Honourable Shufai Wirkitum stand before the Traditional Council and claim that he created Yerr-Bukang Village, prepared allocation letters, and also created roads for the suffering people of Yerr-Bukang. *(Stares briefly at Honourable, shakes his head, then continues).* Honourable, do I need to remind you that Kibaaka paid a heavy price for the so-called roads your caterpillars dug in Yerr-Kibang? Do I? In case you have forgotten, let me refresh your memory: A fertile portion of Government land called Yerr, was ceded to Bukang because Bukang is eaten up by hills that leave the people with no water and little land for farming and grazing activities. I am, however, still to know how you became the sub-chief of this newly created fertile village. You even signed allocation letters of the land stretching to Mboh whereas the neighbourhood does not fall within Yerr-Bukang traditional territory. Nobody knows how you became the traditional ruler, carving out huge chunks of land and giving it out to the very rich. I hear he gives out the land together with plans for the specific kind of house to be built in the allocated plot. As I speak, there is a mountain of sand and another mountain of gravel on the left entrance to Yerr-Bukang village. I hear Wirkitum gave the parcel of land to the Senior Divisional Officer for his cattle ranch. The City Mayor is raising pigs and fowls on another portion of the land. The poor are entirely excluded and Wirkitum calls it development. *(The Elders shake their heads).* Transforming the natural environment into cattle ranches, building sites, residential areas for cattle, building gigantic houses and roads seems to be the only form of development he knows. He perceives land only in terms of its marketability. If we do not flush out this Come-no-Go fast enough, he will sell all our land with its people. He is the one that determines the outlook of the new layout and that is not good for our fondom at all. A foreigner shaping our landscape and our future.

Verdzekov and Chicha Kisito recently bought parcels of land in Yerr-Bukang from Wirkitum *(Verdzekov and Kisito nod in acceptance).* I hear Wirkitum has allocated another portion of Yerr-Bukang land to Fada Anton to build a small church. If we are not careful, Wirkitum will soon sell all our ancestral lands to us and call it development. *(The Elders shake their heads while Wirkitum grimaces).*

Honourable Wirkitum, do you know what you destroyed when your caterpillars tore through ancestral lands, trying to create roads? Pillars planted a long time ago were destroyed. Pa Medzefen's ancestral land was destroyed. *(Medzefen shakes his head, twists his lips, and wipes tears gliding down his cheeks with the back of his hand).* You destroyed our trees. You cut down raffia and palm trees to create roads. For almost five harvest seasons, we have not seen a single palm kernel in our market. We do not have palm wine. We do not have palm oil. We used to sell palm oil and palm wine to people. Today, we buy palm oil and palm wine from distant villages, at exorbitant prices. Our only source of income is destroyed. Gheeh and Medzefen cannot send their children to study at the university. I hear Yuwai is pregnant. Is that the meaning of development?

GHEEH
Bongkisheri and Come-no-Gos are actually our problem.

ABILITY
Bongkisheri must go!

ELDERS
Réngréng!

WIRKITUM
Folks, how can you fight Bongkisheri without attracting legal instruments that protect the rights of women and the minority?

SHUFAI LAIKA
(Cuts in). That's my fear.

WIRKITUM
Have you thought about what Bongkisheri has done, and is still doing for your own people through Mrs Ghamogha? Who created the Community Forest? Who dug the well in that forest? Folks, listen very well. My grandmom told me that if you refuse to harvest the ripe pumpkin plant growing along the shoulder of the road because its seed came from the droppings of a flying bird, a stranger passing along the road will harvest the abandoned plant. His family will eat the precious meal, lick its fingers, and even wish their village had birds. *(Ability leans back).* Let the challenges bring out the best in you, and not the worst. *(Looks at his wristwatch).* Dudes, I have another meeting to attend. I should be on my way now *(Ability's body language reaction to the caution from Honourable including winking, opening, and closing his mouth draws others' attention).*

SHUFAI LAIKA

Honourable, we appreciate you for your contributions.

(Dzekewong carries Honourable's seat on his shoulders and tears across the hall, leading the way, Honourable following).

SHUFAI LAIKA

Sons of the soil, I don't think we should ignore everything that Honourable has said. We can sift his words, throw away the chaff, and make use of what is helpful. We should not pull down the building that provides shelter and a roof over many households. The family will be exposed to rain. What am I saying? We still need Bongkisheri and strangers. They have done a lot for us. Bad things happened. Good things also happened. It is true that Fada Anton and his Christians destroyed all the young raffia trees in the name of celebrating Palm Sunday. We cannot deny that we also contributed to the destruction of our land and they repaired what we destroyed. Every dry season, the men set fire on huge bushes and stood in rings, waiting for escaping animals. The women raised mounds in farmlands and burnt the soils to prepare their farms for planting. We tapped our raffia trees for palm wine until our raffia dried with the water that held its roots in the ground. We destroyed our land by burning bushes to track wild animals. We destroyed our farmlands through soil-burning. Our rivers dried up with their sources, leaving behind only bony stretching chests. Our soils became thirsty and barren. For almost three farming seasons, our maize refused to bear. Women and children trekked long distances in the valleys during the dry seasons, looking for water. It is Bongkisheri that saved our land from hunger and dryness. I can explain. When Manka returned from Beijing and started her campaign on: "Where there are trees, there is life", Bongkisheri women mobilised and created the community forest on the land we have suddenly learned that she bought in her name. They dug a borehole in the middle of the Community Forest. Our women and children no longer travel long distances to fetch clean water especially when public taps go dry as usual. *(The Elders nod).* They simply carry their calabashes and gallons to the Community Forest and fetch clean water from the well. During the dry season, builders fetch water from the same borehole. That is not all. Bongkisheri gave the people of Yerr-Bukang a large borehole and a community grinding mill. For a long time, the Council of Elders has not received any complaints from Alhadji Musa here seated about Bororo women and girls violated or even strangled to death on the walls of Yerr-Bukang Hill because the victim recognised the rapist.

Fathers of Fathers, when we wash a baby who has messed up its buttocks with shit, we do not throw away the baby with the bathwater. No! There are other ways to correct the wrongs of Bongkisheri and to also frustrate the women's protest. The women are still on the streets asking for land rights from *Nwerong*. They have said they will not return home until *Nwerong* signs a contract granting them their rights and demands. This is the only topic we should be addressing now. *(The Elders nod. Shufai Laika steps forward and bends before Your Highness. They discuss in hushed voices for a while and he returns to his seat).* Elders of our land, we will place an injunction on the disputed land and inform Bongkisheri that nobody will have access to the land for now *(The Elders nod).*

ABILITY

Some people are benefitting from the problem we have with Bongkisheri and the Come-no-Gos. Conflict is business. Elders of our land, you all heard the way Wirkitum defended Bongkisheri and the Come-no-Goss. He might go behind and stuff Nwerong's stomach to remove the bamboo and the injunction plant from the land. *(The Elders gasps, staring at Ability).*

GHEEH

(Tiptoes to the door, sticks forward his head across the door, peers in the left and right directions, and then returns to his seat). Ability, give thanks to your fathers because between those walls and the courtyard, Dzekewong is no longer around.

ABILITY

And what would happen if Dzekewong was around?

GHEEH

If it goes out, by the time you finish telling the story of Honourable bloating *Nwerong's* stomach to remove the injunction plants, you would be on exile. Nobody insults *Nwerong*!

ABILITY

Some people talk behind. I talk in public. *Gheeh*, where was *Nwerong* when I spent miserable years behind the bars? And who sent the Vigilante boys to destroy the water tank in Yerr-Bukang village? Who sent members of *Nwerong* to Yerr-Bukang? Who directed the Vigilante boys to incite and start the riot that obstructed the installation of a stranger as the Senior Divisional Officer of Kibaaka? Tell me! Who released the masquerades and followers of *Nwerong* to burn down the small palace and all its jujus on the grounds that two cows cannot drink from the same bowl? Tell me? When the villagers testified in court that the protesters and masquerades who obstructed the installation of the SDO, burnt the small palace and proceeded to Yerr-Bukang to destroy the water tank were just a handful of misguided youths led by Ability, why was Nwerong silent? Huh! I served a seven-month jail term, I lost my job. I am insulted in beer parlours as an ex-convict for a crime I was pushed to commit. Let it be known that prison life hardened me and I am not afraid of anybody!

SHUFAI LAIKA
Ability, broken hearts have been mended.

ABILITY
Our fathers say that the mended pot has scars. Bongkisheri must be banned!

SHUFAI LAIKA
Our people say that when kinsmen gather for a reconciliation ritual, we do not count the heads that were butchered during the war. *(The elders nod in consent).* Verdzekov, Ability, Gheeh, Chicha Kisito, Fola, join Your Highness and I in the inner chamber. *(They drift behind, discuss in muted voices and return to their seats).* Sons of the soil, we cannot ban Bongkisheri. They are a lawfully registered group. It should not be war. Let us go back and talk with the women. *(Turns to Dzekewong).* You and the vigilante boys should guard the contested farmland. Make sure nobody gets in or out of the land until *Nwerong* lifts the injunction plant. *(Dzekewong bows down his head).* Elders of our land, we went behind and hurriedly wrote a letter addressed to the women. *(Reads from a sheet of paper).*

From: The Office of the Council of Elders; Kibaaka.
To: Kibaaka Bongkisheri Women's Association
C/O. Mrs Ghamogha Manka.

Subject: Our Response to Your Request for Land Rights, Others
It has come to the notice of the Council of Elders that some Kibaaka women and others purported to be members of Kibaaka Bongkisheri Women's Association are demanding land rights and related entitlements through street

demonstrations.

The Council of Elders appeals to the good women of Kibaaka to accept peace and the offer of dialogue, and hereby announces the following measures aimed at addressing the women's grievances: a committee led by Shufai Laika has been set up to work with the women leaders and make suggestions for addressing Bongkisheri's grievances. The Committee will create the Women Wing of the Traditional Council, led by a woman, to oversee domestic-based activities. Part of the Royal farmland will be allocated (not sold) to Bongkisheri for their activities, under the custody of Kibaaka Royal Palace. An order reinforcing the ban on cross-dressing and same-sex relationship becomes effective from today. Another order proscribing the use and entry into the disputed land until further notice goes into effect today. A peace plant and two bamboos are thereby planted on the disputed site until it shall become necessary to lift the injunction. Any action or activity that violates the above injunctions shall attract appropriate punishment from the *Nwerong*. The women leaders are hereby invited to a meeting with a delegation of the Council of Elders led by Shufai Laika tomorrow at 10 am prompt in the Palace Hall.

Signed:

Shufai Laika, Kibaaka Traditional Prime Minister, on behalf of the Traditional Village Council. *(Native expressions and clapping of hands to signify applause are heard across the hall).*

SHUFAI LAIKA

Verdzekov and I will try to talk with the women's leaders. We will meet here again once we hear the gong. You may go home now. *(The Elders file out across the door).*

ACT 1

Scene V

AT THE BEER PARLOUR

(Enter Fola, Gheeh and Dzekewong)

(Pa Jacov is seated at a table in a bar wearing dark glasses and a fez cap pulled down to cover his forehead. He quickly lowers his half bottle of beer under the table as Fola, Gheeh, Ability, and Dzekewong approach. Fola releases a fart, twisting his torso and causing the others to roof their nostrils with their hands).

GHEEH
Fola, the moon has not died and you are inviting us again to the bar. *Ngomna* has not paid salaries. Where did you harvest this money that you are spending on drinks?

DZEKEWONG
Na de money weh dem gif Fola make yi take pay Vigilante Guards, ha ha ha ha ha!

ABILITY
What do you expect when you send a rat to guard a bag of groundnuts, ha ha ha ha ha!

FOLA
(Squeezes one thousand Francs CFA into Gheeh's hand, one thousand into Dzekewong's hand, and three thousand into Ability's hand. Like Gheeh and Verdzekov, Ability opens his palms slightly and peers into it, and smiles. The Elders should not know about this! (They nod). Let us join the man wearing face cap. I like the position of that table. It's right inside and nobody will know we are here. (Speaks to the stranger). Shift small, Sir. We want to share this table with you.
   (The stranger shifts his chair to the adjourning table).

FOLA

Praarrrh, pfeeh, pfeeh, mpuuuum… (Fola's stomach grumbles and rages as he farts, moving his buttocks. The stranger, Gheeh, Ability, and Dzekewong swiftly roof their nostrils with their hands, while Fola rushes to the toilet as if ants are biting him).

GHEEH

Something is wrong with Fola. He was not like this before. He even looks like a tiny grass growing on the top of a distant hill.

DZEKEWONG

Everywhere *Fola go, you go de hear ntuuuut, mpooot, mpaaah. ha ha ha ha ha. Fola don carry dat bad sick.*

FOLA

(Releases raging farts as he excretes). Ntuuuut, ntuuuuuut, pfseh, pfseh, mpuuuum…

ABILITY

That should be Chicha Kisito's car hooting outside. When a moving car starts snoring like an old man, whispering and grumbling at the same time like water flowing between rocks, and then changing gears on its own, my friends, it is a sign that the engine is weak and needs serious repairs. I had a car before, so I know what I am talking about.

GHEEH

(Sniffs the air repeatedly). That sound is coming from the toilet.

FRIENDS

Ha, ha, ha, ha, ha.

DZEKEWONG

Fola don condemn already.

ABILITY

You can say that again. I wonder whether his wife and Regular are aware that his manhood is now like a muddy trash can housing twerking ants and maggots.

GHEEH
Ability, you will never change! What do you mean?

ABILITY
Are you a stranger in Kibaaka? Haven't you heard that... *(The door of the toilet opens slowly diverting attention to Fola. He steps out and walks up to the table).* Fola, so it was you excreting and changing gears like a moving lorry! Ngiri!... *(They shiver with laughter).*
  (A slight sharp noise under Pa Jacov's table divert attention to Pa Jacov. He has accidentally knocked down the half drink hidden under his table).

FOLA
(Opens his mouth and eyes wide as he stares at Pa Jacov). Is that not Pa Jacov sitting over there!

GHEEH
(Opens his mouth). Man of God, I could not even recognise you, perhaps because you are wearing a fez cap and dark glasses.

DZEKEWONG
(Dzekewong wipes his eyes twice, shaking his head as he stares at the Catechist).

ABILITY
I have never seen him dressed like this before.

PA JACOV
May the peace of the Lord be with you...

DZEKEWONG
Amen!

PA JACOV
(Belches and releases a copious stench of alcohol which wafts across the room. Fola, Ability, Gheeh, and Dzekewong, look at each other and then away, as they sniff the smell of alcohol in the air).

ABILITY

Bar Girl, bring me two bottles of big Guinness…

DZEKEWONG

Bar Girl, bring me that drink that burns the tongue and the throat, like dat, de one I always take, *Kitoko*…

BAR GIRL

Sar, good palm wine dey, too. *You go laikam plenti ohhh.*

GHEEH

Bring five litters!

FOLA

Bar Girl, bring me Guinness.
(*A slim girl wearing a short blouse over a mini skirt comes over with drinks in a tray and begins to place them on the table. She rolls her eyes as she serves Fola and Ability*).

PA JACOV

(*Opens his eyes and mouth in gesture of surprise and protest, shaking his head as he stares at Fola*). Big Guinness! Kitoko!

GHEEH

Pa Jacov, was that not the smell of alcohol coming out from your mouth like that?

FRIENDS

Ohorrrr!

PA JACOV

(*Follows the Bar Girl to the counter, settles his bills and leaves*).

GHEEH

(*With a fixed stare at the Catechist walking off*). So, he drinks the same beer that will take us to hell fire as he preaches in church on Sundays!

ABILITY
Don't mind them.

DZEKEWONG
Beer is sweet only in his mop! Ha ha ha ha.

FOLA
(In a drunken voice, Fola confronts Ability). Ability, how can you take what I told you in secret to the public? Have you not been seeing Regular too?

ABILITY
Fola, I did what I did in your interest…

FOLA
How did you serve my interest by telling an old jealous man that I said his wife is a tigress in bed? Do you know my life is at risk because of your utterances?

ABILITY
Fola, have you not been borrowing drinks from Regular? By the way, exposing or taking your bravery to the public is psychological intimidation. Bravery and callousness scare away enemies and potential threats, take note! *(Fola smiles. The men begin to sing).*

> *(As the men sing and sway, Ability hurriedly grabs the jug Gheeh had just requested on its neck lifting it toward an opened mouth in an upside-down manner, slightly throwing his head behind. A rushing waterfall of palm wine plunges into his throat which he guzzles down until the last drop attracting protesting looks from Fola, Gheeh and Dzekewong. Fola releases a crackling fart and rushes to the toilet again. After a while, he returns to his seat, twisting his body).*

FOLA
I'm not feeling fine, at all. I can't sit here any longer. I need to see a Doctor. *(Tugs money from his pocket and gives to the Bar girl, squirming in pain).*

ABILITY
I will go with you, my man. *(Ability holds Fola by the hand as they walk through the door).*

ACT 2

Scene I

AT THE CLINIC

ABILITY
(Leans on the window from outside, trying to eavesdrop on the conversation between Fola and the Doctor).

DOCTOR
What is the problem?

FOLA
F-f-f-frequent runny stomach, and sharp pain under my navel.

DOCTOR
How many times do you pass out stool in a day and how is the stool like? *Emmmrr,* is it liquid?

FOLA
More than *(gasps)* six times. It is always watery.

DOCTOR
When did it start?

FOLA
Two days ago.

DOCTOR
Are you on medication?

FOLA
I have been taking herbs…, at times, it stops, later, it continues.

DOCTOR
Are you married?

FOLA
Yes.

DOCTOR
Have you done HIV test before?

FOLA
(His hands tremble). N-n-n- no.

DOCTOR
I will run the HIV test on you and your wife *(Fola shrugs).* HIV is just a disease like any other. If you are positive for HIV/AIDS, and you take your medications as prescribed, and follow the Doctor's instructions, you will live long even with the disease. I will collect your blood sample now to run the test. *(Ability props his head against the window).* You will also bring your wife later for the same test. *(Collects blood sample from Fola's arm and walks into the laboratory and returns later with the results).*

DOCTOR
Fola, remember what I told you. I have here your results sealed. *(Fola shivers and wipes sweat gliding down his cheeks. His chest is rising and falling. Meanwhile, Ability keeps ear-hugging the window. The Doctor hands the sealed envelope to Fola's trembling fingers).* Open it.

FOLA
(Opens the envelope, stares at the sheet of paper from the side of his eye and drops his head).

DOCTOR
Fola, the results shows that you are HIV positive… *(Ability opens his eyes and mouth wide and quickly shifts away from the window).* But this is not a death sentence, right? *(Fola nods).* Don't smoke. Don't drink alcohol. I can get the strong smell of alcohol from your mouth. Don't keep extra-marital relations. Eat well. Eat much vegetables and drink a lot of water. Take fruits as well. *(Fola nods).* I would like to examine you after one month. You will be

fine. *(Fola nods, twisting his buttocks. The Doctor scribbles something on the sheet of paper he hands to Fola).* These drugs are found in our pharmacy. Go and buy them. We have counselling resources for you. Tell the next person to come in. *(Fola walks out).*

ACT 2

Scene II

IN THE PALACE HALL

(Your Highness and the Elders are seated in the hall).

YOUR HIGHNESS
Shufai Laika, what is the message from the women?

SHUFAI LAIKA
Your Highness, Elders of our land, the women said they will only stop the protest when *Nwerong* has granted all their demands without preconditions *(the Elders hang their mouths open)*. Manka has become something else. She said the women will not attend any meeting with the Council of Elders until *Nwerong* writes officially to Bongkisheri stating that women can now buy land and get land titles issued in their names.
(There is a thick silence in the hall for almost a minute).

VERDZEKOV
This matter is getting out of our hands.

ABILITY
Isn't it obvious that the bird calls itself Head of House because the house owner allowed it to build its nest in his roof? We allowed locusts to settle in our land, and now they are preying on our crops.

YOUR HIGHNESS
(Shakes his head, clenches his fists and leans back on his seat). What do we do now?

ABILITY
Your Highness, *Nwerong* should levy land tax and also Settler's Tax on all the Come-no-Gos. If we do that, Bongkisheri will miss the support they are getting from the women.

YOUR HIGHNESS
Has anybody understood Ability?

ELDERS
Kah-Mbeeh (A native Lamnso expression for answering the Fon in the negative).

ABILITY
Your Highness, Elders of our land, what I am saying is, if *Nwerong* should impose Land Tax, Settlers' Tax on Come-no- Gos as it is done in other lands, and Business Tax on NGOs and businesses operating in Kibaaka, specifically those owned by strangers, and call it compensation to indigenous Kibaaka women and communities, the first effect will be to divide Bongkisheri. The Come-no-Gos will also be affected. True daughters of Kibaaka might see that they stand to gain. When that happens, the rest of the Bongkisheri and Come-no-Gos will be faced with two choices: either they stop asking for land ownership rights, or pack their bags and return to their land, and leave Kibaaka to sons of the soil because they will definitely not have the money to pay the heavy taxes.

ELDERS
(Various consensual expressions and reactions echo across the hall as Elders nod, clap hands and make dance steps).

YOUR HIGHNESS
Ability, you truly deserve a red feather. *(Ability smiles).*

ABILITY
Sons of the soil, I can assure you that the strategy of strangers' tax and the idea of giving the proceeds to indigenous women might sound convincing to a faction of the women, but the high tax would also scare away the non-indigenous Bongkisheri women from pursuing land rights. This strategy might divide the women; after all, our people say that women are many, but friends are few. As our ancestors used to say, woman is woman's enemy. If we divide Bongkisheri into two, that will be the beginning of the end of this toxic group and in the absence of that dangerous NGO, our women will listen to us. Your Highness, when that strategy works, your throne will no longer be threatened.

YOUR HIGHNESS
Elders of our land, we need to hasten the procedure for Ability to take his Red Feather *(Ability smiles as the Elders nod with the exception of Shufai Laika, Honourable and Alhaji Musa).*

WIRKITUM
Ability, listen very well. You don't have more rights in this marriage than I do.

SHUFAI LAIKA
Honourable is right. Ability, nobody wins a war against his own people. Nobody fights his in-laws. The people we call *Come-no-Gos* are not total strangers. That breed has our blood flowing in their veins. They are like grafted-skin plants. Their ancestral lands are known by all of us. The stumps of their ancestral trees and compounds are in Kibaaka. The fact that some of them were born in other lands does not mean that they do not have our blood flowing in their veins. They have our blood in their veins no matter how tiny it may be. That is why our fathers called them plaited ropes. Nobody has the right to deny them their origin. Some of the Come-no-Gos are our in-laws. They are marrying and having children with our daughters. Our children have their blood in their veins. Birth right has joined us together. Marriage is a cobweb of relations. Marriage has joined us together. Our Queen is part of us by marriage. Alhaji Musa is one. Honourable Wirkitum is a bridge in the Kibaaka bloodline and a fibre that links us to Motherland. He is a branch on the family tree. He has our blood in his veins. *(Wirkitum nods and smiles).* He belongs here. Which of you questioning the ancestry of Honourable will deny an opportunity to travel abroad? Tell me. Let us be careful how we treat others because we may face the same discrimination as we climb the ladder of life.

WIRKITUM
Thank you, dude.

ABILITY
Our fathers say, the he-goat should not insult his mother because he has double rights over her as son and husband. Shufai Laika, look at Honourable Wirkitum again and tell me if he looks like us. I have matted black hair. Matted black hair runs in my family. My skin is dark. Wirkitum has red-brown skin and a sharp pointed nose just like his brother, Savage. His hair is long and weak and looks like the hair of corn. He speaks through his throat. His brother's hair

is brown and looks like a bunch of bouncing bees hanging down from a tree. How can someone have our blood and yet look different. Shufai, are you sure you are not propagating the story of Wirkitum's roots to separate the Come-no-Go from his real origin?

WIRKITUM

Ebilidy, my father's people gave Kibaaka roads, electricity, and water. The first bridge in Kibaaka was built by them. The first railway in Kibaaka was built by them. We gave you a language. We gave you a school. I deserve some level of respect for that.

ABILITY

There, he goes again! Wirkitum, what the Come-no-Gos took from us is more than what they gave us. The families of Dzekewong, Medzefen, and Gheeh became jobless during the day and homeless during the night because their ancestral family lands with raffia and palm bushes were seized and transformed into railway lines and road lanes *(The expression on the faces of Medzefen and Gheeh saddens)*. And what was the outcome? Pillars, iron rods, and pipelines are today affectionately lodged in the warm embrace of our soils smuggling our petroleum into their land while the uprooted families and miserable hunters continue to lament and grumble under the weight of hunger, joblessness, poverty, and frustration. They drink bottled water which comes from their land and is sold very expensively. We cannot afford it. Our women and children trek long distances to get water from valleys because the borehole in the Community Forest cannot satisfy the entire land. During the dry season, our lips would get dry and crack. And this Come-no-Go called Wirkitum sits here talking about the things his father's people brought to Kibaaka! Perhaps your grandfather handed over to you the job of paying the long-promised compensation to the families whose lands were taken away. You only know what your father's people brought to Kibaaka but forget all they took away from Kibaaka. *(Insults) Nyamfuka*!

WIRKITUM

Ebilidy, prison life is not good. The only thing you do so well is projecting your frustration on others.

ABILITY

Wirkitum, Bongkisheri and all the Come-no-Gos must pay land tax to live in

Kibaaka, or pack their bags and leave our land…

ELDERS

Réngréng.

VERDZEKOV

(In a tone ladened with mockery). Ability, we cannot ask them to go back to their land. They may not still be recognised in their father's land. We know how they came here. Some of them traced their roots to Kibaaka when the white man made it clear to them that a butterfly cannot become a bird just because it flies in the sky. Some of them escaped from intertribal conflicts *(shoots a glance at Alhaji).* Where do you want them to go?

ABILITY

I don't care how they came here! We need to weed them out! Kibaaka should not be paying the price of rejection and instability in neighbouring tribes and other lands. Who does not know where war survivors run to? *(Turns to Wirkitum)* Does Kibaaka look like a refugee camp to disposable children? Does Kibaaka look like a dumping ground for half-bloods? *(The Elders throw their hands open).*

YOUR HIGHNESS

All the Come-no-Gos will pay land tax to live in Kibaaka!

ELDERS

(Some Elders applaud). Bvere'eh! *Réngréng! Nchangchang!*

ABILITY

Thank you, Your Highness. All title holders who are not full-blooded *Kibaakans* will also rent their titles or, hand them back to the throne.

ELDERS

Réngréng.

WIRKITUM

Ebilidy, I inherited what belonged to my great-grand parents, including his title. I don't owe anybody anything.

ABILITY

Mr borrowed feathers, the question you should be asking these Elders is how much for occupation tax, land tax, Title Tax, and tax for hiring out a title we should charge you and the other Come-no-Gos littering our land. *(Laughter erupts from Elders).*

SHUFAI LAIKA

Ability, stop it now! How many times will I tell you that the people you call Come-no-Gos are our bloodline and in-laws?

ABILITY

When a viper has hatched, eliminate it with all its hatchery, else they will grow up and bite. We are fighting a system with all its offshoots, strains, and outgrowths. I am sure our fathers thought the same, and told each other, "It's enough, they are our bloodline and in-laws". The result is that we got up only to find our streets invaded and occupied by the same people we call in-laws and bloodline, with even those among them to whom we gave noble roles like queen mother instigating their kind against us. Truly, when you give a lepper a handshake, he or she asks for an embrace the next time. No one says they are not our in-laws or bloodline, but marriage is not by force; now we want a divorce; is it a crime?

VERDZEKOV

That is the question!

ABILITY

Have we all agreed that this Come-no-Go and all titled *Come-no-Gos* will pay occupation tax and also taxes on their titles to avoid having the titles withdrawn?

ELDERS

(Some Elders echo across the hall). Réngréng.

WIRKITUM

You keep calling me Come-no-Go and your accomplices clap for you. Let me ask you a question, is 'Come-no-Go' a Lamnso word? My people captured you and tamed you and yet, you use the same language we gave you to insult me.

ABILITY
If your people truly captured us and tamed us, why did they not capture our language? Tell me. Why would you capture us and yet join us to speak our language?

WIRKITUM
You were in the majority. That is why the native Lamso language which your people spoke at the time survived. Read your history.

ABILITY
Were you not told in school that even history is invented? Are you sure the history you are reciting here is not a Come-no-Go version? Wirkitum, let me tell you what you don't even know. The so-called English language is spoken only in schools, offices, and in church. Visit any home in Kibaaka and tell me how many parents speak to their children in English. That thing ends only in books.

WIRKITUM
I am happy you acknowledge the fact that English Language survives in books while your native Lamnso is spoken only at home. That is victory. Now, tell me, who should pay tax to whom? *Mehn*, your children will soon join me to speak an imported language when yours dies. Besides, be reminded that the National Assembly has banned hate speech.

ABILITY
Wirkitum, this is Kibaaka! Get ready to pay your taxes beginning with Title Tax. If we do not impose these taxes on the strangers and Bongkisheri, Your Highness and tradition will pay the price.

ELDERS
Réngréng! (Honourable puckers his face).

ABILITY
(Stretches his hand forward staring fixedly into Honourable Wirkitum's eyes). Mr Come-no-Go, remove the beads around your neck, and the Red Feather on your head, and return the items to the Council of Elders until you settle your taxes and your asylum status is regulated.

ELDERS
(A few Elders nod their heads). Réngréng. (Wirkitum looks sad).

ABILITY
Wirkitum, are you by any means trying to tell us that nobody has ever insulted you in a bar as a *Come-no-Go*, or half-blood?

WIRKITUM
Mr Ex-convict, how many of your people have settled in other lands, and even own houses and properties there? How many are living, working, and investing in other places? Have you thought about the fact that other host communities can also ask your people to return to their lands? Do you think you have a monopoly on rights and decision-making? Have you heard that Kibaaka people pay taxes to live in other communities?

ABILITY
Wirkitum, have you heard of settlers in other places stirring up trouble and asking for rights as your kind does in Kibaaka? *(Some Elders throw open their hands).* You and your Come-no Gos are the reason why the criteria for attributing land and titles should be revised. *(Your Highness nods, an action that attracts a look of surprise from Honourable).*

SHUFAI LAIKA
Ability, this is not what brought us here! Apologise to Honourable Shufai Wirkitum now!

ABILITY
The greatest casualty of blood pollution takes place in *Kibaaka*. The only place where climbers, disposable people and Come-no-Go would join women to take their kitchen rebellion to the streets is Kibaaka. The only place where a Come-no-Go under the guise of an NGO would push Bororo women and the sexless likes of Savage, Katika, and Livinus into the streets to ask for land ownership rights and the right to become who they want to become, is Kibaaka. Women and strangers have taken advantage of our silence on their excesses to buy land and stage street demonstrations against our ways. I am asked to apologise for crimes Wirkitum and Come-no-Gos have committed against the land. *(Shakes his head).* It is only in Kibaaka that people are asked to apologize to their offenders.

WIRKITUM

I'm really surprised that surviving embarrassments in the life of this tragic hero *(points to Ability)* have not even taught him lessons the classroom denied him.

ABILITY

Wirkitum, do I look like someone who needs a lecture on ethics?

WIRKITUM

Ebilidy, this gathering is for men.

ABILITY

Are you a man? Has anyone ever heard the cry of a baby in your compound? *(Wirkitum bites his lower lip).* At least I have a son and a daughter.

WIRKITUM

You have a son and a daughter, but you are neither a father nor a husband.

ABILITY

What did you just say?

WIRKITUM

Let me remind you. Tragedy befell you in your career and marriage. It will appear it has also befallen your so-called daughter who sells her body to men in the streets of Buwala. *(Ability hangs open his mouth).* Am I the one who said the sins of the father shall visit their children and their children's children?

ABILITY

One more insult from you and you will not like my reaction!

WIRKITUM

Mr. Ex-convict, I need to know how you were raised.

ABILITY

Get ready for a lesson on how I was raised. *(Ability begins to fold the sleeves of his shirt, taking a step towards Wirkitum).*

WIRKITUM

Ebilidy, you know the price you paid when you incited and led a rebellion to obstruct the installation and official duties; you know the price you paid when you destroyed the water tank and burnt down the small palace; you know the price you paid when you impersonated your late friend's identity to collect his pension from the bank. You equally know the role I played in fishing you out of your filthy hiding. Dare do something stupid and you will pay a harder price!

ABILITY

Wirkitum, don't make it look like a comedy *(screws up his nose in anger)*.

WIRKITUM

Ex-convicts *(pointing to Ability)* never learn. *(Laughter erupt from lips)*.

ABILITY

Repeat what you just said if you are a man!

WIRKITUM

If you are not an all-time tragic figure, why are you not in service at your age? By the way, where is your wife?

ABILITY

This is the climax!

WIRKITUM

Of course, you are living the climax of your domestic tragedy.

ABILITY

You cannot reduce me to a subject of ridicule and get away with it.

WIRKITUM

You are no stranger to crime.

SHUFAI LAIKA

It's enough!

ABILITY

The grave is already dug. One of us must occupy it.
>   *(Ability suddenly leaps over and hurls his hand to hit Honourable on the chest but the elders intervene in time, forming a fence with their*

out-stretched hands between the disputants. Ability suddenly hurls a clenched fist over Ndzewiyi and punches Honourable hard. Honourable staggers to the floor. Ability tries to grab Honourable but is hemmed in on all sides by the Elders).

SHUFAI LAIKA
Ability, you started this thing. Have you forgotten where you are?

ABILITY
Wirkitum, you will not always have this fence around you. Come-no-Go!

WIRKITUM
(Stares at Ability, and then, at the elders, shakes his head). I've had enough. I'm no longer a member of this group. I can do without you. *(Turns and walks out through the door).*

SHUFAI LAIKA
(Watches Honourable as he storms out). Ability, do you realise the harm you have caused?

ABILITY
I have no regrets.

SHUFAI LAIKA
(Rages). Ability, shut up! Shut up! You can't always have it your own way! This is not the first time you start a fight during our gathering. You have a fine to pay for causing a fight in the Palace…. Ability, you will bring a twenty-litre calabash of palm wine during the next gathering *(Ability puckers his face).* Elders of our land, Ndzewiyi and I will go and tender an apology to Honourable Wirkitum on behalf of the Council of Elders….

VERDZEKOV
Apology! *(Hangs his mouth open)* Who should apologise to whom? *(Some Elders throw their hands open).*

YOUR HIGHNESS
Is it not because of Wirkitum's wife that the women are sitting in my backyard asking for land rights? *(Ability nods his head).*

SHUFAI LAIKA

This discussion cannot continue without Honourable Wirkitum. I know what I am talking about. It will be difficult to get the women to end the protest and come to the negotiation table without involving Barrister Johnson, and Honourable is her husband, and the only person she would likely listen to. If we chase Wirkitum away, he can instigate his wife to use the law against us. We have seen her works in the past. If she could get the likes of Savage, Katika, and Livinus released from jail, then, she can do anything. *(The Elders nod their heads in consent)*.

YOUR HIGHNESS

Shufai Laika is right. We need to bring him back.

SHUFAI LAIKA

(Beckons Gheeh and Verdzekov. They step up and he whispers in Your Highness's ear). Your Highness, Elders, Ability is a problem and not a solution as we may think. If we will ever get somewhere, we need to find a way to contain his excesses.

YOUR HIGHNESS

How can you say such a thing? We can't do without Ability. *(Gheeh and Verdzekov nod in approval)*.

SHUFAI LAIKA

Your Highness, Elders, I am a politician. I was once the Mayor of Kibaaka. A dog barks because there is no bone in its mouth. If we give Ability a post of responsibility in the Elders' Council, that may curb his excesses and limit his attacks on Honourable Wirkitum. Honourable will likely not agree to return and give us the collaboration we need to save the throne except there is a guarantee from us that Ability will stop attacking and humiliating him. Besides, we need to strengthen the Security unit. He studied Information Gathering. He is the right person for that position despite his outbursts. *(Your Highness and the Elders nod with curiosity. Shufai and the Elders return to their seat. Shufai coughs and takes a major decision)*.

Elders of our land, we need to put order in the Council of Elders before anything can work. If we must succeed to get the women to listen to us, we need to put order in the Vigilante group as well. Fola, from this moment, you are no longer the Coordinator and President of the Vigilante group *(Fola hangs his mouth open).* We all know why Fola is punished. Ability, you are henceforth in charge of coordination. *(Ability sticks up his head, and smiles).* You are also one of the advisers to the Fon. Your job includes advising and guiding the Fon on cultural matters, offering suggestions, buying materials like raincoats and rain boots, and paying the salaries of the vigilante boys. *(Ability smiles).* We also expect you to ensure that the ban on access to the disputed land is respected. From this moment, a Disciplinary Division is created in the Traditional Council headed by Ability. Meet the Vigilante boys this evening and talk with them. Assign three or four of them to keep guard at the premises of the land that Manka bought in her name. Nobody should be allowed to enter, or to use that land and its facilities until the Traditional Council has lifted the ban. Follow up and give us a report. Fola, return the 300,000frs we gave you last week to Ability. *(Fola shrugs, bites his lower lip).* Ability, I will transfer security funds to you immediately. *(Ability's appointment attracts applause across the hall).*

ABILITY
(Aside. This appointment gives me the legitimacy I needed to settle scores, to get what I want. To the Council). I am honoured to serve my fatherland.

SHUFAI LAIKA
Elders of our land, go home now. We will all gather here when we hear the sound of the gong *(The Elders nod and begin to walk out through the door).*

ACT 2

Scene III

AT THE PALACE

OUTSIDE THE PALACE

ABILITY
Fola, Dzekewong, Gheeh, you must support everything I say if you need free drinks. *(The Elders nod, smiling).*

FOLA
Consider it done! *(They laugh and walked into the inner chamber where the Fon is seated).*

YOUR HIGHNESS
(Hangs his mouth open), atarwong *(fathers of fathers)* …,

ELDERS
(Cup hands to their mouths and answer). Mbeeh.

YOUR HIGHNESS
Did you forget something? What brings you to my palace? Is there another meeting?

ABILITY
Your Highness, I have started my work *(The elders nod).* Our people say that a mountain does not crumble without leaving behind the stump of the fall. A hero does not crash without relics of the crash.

YOUR HIGHNESS
Go straight to the point.

ABILITY
I was surprised when Your Highness joined Shufai Laika to reject my proposal

to take new measures that can weaken Bongkisheri and save the throne. I am talking specifically about the Stranger Tax which I proposed. *(The Elders nod their heads).*

YOUR HIGHNESS

Ability, were you not at the same meeting when it was said that if we take Bongkisheri to Court, it is the Law of Government and not the Law of Nwerong that would decide the owner of the land my wife bought?

ABILITY

Your Highness, that's why we are here. We need to try another strategy.

YOUR HIGHNESS

Which is?

ABILITY

Divide and rule. *(Fola nods in approval).*

YOUR HIGHNESS

What do you mean?

ABILITY

Bongkisheri is planning to hold Elections soon. After that, they will be celebrating Women's International Day. Manka should not enjoy another term of office as the President of the women's group. We need a woman who will listen to us, a native of Kibaaka. We need someone we can easily manipulate to create a Kibaaka women's faction within Bongkisheri. *(The elders nod, Your Highness stretches out his neck and nods).* Even though Manka remains our wife for life, Kibaaka women will not hesitate to prefer a Kibaaka woman for the post of the President of Bongkisheri. *(The elders nod and Ability smiles).* Your Highness, Manka is very powerful, she's very influential. She's loved by all the women. If we remove her as leader, the strength of the group will be weakened.

ELDERS

Rengreng!

ABILITY

A born and bred Kibaaka woman fears Nwerong and would listen to us. Once

Manka finds herself abandoned by the very women who are supporting her and even clapping when she farts, she will have no choice than to accept to transfer ownership of the Land Title to you.

ELDERS

Rengreng!

YOUR HIGHNESS

(Nods repeatedly). Ability, Elders, that's a good suggestion, but… *(a long pause)*. Ability, these are the same women who boldly told Shufai Laika that they would not stop the protest until Nwerong grants land ownership rights to women. How do you then intend to tear them from 'Mother of children' when they see her as the shoulder on which they can lean?

ABILITY

Your Highness, our fathers say that a dog barks because it has no food in its mouth. What am I saying? Our wives and the Bororo Come-no-Gos live from hand to mouth. They will not hesitate to cooperate in voting for the candidate of our choice when pregnant envelopes exchange hands under the table. *(The elders nod)*. Money is power. Election is business. Money will decide the winner of the election. Manka will listen to you when she finds herself voted out of office and abandoned by her supporters.

YOUR HIGHNESS

Ability, Shufai Laika did not make a mistake to appoint you as one of my Advisers. Now, which of the women do you have in mind for the post of the President of Bongkisheri?

ABILITY

Dzekem is a native of Kibaaka. She will easily earn the support of daughters of the soil. Apart from that, she loves money more than a witch loves blood. *(Fola nods)*. What I need is 500,000frs…

YOUR HIGHNESS

Ngiri! (Drops his chin and stares at Ability open-mouthed).

ABILITY

Your Highness, do you still want the throne?

FOLA
That is the question!

ABILITY
Your Highness, you are just one finger away from losing the throne. Have you considered that? *(A long pause).* We need money to save the throne. Election campaigns need a lot of money. We are only doing this to spare you the humiliation of losing the throne. You can take a loan. I believe there is much money for security. *(The Elders nod in approval).*

YOUR HIGHNESS
(Muses for a while, withdraws and returns with an envelope which he stretches out to Ability). Ability, this is 200 000frs, take it. This is all I have for now. I will struggle to complete the rest. What we do here remains here. Am I understood?

ABILITY
Dzekewong, hold your lips together.

DZEKEWONG
(With the thumb and forefinger, Dzekewong holds his lips in a squashed).

ABILITY
Dzekewong, you heard the Fon!

YOUR HIGHNESS
(To Dzekewong). If it goes out, you will lose your job!

DZEKEWONG
Your Highness, I no de carry *sikiriti* waka share again.

ABILITY
Your Highness, we will be on our way now. *(They exit).*

YOUR HIGHNESS
(Muses). Will Dzekem accept to challenge Manka in the election? Will the women even accept to vote Manka out of office…? After all she has done for them! Can I really rely on this strategy to save my throne…! Well, our people say that a drowning man can clutch at straws or at a snake.

OUTSIDE THE PALACE

ABILITY
There is still one bridge to cross. We need to convince Shufai Laika to stop throwing his weight behind everything Honourable says *(The friends nod as they walk away).*

ACT 2

Scene IV

AT A ROAD JUNCTION

(Shufai Laika and Ndzewiyi meet Ability, Gheeh, Fola and Dzekewong).

ABILITY
Shufai Laika, we are on our way to your house.

SHUFAI LAIKA
Ability, is there another problem?

ABILITY
Mmmmm. Shufai Laika, you are the pillar of our Fondom and should join the Fon to support our tradition and customs.

SHUFAI LAIKA
That's just what I'm doing, or did I do anything wrong?

ABILITY
Shufai, why are you easily misled by Wirkitum who knows nothing about the ways of Kibaaka land? Were you not against the idea of imposing Taxes on land and on Titles conferred on the Come-no-Gos? It is done in the White Man's country.

SHUFAI LAIKA
Ha, ha, ha, ha. Ability, how many times will I tell you that Honourable Wirkitum is a branch on our family tree? He has our blood flowing in his veins no matter how tiny. By the way, I am a retired Civil Servant, and I know the laws of this country. The people who must pay whatever form of taxes are decided by Government, not Nwerong, not the Traditional Council.

GHEEH
Shufai Laika, before Government came to Kibaaka, we had our ways

(Dzekewong, Fola and Ability nod assent).

SHUFAI LAIKA
Things have changed. Government is bigger than Nwerong. Nwerong is just a room inside the house, and Government is the house. Only Government makes the laws. We cannot start collecting taxes from people we consider to be strangers. Kibaaka people are also living and investing in other lands. Should the host communities ask them to also pay strangers' tax? Let us not start another fight with Government and our neighbours. Remember the raging 90s. Remember what happened when we destroyed the water tank, burnt down the small palace, and obstructed the installation ceremony? Let us find a better way to make our wife understand that in Kibaaka tradition, land belongs to the man *(Ndzewiyi nods)*.

ABILITY
Nobody teaches me how to use my rights and authority.

SHUFAI LAIKA
Ability, why have you refused to learn from history? Why? I still remember the *Kibaaka* water incident. Kibaaka people ordered Snake to park their bags and leave and allow the management of *Kibaaka* Water to *Kibaaka* people. Ability, you led the demonstrations. You should not forget so soon what happened when you led the Vigilante boys to the catchment site in Yerr-Bukang, destroyed the water tank and pipes, and burnt down the homes of the people you suspected were collaborating with Government to identify your group. That's not all. You spent additional years behind the bars and what was the reason? After the water incident, you led the followers of Nwerong and the Vigilante boys to neighbouring Bukang village. You set fire on the Small Palace. You seized their masquerades and their Nwerong regalia, alleging that the people of Big Compound were strangers and had no right to build a palace within a paramount Fondom, no right to a Nwerong cult, and no right to farm on non-farming days you called Kibaaka 'country Sundays'. Ability, should I remind you again about the bloody fight that erupted and how we ran into bushes? We spent days, weeks, and months, hiding in bushes and in neighbouring villages. Water mixed with sand was sprayed on us. Women screamed from bushes in childbirth pains. We yawned and stretched in long queues in front of bakeries because people had escaped to bushes and businesses were shut down. Ability, do you want to go back to jail…? Ability, Fola, Gheeh,

Kewong, are we ready for another fight with Come-no-Gos that could attract the anger of Government?

ELDERS
(Lift and drop their shoulders in protest). Ngang!

ABILITY
I have even forgotten that the easiest way to fail before you start is to involve Shufai Laika in your plans. He behaves like a woman. Fola, Taa Gheeh, Kewong, let us leave this woman with balls between his legs, follow me. *(Ability and his friends walk away).*

(A Few Hours Later)

AT THE PALACE HALL

(Enter Shufai Laika and Ndzewiyi)

SHUFAI LAIKA
Your Highness *(the Fon nods)*, Honourable Wirkitum accepted our apologies. When we met him, he was hurrying to join the Governor, the Senior Divisional Officer, and the Mayor in a meeting with the women leader. They want to convince the leaders to call off the protest and accept dialogue with the Elders. That is what he said. *(Your Highness relaxes his tense facial appearance).* Your Highness, while Government is doing their part to end the protest, we should be strategizing because we are the solution to this problem and not Government. That is what the women think. The bedroom is the best dialogue table. Our people say that if you want to catch a fowl, throw grains of corn to the ground. Your Highness, we will be on our way now *(Shufai Laika and Ndzewiyi take their leave, Your Highness stares vacantly across the room).*

ACT 2

Scene V

BEHIND ABILITY'S COURTYARD

ABILITY

(Musing). I am now the Coordinator of the Vigilante group. Hahahaha! This appointment gives me the legitimacy I needed to get back what is mine, to make money from the protest. I have nothing. And who is the cause? Three of them. My father was given the Shufai title, just to tear his family from the Royal line of succession. I should have been the Fon of Kibaaka and not Ghamogha, if my father was not deceived with the Shufai title. That is not all. Far back in our High School days, I had plans of settling down with Manka, she was very intelligent. I should have been the one enjoying the money she makes from her *toghu* business and teaching career. But she rejected my marriage proposal, claiming that she could not handle my excesses, whatever that meant. She suddenly noticed my excesses just when the Crown Prince, Ghamogha, proposed marriage to her. As if that was not enough, I lost my job leading demonstrations on the directives of Nwerong and the Fon, who wanted to restore the management of Kibaaka administration, its Water Tank and water sources to the hands of Kibaaka people. Manka dragged my wife into her Bongkisheri NGO and told her that polygamy is a killer disease and cooking pot for diseases. She left me, she abandoned her own children. The same Manka sits back to enjoy her own marriage that is also polygamous. I bathe in cold water. Nobody calls me father. Nobody cooks for me. I do not have a job. These are the things that make a man a man. People who smoke maize tassels in the village greet me with a snap of their fingers and shake hands with me while some wave me down just to greet me - a thing they would not do with Wirkitum and Shufai Laika. The children of my age mates are graduates from the university, with good jobs. I hear my daughter is in the city and hawking her thing for money. His brother sits at home, hunting birds. I have lost dignity and authority. And who is responsible? Bongkisheri, Wirkitum, Manka, and the Palace. *(Shakes his head)*. By the time I am done destroying them one after another, we shall be on the same level, measure for measure. Let me see how Manka's marriage will continue to enjoy a prolongation while mine is broken. And when I am

done tearing Manka and the Fon apart and destroying Bongkisheri, Wirkitum is next. He called me a criminal, an ex-convict, and a failure right in front of my wife. Who insults a man in the presence of his wife? Who does that? Haven't I been sufficiently humiliated by Wirkitum whose wife planted Bongkisheri NGO that used Manka to tear my marriage apart? He even led Police to my compound to arrest me right in the presence of my wife and my children. When I returned from jail, lost my job, and went to beg him to employ me in one of his companies, he told me he had two vacancies for me. And what were they? Market Master; Chairperson of his Church Committee. I went to Wirkitum's house to watch the finals of the African Nations Cup eager to cheer Eto'o Fils, Song, and Mboma Patrick to victory, but he directed his 'Gate Man' to open the window for Fola and I to watch the march through the window. *(Shakes his head)*. As if that was not sufficient insult, that Come-no-Go reduced me to a beggar right before my wife again. And what was my crime? Dzekewong served me extra food and palm wine in his house during his birthday party and he shouted in anger, *(tries hard to remember as he mimics)* "Zekewong, you cannot transform my house into a Charity Organization. *Ebilidy*, when is your own turn to feed the people of this community in your own house?" Just because I asked his domestic servant for a takeaway meal and he filled my gourd with palm wine and also gave me fried chicken and loaves of fufu, I became the reason why charity organizations exist. He even ordered me to return the takeaway meal on mere allegations that I had gone to the table twice and had another wrap of food in my raffia bag *(Shakes his head with his lips twisted)*. After embarrassing and reducing me to a subject of ridicule right in the presence of women, it was the turn of my son, Ntumfon who sat eating quietly. *(Ability imitates what Honourable said about Ntumfon)*: "Young man, each time you struggle to tear meat from the bone, I see a thousand veins and furrows lying prostrate on your chest while some are fighting for space on your forehead. Hahahahaha! Are your parents still alive?" *(Shakes his head)*. I cannot wait for death to fight my battles when there are no indications that people like Your Highness, Manka and Honourable will die soon. No, I cannot wait for Nwerong and the Council of Elders to fight my battles when, at the mention of Government, Bongkisheri, Wirkitum, and Barrister Johnson, they tremble like chickens in the presence of a hovering hawk. I must get rid of the injury. And I will stop at nothing until I beat Satan's records. I will continue where the likes of Hitler, Covid-19, and locusts ended. *(Bites his lower lips with his upper teeth, smiling)*.

ACT 3

Scene I

IN THE SITTING ROOM OF THE PALACE

YOUR HIGHNESS
(Closes his eyes trying hard to remember). "Our people say that a mountain does not crumble without leaving behind the stump of the fall. A hero does not crash without relics of the crash." "Your Highness, think about the throne." *(A loud voice awakens Your Highness to the television screen where his wife is granting interview.* Mrs Ghamogha *is wearing a skirt of plantain leaves around her waist, with another strand covering her bra, made in a sheet and torn into pieces).*

JOURNALIST
…the interview with Mrs Ghamogha and Miss Binla continues after the update. *(Reads).* The President of the Republic of Kibaakaba signs a decree to put First Class Paramount Rulers on Civil Service Payroll. *(Your Highness sticks out his head, his mouth gaping).* With effect from today, all Paramount Rulers, or First-Class Chiefs, who have been granted Special Status in the House of Chiefs as auxiliaries of Government Administration, will receive a monthly salary of 200 000 frs CFA. They shall also be entitled to a service car… *(Your Highness opens his mouth and eyes wide as his face beams with a smile).* Bongkisheri Kibaaka Women's Association holds their Elections next week. Earlier this morning, the President of Bongkisheri Women's Cultural Association, Mrs Ghamogha, issued a communique suspending their land ownership rights' protest, promising to return to the streets if the traditional authorities do not lift the ban on women's rights to land ownership. *(Your Highness frowns).* We have come to the end of the news updates but do not go away. The interview with my special guest, the President of Bongkisheri women's group, Mrs Ghamogha Manka, and Binla, on the programme "Women and Development," continues. As a reminder, they are here to explain to the public why the women were protesting. *(Your Highness adjusts himself on his seat, his eyes glued to the television screen).* Welcome back on the show.

MANKA

Thank you so much *(Binla nods, smiling)*.

JOURNALIST

Mrs Ghamogha, you are the President of Bongkisheri Cultural and Development Association. What does Bongkisheri stand for?

MANKA

Thank you, *euuuh*. Bongkisheri means it is good to be happy. The word also conveys a happy, *euuuh* satisfactory, and joyful state of mind which could be an expression of what is good, for the general good. As a group, Bongkisheri is a socio-cultural association, or the women organ of the Kibaaka community all over the world. The group is governed by the law on socio-cultural liberty. This takes us to the inspiration for the group which is diverse: the Kibaaka woman needs a place in the community, she needs a place to express herself, her rights, and obligations not just from a Kibaaka ancestral cultural perspective. The group was also created to empower the woman and the girl child for social promotion; to promote cultural ancestral values from the Kibaaka ancestral cultural perspective; to promote cultural emancipation for the Kibaaka woman; to raise money for social promotion; to fight for the rights of the marginalised through empowerment and sensitisation programs; to promote development and emancipation of the woman; and to promote solidarity and social responsibility among the men and women. *Yeurrh*. The group seeks to work in collaboration with Kibaaka Traditional Council (the Kibaaka men's organ as well as the umbrella of all Kibaaka cultural groupings all over the world).

JOURNALIST

Interesting. You said Bongkisheri is working for the women and the girl child and you cited empowerment, social promotion, development, cultural emancipation, social obligation, and solidarity as some of the areas of interest. What makes you think they need these things?

MANKA

We didn't just decide for them. We visited villages, *euuh* the disadvantaged and women's groups across Kibaaka and talked to them and to the women and girls about their challenges and how they think we can help them.

JOURNALIST

Manka, you are dressed in skirts made of leaves and barks of plantain trunk, with camwood and wood ash smeared on your body. And you and Kibaaka women marched naked. What does nakedness and this attire signify?

MANKA

Mme Journalist, wood ash, Camwood, and the leaves around my body indicate deprivation. They are cultural symbols, and in this context, they are signs that we are protesting. They carry a message. Women are denied their basic human rights. We feel frustrated and marginalised as women and that feeling is suggested by our poor dressing. So, the Camwood, the wood ash, the leaves, and our nakedness indicate our frustration and marginalisation, *euuuh* the deprivation which Kibaaka women are experiencing because of certain traditional customs imposed on women and denying them the enjoyment of their full rights. Of course, if I came here dressed well, I would be giving the impression that all is well, but all is not well.

JOURNALIST

What specifically do women want?

MANKA

We want land ownership rights. We don't want to be victims and objects of pity. We don't want to be seen as guests in the house. We don't want to be seen as consumers and beggars anymore. We want to be producers. Madame Fonyuy, yesterday you were in town doing interviews with the women. I saw you taking pictures of our posters and banners. Our message is still the same *(recites)*. "The Lock on our Lips is removed. Give Back our Land Rights. This is the woman's turn. Power to the woman. Of course, we want equality and justice for all."

JOURNALIST

Who are you talking to?

MANKA

Government says the woman has the same rights as the man, including the rights to inheritance and land ownership. On the other hand, tradition says land belongs to the man. So, we have chosen to talk to the traditional authorities first.

JOURNALIST
Why did you take your protest to the backyard of the palace?

MANKA
The solution to our problem is the cause of our problem. The palace is the headquarters and the seat of traditional institutions that take decisions on the ancestral cultural values of the land. The Fon is the custodian of ancestral cultural values.

JOURNALIST
Interesting. Mrs Ghamogha, I can see the link now. Let me ask a related question. Kibaaka women have much respect for their ancestral traditional customs and values. Don't you think they may interpret your land right protest as a fight against tradition and decide to withdraw their support?

MANKA
Fonyuy, anyone who thinks we are fighting tradition is not reading our words the way s/he should. That's why I'm here to clarify misconceptions about the fight for women's rights. Bongkisheri is just asking for restraint and fairness in the practice of traditional customs especially when we consider that some penalize or punish the woman. The women are only asking for opportunities to explore and put their talents to good use in the interest of their families, their communities, and their nation. The woman can be a key partner in driving development forward if she has the right tools, the right platform, and the collaboration of society.

JOURNALIST
Mrs Ghamogha, it is rumoured that you bought land in your name. Are you not afraid of attracting punishment from Nwerong? Or don't you think your action could be seen as a violation of Kibaaka ancestral tradition that says land belongs to the man?

MANKA
Why is ancestral tradition still a problem to the woman even when Government has granted land ownership rights to women? Why is the human rights clock of Kibaaka still behind time, why? Mme Journalist, we still have disturbing reports and experiences of women denied their own share of family property or inheritance, including land; we have seen women forced to drink water that

was used to wash the corpses of their husbands just to prove their innocence relating to the death of their husband; we still find in-laws storming into the compounds of their late brother and seizing everything, including the house, land, the bed and mattress, television set, properties, and bank documents, leaving the widow and children in miserable conditions. It happened to my cousin. Almost daily, we have alarming reports of young girls brutally butchered down there with infected razor blades in the name of circumcision, leaving them leaking like a leaking roof; we have reports of women beaten, left with broken nostrils, and with wounds all over the walls of their bodies by their husbands. In Kibaaka, the woman and the girl child are not allowed to share in family inheritance. Why is it a taboo for a girl or woman to inherit what belongs to her father? Why? Some of them are often the most useful members of their families. The woman always remembers to send palm oil, bags of rice, fish, groundnut oil, drugs, money, and other essential items to her parents during festive seasons. She provides for their upkeep. Always, yet, it is a taboo for her to share in the family inheritance. In Kibaaka, land belongs to the man. It hurts. It hurts. Bongkisheri is dealing with these problems and more almost daily. The ancestral customs of Kibaaka do not favour the woman, especially when it comes to inheritance and land ownership rights. Mme Journalist, what the women are going through is simply a replay of collective thinking which we believe can be changed or given some degree of restraint or moderation, if our cultural institutions are involved in the fight to curb the excesses of ancestral traditions. *(Fonyuy nods, smiling).* We simply want change, the kind of change that needs to start from within because that's where it emanated. We believe that if the excesses of ancestral traditions are addressed from within, or by our traditional authorities, the solution would be better accepted, sustainable, and also workable.

JOURNALIST

You are absolutely right. I hope the custodians of ancestral traditions are listening to the President of Bongkisheri and will act on that. Manka, it is rumoured that Bongkisheri women are trying to compete with the men. Some people say you are trying to take up male roles. How do you respond to that?

MANKA

Mme Journalist, the woman should be relevant and not just an appendage. The woman needs her own purse. We want to be useful, and to be relevant and not only to be used. We need self-building opportunities without fences.

Complementing each other is the right word here. We want to take up leadership positions that suit our talents, not subordinate roles, not sympathy and not compensatory positions as has always been when it comes to political decisions and appointments. Competence, skills, and potential should define the woman and not her sex.

JOURNALIST
(Smiling). When I listen to you, what I seem to get is that the men of Kibaaka are greedy and want women to occupy back seats while they sit in front. What is Government doing to achieve gender equality?

MANKA
Mme Journalist, Government needs to do more. Why are women still absent where major decisions affecting their lives are made? Has any woman ever been the President of Kibaaka Development Association? How many women are in key positions in Kibaakaba? The last time I checked, the woman has been Vice President, Minutes Secretary, Social Welfare Officer, Publicity Secretary, Principal, Minister of Culture, Education, or Women's Affairs. Educating a girl child or giving a woman a top post of responsibility at any level on the social ladder shouldn't be seen as a favour or compensation. Give her the post that suits her talents. The woman should be a key partner in development. Let us be reminded that the person who founded Kibaaka was a woman.

JOURNALIST
What if Nwerong refuses to grant land ownership rights to Kibaaka women?

BINLA
We will resume the protest.

MANKA
(Nods her head). Mme Journalist, we have done and are still doing a lot of sensitisation and education about equal rights to land ownership. Everybody needs to play a role, including the media, in educating the traditional public that gender equality is just about giving equal access and equal opportunities to both the boy and the girl child to discover their talents and explore them in meaningful ways.

JOURNALIST
What is Bongkisheri doing differently from what the Traditional Council is doing?

MANKA
The main objective of Bongkisheri is to help women to discover their talents and to build skills in women through empowerment projects. We have trained women to mark *toghu* and other African wears, which we sell abroad through Fada Anton. The women have also offered a Community Forest with a giant borehole to the people of Lower Kibaaka.

JOURNALIST
Interesting.

MANKA
That's not all. We have equipped many women with sewing machines. Part of the funds Bongkisheri makes from the sale of toghu are used in training talented orphan girls in technical education abroad with the help of Fada Anton who looks for the scholarship opportunities. This is just one example. We want the women to stop depending. And we are doing a lot when it comes to empowering women with skills. I will offer you some of our magazines so that you can see what we are doing. I can cite more examples. Try to compare the situation of Bukang-Yerh women, including their village, before and now. The Presence of Bongkisheri is felt across Kibaaka, specifically in the mountainous village of Yerr-Bukang, thanks to the land that is hosting the projects of Bongkisheri and also the Community Forest. Before a motorbike conveying you to Bukang-Yerh village approaches the main entrance to the market, you are welcomed by a thick strangling smell of rotten crumbs of food wafting from the mountain of garbage heap. You were greeted by flies taking off and landing on tiny mountains of excreta littering the shoulders of the road especially around taverns. Many of the squatting houses you find on the shoulders and walls of Bukang hills do not have toilets. The situation is gradually improving, thanks to Bongkisheri. Before the Council built toilets in Bukang-Yerh Market, Bongkisheri had been distributing toilet bags to the Bororo community and the herd boys. We also offered them a Corn Grinding mill. Mme Journalist, many of the wives of Fulani men and their herd boys are now registered in Bongkisheri, benefitting a lot from the group. Abiba now has a sewing machine bought for her by the women's group. She marks and sells

toghu in the local markets. She sponsors her children in school. Some of them can now communicate confidently in English after attending Adult Evening Classes for about two years. Bongkisheri has also constructed a borehole in the Bororo Herdsmen settlement where houses that look from a distance like coffins are scattered across the chest of the hills. We no longer hear people dying of cholera as before. We are able to do some of these things because we have land to host the hall where we train women. We produce stuff like toghu, beads, bags, and *omo*, and sell. Women do not spend money buying school bags for their children any longer, they stitch the bags themselves, they weave shoes from raffia fibre thanks to the training they receive from Bongkisheri. We also teach women poultry farming and piggery. We raise pigs and fowls for sale and use the money in the interest of the group and our communities. We create the Community Forest. We pay the young man and his wife who take care of our pigs and fowls. We provide free training to women in food processing, bakery and cookery. So, Mme Journalist, how can anyone qualify these philanthropic and self-building activities as a fight to become a man or a violation of tradition? Women are better today than they were yesterday.

JOURNALIST

You just mentioned the Community Forest, the distribution of grinding mills and boreholes among the projects that Bongkisheri has done for the people of Lower and Upper Kibaaka. What's your source of funding, and where is your inspiration coming from?

MANKA

During one of our conferences in Beijing, we, the participants, were asked to organise ourselves into collaborative networks, NGOs, and cooperatives to lobby for development when we return to our respective countries. There was also a striking presentation on the role of women in climate change and one of its recommendations was: "One woman, one tree." Remember that this conference on "Women and Climate Change took place at the time Kibaakaba was facing prolonged dryness, heat, hunger, and disease. The soils were dry and hard. Rivers dried up everywhere. Crops did not do well. Even when the rainy season came, there was little rain. Women and children trekked long distances in valleys, looking for water to carry. When I returned from Beijing, I discussed the recommendations with Bongkisheri women and we started the project, "Water is life," and also encouraged men and women to plant trees…

JOURNALIST
(Cuts in). I hosted you on my TV Talk to discuss that project…

MANKA
Exactly. We got financial support from the Ministry of Forestry, and from Forum for African Women Scientists and launched the project: "One Woman, One Tree; Where there are trees, there is life; Water is life" *(Smiles)*. The funds helped us to hire experts, buy young trees, and paid our workers. That is how we were able to create the Community Forest and the giant borehole in that forest. We offered the forest to the people of Kibaaka and I am happy we were able to solve one problem. We no longer see herdsmen, Bororo women, and girls winding their way through slim passages between hanging boulders on Yerr-Bukang Hill, looking for water to carry. Our women no longer trek to the valleys, looking for wet surfaces to dig and scoop out water. We do not see Yerr-Bukang women sweating under heavy pots of water or bags of corn to grind in Kibaaka town like before.

JOURNALIST
Your last word.

MANKA
Women are like actors on stage, acting the script written by men. The rights of women are still in chains regarding land ownership and we are appealing to Nwerong to lift the ban on that right. I appeal to the traditional authorities to exercise moderation in the practice of ancestral traditional customs that are harmful and tend to limit the rights and ambitions of women and the girl child. We are builders, not fighters.

JOURNALIST
Thank you, President of Bongkisheri and Miss Binla, for accepting our invitation to come and clarify why the women are protesting. On the anchor, I am Fonyuy Leinyuy, on the programme "Women and Development," broadcasting live from Kibaakaba National Television station.

IN THE FON'S SITTING ROOM

YOUR HIGHNESS
Manka is bent on having her name on the land title…! How can I remain the

man and the Fon when my wife is in control? That land is my manhood. If I lose the land battle to my wife, I lose the throne. Power and authority will abandon me. I will miss the monthly salary, and the service car… No, no. I will die fighting. *(Gets up, walks back and forth, across the yard and returns to his seat).*

ACT 3

Scene II

IN THE FON'S PRIVATE ROOM

(Your Highness is sitting on his high back stool. Manka walks in dressed in plantain leaves wrapped around her chest and her waist. She has a cool, drained look. She bends her knees forward in a gesture of greetings).

MANKA
Greetings, owner of my household…

YOUR HIGHNESS
(With his mouth pouted and face twisted in a scowl, he silently slides a chair over and points to it, staring away. Manka steps forward and perches on the chair. With a disarming voice, he confronts her). Manka, where are you coming from? And who is the owner of your household? … One more time. Are you my wife or my husband?

MANKA
Father of my children, at home I am your wife…

YOUR HIGHNESS
(Interrupts). And outside of home, you are….? *(Manka remains silent).* Manka, am I still a man and a husband? Where on earth have you seen a husband getting out of bed while the supposed wife is coming back from the streets? Manka, when did this supposed husband last perform his duties as a husband? Between the two of us, who married who? Who paid whose bride price? Tell me! Who owns who? Just look at you. What's the difference between you and a stripper? You call yourself a wife, and yet, you went marching in the streets bare body, exposing what is mine to public eyes? Is this what I bargained for? This is not the woman I married! How am I even sure if the delay in giving me children was not a decision! Manka, where is my dignity when palm wine tappers and bird hunters have seen what is mine? Tell me. Did you have to carry bedroom battles to the streets? Which woman with integrity does that?

Huh! Manka, why did you lead women to march naked in the streets?

MANKA
Father of my children, the women deserve to know their rights.

YOUR HIGHNESS
By taking off their dresses? Does refusing to grant you rights also imply denying you the right to dress properly?

MANKA
We are only asking for land ownership rights.

YOUR HIGHNESS
(Rages). On which land do the women intend to get these ownership rights? I ask because, myself, you and the gods know that it is not and can never be in Kibaaka! Manka, you are the one who jumps out of this palace every Sunday, saying *(mimics),*" *I* am going to church. I am a member of the Catholic Women's Association". Please, ask Fada Anton Morgan who, between Adam and Eve owned Eden. Even in that religion of yours, were you not taught that God made man master of all his creation? That God made man master of woman, not woman master of man? Do not forget that it was disobedience brought by debased womanhood that debased mankind in God's sight… Is that what you want to repeat? Why are women turning the world upside down? Now, listen very well. The Elders have been informed that you bought land in your name…! As usual, I will always be the one to clean up your mess. Afterall, as head of the family, I must protect my own. I will offer you the one narrow escape route from the wrath of our tradition. You must sign a new document to transfer ownership of that land to me, immediately.

MANKA
Father of my children, we agreed to call off the protest on the understanding that the Fon and the Elders are ready to sit down and talk with the women.

YOUR HIGHNESS
Land belongs to the man. It is not me speaking. I did not create tradition.

MANKA
The same tradition is the reason I cannot transfer ownership of my land to

my polygamous husband.

YOUR HIGHNESS
Do you want to become a man?

MANKA
Owner of my household, your biggest threat is your stubborn pride.

YOUR HIGHNESS
Ngiri!

MANKA
There is a problem that you and I need to solve before things get out of hand. When I agreed to get married to you, it was on the grounds that we would go in for monogamy.

YOUR HIGHNESS
And that is what we signed…

MANKA
(Cuts in). But not what you are practising.

YOUR HIGHNESS
Have I married another wife since I got married to you?

MANKA
You are the Fon of Kibaaka, and by our culture and tradition, a polygamist. Father of my children, the moment you became the Fon, you automatically became a polygamist. I have to share you with other women because the Fon belongs to all his wives and to all his children, including everything he has.

YOUR HIGHNESS
I didn't choose to be the Fon of Kibaaka. My late father chose me to succeed him. When tradition decides, we must obey. Nobody quarrels with tradition.

MANKA
Tradition didn't just impose a choice on you. It imposed problems that come with polygamy. And that is why we are where we are today. That is why I had

to buy land in my name to separate what is mine from what belongs to everybody, following traditional polygamous customs.

YOUR HIGHNESS
(Interrupts) You married me and my problems.

MANKA
That was when you were the prince. Remember I married the prince and not the Fon.

YOUR HIGHNESS
I married Manka and not an anti-tradition activist.

MANKA
I am tired of hearing people calling me a guest in the house. We need a society where nobody will call another guest in the house, stranger, Come-no-Go. I don't want my children to be treated the same way.

YOUR HIGHNESS
Since you went to Beijing and came back, you do every other thing well except the reason for which you became a wife. Manka, are you giving me the land or not?

MANKA
Your Highness, convince the Elders to exercise restraint with ancestral traditions that impose choices on people and deny women the right to land ownership and my land will be yours.

YOUR HIGHNESS
(Holds and presses his lips tightly together, clenches his fists, before letting go, and then speaks in a hushed voice). What you just said can fetch you a curse! You will not like the reaction of the Elders and Nwerong if that thing you just vomited from your mouth enters their ears! What has come over you? You bought land in your name! As if you had not wreaked enough havoc in my palace, you led women in a bare-body protest to fight the ways of Kibaaka land. I have not even started solving the problems you created, and now, you want to light a new fire on my rooftop. Do you think you are safe after buying land in your name? Let me remind you again. Nwerong will take away my throne and all

its entitlements if you remain the owner of that land. Is that what you want?

MANKA

Father of my children, have you for once thought about the birth-right entitlements my children will be robbed of in this imposed polygamous union if I were to cede ownership of my land to you because tradition says land belongs to the man?

YOUR HIGHNESS

Ngiri! Manka, who pays the damage if you keep that land in your name? Do you know someone has got to pay for this and that person cannot be me? *Huh?* How many times will I tell you that land belongs to the man?

MANKA

Father of my children, if land belongs to the man as you insist, what happens when a polygamist like you becomes the owner? The answer is simple. What belongs to the man belongs to all his children. What that means is that the land I bought for my children will become family property to be shared to all your children because you have other wives and children including the ones you inherited from your father, the late Paramount Fon of Kibaaka. That's what I am trying to make us understand. Father of my children, that land belongs to me, you, and our children, but it cannot bear your name for obvious reasons.

YOUR HIGHNESS

(Thunders). This is *Kibaaka!* Nobody sings out of tune.

MANKA

Government has signed a Decree granting both inheritance and land ownership rights to women.

YOUR HIGHNESS

A caterpillar can never become a bird simply because it transformed into a butterfly and started flying in the sky. You will have to do a new Land Title in my name! *(Lifts his finger to the wife's face).* Let me warn you, I don't want Nwerong to be the one asking you to transfer ownership of that land to me because you will not like their method.

MANKA
Father of my children, we need change.

YOUR HIGHNESS
What do you want to change? Your bare chin or your full chest?

MANKA
Look at my potential and not my sex.

YOUR HIGHNESS
Human potential can never go beyond that of the sex to which he or she belongs. You are a woman. You have crossed the boundary. We do not drag a rope with Nwerong.

MANKA
Father of my household, how credible is Nwerong when all its members are men? *(Your Highness shrugs)*. Is it not the voice of Nwerong that continues to say that land belongs to the man even when Government has granted property rights to the woman? Why was tradition made by men and for men? Why was the woman's opinion not consulted? Father of my household, let's join hands and build Kibaaka.

YOUR HIGHNESS
Live in what has been built before! I have spoken to you as a husband can speak to a wife. Next time I will speak to you as the institution that I am.

MANKA
Your Highness, is it hard to understand that you are a polygamous husband with many children from different wombs who are all entitled to inherit what belongs to their father? Will they not argue that what carries their father's name belongs to them? I am only trying to prevent future problems, problems that often arise from inheritance....

YOUR HIGHNESS
Then, transfer ownership of that land to Bame, or Fomu.

MANKA
Father of my children, it is not just about the entitlement mentality of

polygamous homes. I have three children and not just two. Kila is a girl. Bame and Fomu are boys, and they will grow up and get married one day. What is the guarantee that Kila will get her own share of the land when we are no more alive? What is the guarantee that Kila will not hear such declarations as: "You are a girl, you are not entitled to inherit what belongs to your father"?

YOUR HIGHNESS

Do you want to transfer this problem to my daughter's home as well? What will Kila want to do with land? You think this madness of yours is genetic or hereditary? Orrh! You want to give land to Kila so that she will carry it to another family when she gets married? Hurh! You want Kila and her husband to continue this squabble between us over land? Manka, why are you so bent on castrating the men in my land? Let me warn you that if you don't do what is right regarding that land, you will not like the outcome of the rope you are dragging with tradition! *(A long pause)*. Manka, we need to know the name of the person who sold that land to you. I doubt if Lukong or the land dealer sold that land to you, who did it…? You have to tell me now… *(Manka is quiet)*. Manka, you mysteriously acquired land belonging to either Lukong or the land dealer and up till now nobody knows how that happened in a place like Kibaaka. And you seem to see nothing wrong with that…? In any case, before you are dragged before Nwerong to explain how you acquired the land, I want us to go to the Department of Land Tenure tomorrow and do a certificate of transfer of land ownership!

MANKA

Why is tradition still a problem to women even when Government has granted women the right to own land?

YOUR HIGHNESS

We do not question tradition. Nobody has the option to obey or not obey tradition. It is not Bongkisheri or whoever that decides who inherits land; it is tradition.

MANKA

Your Highness, listen to the cry of the woman.

YOUR HIGHNESS

My word is law.

MANKA
A woman needs her own purse.

YOUR HIGHNESS
I do not rule Kibaaka on the weight of sentiments. And I don't want to remind you again that you are unroofing your own house to build Bongkisheri.

MANKA
You are equally part of the house I want to build. Your Highness, have you noticed that almost all Kibaaka women attending Adult Education classes, including your mother, speak English now? The last time I went to give food to Mama, I was amazed at how she was bargaining upward the price of a bag of beans with her customers from the city. I know you will always argue, but that is just one of the ways Bongkisheri and I are using the land we are talking about to build the house that belongs to all of us. Even if you cannot appreciate the work Bongkisheri is using the land to do, at least give thanks to the group for teaching Mama how to speak English.

YOUR HIGHNESS
Why are your justifications for your crimes against the ways of our land always around the English language? And why do you and Honourable seem to agree on every point? Huh? Can language help me recover what I am about to lose? Manka, was there no language in *Kibaaka* before the arrival of Bongkisheri? Was the language we spoke at the time insufficient to address our needs? Was there anything that did not have a name and needed Bongkisheri to come and give it one? Tell me. Before we heard about English, how did our people speak to the world? What makes you think that *Kibaaka* people needed another language? Why is it difficult for you to notice the price we are paying for embracing Bongkisheri? Thank you for bringing up the issue of Bongkisheri. I learned the women were seen together with Savage, Livinus, and Katika. Is it not because of this same group that human riders are asking for their own rights? Do you know why Nwerong banned them from our land? Do you know it is the court's ruling that brought them back from the city to Kibaaka? Let me remind you. Government does not even want the strange humans in our land. What the Court said was that Nwerong did not follow due process in sending them on exile. And one of the reasons the Elders are planning to drag you before Nwerong is that you are leading a group that has ties with human riders.

MANKA

Your Highness, I knew Jessy before he became Savage; I knew him before he became a woman; and I knew Katika and Livinus before they became human riders. Savage had a flat chest area when I knew him, but that is not even the issue for now. If Bongkisheri does not go closer to them, how can we change them, their behaviour, choices, preferences, and their actions? I work with them only to change them, and we are succeeding. Except for Livinus, Savage, and Jessica who have recently undergone surgery to increase the size of their buttocks and breasts, and still wear earrings and short skirts, all their new converts have left the group, thanks to our counselling. Henry does not dress like a girl any longer, he does not wear earrings, he does not plait his hair and doesn't hang handbags on his shoulder anymore. He is now taking lessons on sewing and toghu marking at the Bongkisheri Centre. He recently got married and he and his wife are the ones we have employed to stay in our premises and take care of Bongkisheri pigs and fowls.

YOUR HIGHNESS

(Closes his eyes, trying to remember what Shufai Laika advised earlier). "Your Highness, our people say if you want to catch a fowl, throw grains of corn on the ground." *(Opens his eyes and steps down to the floor).* Mother of my children… *(holds her fingers and squeezes them gently with a vague smile on his lips. He then bends her head over to his shoulders)* … my own gift from the gods…, that land is my manhood. I will lose the throne if the land remains in your name. Honey…, say something nice, something that can make me feel like a man again.

MANKA

(Wipes tears gliding down her cheeks as she muses). I love my husband…. But…, if I give him the land, it becomes family property. That's not all. I would remove food from the mouths of many whose livelihood depends on Bongkisheri and the land hosting our activities and projects. I am what I am because of that land. *(Speaks).* My children will be dispossessed of their land. Let's reason together…

YOUR HIGHNESS

So, it is true you want to put on a thinking cap. Did you come to my house to reason with me? You are not here to reason, woman! I didn't pay all that huge bride price on your head for you to come here and reason for me! I do all the reasoning for you and every other person in this house! No more of that rubbish in my palace! *(Storms out of the sitting room murmuring to himself)*. She really wants to share the leadership role with me in this palace.

(An Hour Later)

SHUFAI LAIKA AND MANKA

SHUFAI LAIKA

Mother of children, have you spent the day well?

MANKA

(Bends forward and cups hands to her mouth). Have they come?

SHUFAI LAIKA

Our wife, thank you for listening to our plea to stop the protest and embrace dialogue and peace. Our people say that we do not wash our dirty linen in public. I brought a message from the Council of Elders. Give that land to your husband, His Royal Highness. Land belongs to the man. The woman can only farm the land and harvest the crops. Your Highness will be dethroned if that land remains in your name. You need to suspend all the activities of your group on the disputed land until *Nwerong* has spoken. Bongkisheri must stop any links with Savage, Livinus, and Katika.

MANKA

Messenger of our land, we agreed to stop the protest because we were told that the Elders were willing to listen to us. I am surprised that it is not the case. All the same, I want us to think together. That land belongs to Your Highness, my Children, and I when it bears my name. But it belongs to all the children conceived on the leopard skin when it carries the name of Your Highness. The Fon has many wives and children. My children's half-siblings have the right to demand their own share of what belongs to their father. Besides, stopping our activities on the land is stopping our assistance to the women.

SHUFAI LAIKA

(Silent for a while). Our wife, I will take your response to the Traditional Council. They will likely take your case to Nwerong. If you change your mind, inform me. *(Turns and walks away)*.

MANKA

The protest must continue if things remain like this. I need to inform the women leaders about the decision of the Traditional Council. That should be after the Town Hall meeting with the Governor.

ACT 3

Scene III

AT A ROAD BEND

(On their way back from school, Bame, Fomu, Kila, and Jaidzeka see Savage, Livinus, and Katika approaching from the opposite direction. Like the other school children, they quickly drift into the shoulder of the road and spread their fingers across their faces, whispering, while peering at the three friends through the tiny windows between their fingers. Katika is limping. Livinus, Savage, and Katika look at the children, and then, at each other).

KILA
(In a muted voice). The human riders are coming. *(The children stare at Katika's lifted buttocks as he limps).* People say that there are maggots inside his buttocks. *(Kila whispers, pointing to flies taking off and landing on Katika's lifted buttocks).*

FOMU
(In a hushed voice). That's true. He can't even walk well. He walks like a woman. I will never increase my buttocks.

BAME
They look different now.

LIVINUS
(Like Katika, his buttocks are rounded and high. He waves at Kila while smiling). Hi.

KILA
(In a whisper). Greetings, Uncle Livinus. *(Waves).*

JAIDZEKA
(In a muted voice). He is now Auntie Livinus! *(Lowers her hand and waves to Livinus).*

(Bame and Fomu lean back, look at Kila and Jaidzeka, and then, turn and look away. The children continue their discussion in muted voices as the three friends walk past).

BAME

Did Mum and Your Highness not say we should not greet the uncles and aunties who wear half clothes and short dresses and make their bum bum to move up and down when they walk in the streets? Kila, Jaidzeka, I will tell Your Highness that you greeted Livinus!

KILA

I only waved back. My mouth was closed. I did not greet with my mouth.

FOMU

Your Highness must hear this!

KILA

You greeted Aunty Regular. I will report you if you report me. *(Kila argues, running behind the others, looking frightened).*

Further Down the Road

(Ability, Fola, Gheeh, Dzekewong, and Verdzekov sight Livinus, Suvuge, and Katika at the road bend and quickly drift into the sidewalk, roof their nostrils, making comments as the three walk up the path. Katika pushes back his bouncing hairs that look like a bunch of bees. Livinus blows up the chewing gum he is chewing to float above his red lips like a small balloon, allowing it to burst while he dangles his earrings).

GHEEH

(Fixes a stare at the pumpkin-shaped breasts that stick out from Livinus' chest as he walks winding his waist like a winding road). He looks different. He is flat down there, I am sure, but still the same. Look at what our own son has become! His hair is plaited flat to the scalp, like corn rows. He wears clothes meant for women. Look at earrings dangling from his ears. He wears high heels. He now has big breasts. Livinus has a white mind in our black skin. *(Points to Katika as he speaks).* Look at that thing. He walks and twists his pumpkin-shaped buttocks like the road with many bends.

ABILITY

He can't even walk like a man. He staggers like a pumpkin stem clambering over plants in a farmland. Ha ha ha ha. I hear that his buttocks are infested with maggots. *(The Elders erupt with laughter while Katika drops his head, struggling to catch up with the rest).*

GHEEH

One will live long and see everything. What is this world turning into?

ABILITY

Livinus and Katika were not like this before the climbers came to our land.

DZEKEWONG

(Points to Savage with his lips pushed forward). He is their *Chicha* (teacher).

GHEEH

No doubt. He wears long black eyelashes that look like the tail of a bird, and a blouse over a short skirt.

VERDZEKOV

Where are they going to, dressed like this?

ABILITY

They are looking for more young men and women to convert to their man-marry-man and woman-marry-woman religion.

GHEEH

We will send *Nwerong* behind the riders. *(The others nod).*

ABILITY

How can a man enter the house through the backdoor like a thief? How can a man ride his fellow man? Who is the man and who is the woman? Tell me, who lies beneath whom? Who among them climbs his fellow man through the back door? *Hei!* How does it feel to be trapped to your fellow man like the blade of a sword clawing into a sheath.

ELDERS

Ha ha ha ha ha ha!

GHEEH
Have they ever thought of God's purpose in creating a man and a woman?

VERDZEKOV
That is the same question I have been asking.

FOLA
No one needs to lie beneath the other. That is why Kibaaka people call them riders and climbers.

GHEEH
Does Livinus still have balls between his legs?

VERDZEKOV
I wonder what he looks like down there.

ABILITY
He is now flat down there.

GHEEH
Ngiri! How can someone throw away grains to chase chaff? Something tells me that the curse that took away the life of *Kiletur* Lukong has visited *Livinur*. Does he still stand up to urinate as men do or he bends his knees and squats in the grass like a woman. *(Tries to demonstrate the action).*

ELDERS
Ha, ha, ha, ha, ha, ha.

GHEEH
I can now understand why the mother of Livinur took away her own life. The shame Livinur brought to that family was too heavy. Everywhere she went, people refused to shake hands with her. Will *Kiletur* Lukong still know his own son when he joins him in the other world? *(Tightens his lips and groans).*

ABILITY
Full-blooded men who should shout, bark, thunder, and watch their wives shiver like jackets of leaves shamelessly throw away their pride and authority for crumbs. Who does that? They have thrown away the thing that makes

someone a man.

GHEEH
If all men became women who will give us children for our names to stay alive and stretch like a river when we are no more? Who will bury us when we join our ancestors?

ABILITY
I don't know whether I should call Livinus he or she. *(Points to Savage with protruded lips and describes)*. How does he see through those long eyelashes that look like the wings of a bird coloured with charcoal? Just look at the heavy metal chain around his neck, and the beads around his waist. His hair looks like a gathering of bees falling over his shoulders. I will rather not have a child than have something with a beard on the chin preferring to twist his grafted buttocks when he walks and reasoning like a woman. Cursed generation! Our people say that where the road passes, development follows. Our own road has brought ant-infested wood and we must now entertain lizards as guests. Their fingernails look like talons. See how they have painted their lips red, just like women. The other one who has bleached his skin now looks as if they dipped him in a swimming pool of red oil before removing him.

GHEEH
I wonder how they got breasts and those buttocks that protrude below their waists like pumpkins.

ABILITY
There are hidden places in the city where Doctors cut and sew human skin like clothes. They call it 'buttocks grafting', some call it *nyash*. Do you remember the private clinic in the city that Government recently closed down and arrested the Doctor?... I am talking about the man who grafted the buttocks of one lady and the lifted area later started decaying and she bled to death. *(The Elders nod)*. That is how it is done.

VERDZEKOV
If it continues like this, we would not recognize our children in the next two years. Boys dress like women. They wear shoes with high heels, hang handbags over their shoulders, and hold the left hand slightly tilting forward like the cocked head of a snake targeting a prey. When you meet some, you cannot

tell the boy from the girl just by looking at their attire.

ABILITY

That is the species of people that Wirkitum brought to our land. It is Savage that brought this thing to our land. My friend Fola standing here almost emptied his savings on Livinus, only to discover in the hotel room that he was with a man. *(The Elders stare at Fola who has quickly turned his face away)*. If Kibaaka was still Kibaaka, things like this would not be happening. Nwerong used to arrest riders and cross-dressers and lock them up in the palace for two weeks before releasing them. See what Bongkisheri has done to us.

VERDZEKOV

Government does not want to see them.

ABILITY

Why are they still parading our streets if Government does not want to see them?

GHEEH

If you ask me who will I ask?

VERDZEKOV

Ability, have you forgotten that it was Barrister Johnson that fought for their release when they were arrested and detained?

ABILITY

The same Government that hates them released them. Is Government afraid of Barrister Johnson?

VERDZEKOV

The Court ruled in their favour because Nwerong did not follow due process. That was what we were told. *(Dzekewong stares vacant)*. Dzekewong, due process means you should do things following the right method or the right way according to the law of Government *(Dzekewong nods)*.

ABILITY

Whose method is the right one? And who determines whose method is the right one? Whose law is the right one? And who determines whose law is the right one? *(The Elders throw their hands open in questioning gestures).* Whose criteria did they use to reach such a conclusion that Nwerong did not follow due process? And whose due process? Did we not have laws before Government came to our land? What happened to our own ways?

ELDERS
Ohhorrr!

ABILITY
This is just one of the consequences of opening Kibaaka doors to Bongkisheri NGO and the likes of Barrister Johnson and Savage. I knew Kibaaka was going to pay the price when that group started talking about human rights, equal access, the emancipation of woman, and about the rights of women and the girl child. Today it is land rights for women; tomorrow it shall be rights for people who hope to make children through the anus; who knows what Kibaaka will see next?

GHEEH
I saw it coming and warned my wives and children to avoid greeting people like Savage, Katika, and Livinus.
(They stop lamenting when the three friends have disappeared at the road bend).

LIVINUS, KATIKA AND SAVAGE

LIVINUS
They hate us. They run away from us whenever they see us. They will never accept us. Did you notice the way they kept staring at my chest and buttocks?

SAVAGE
Who cares! I was trapped in the wrong body.

KATIKA
I regret grafting my *nyash* (*touching his buttocks as he speaks*). I feel pain everywhere. I can't sleep. I'm tired. I need to rest. *(He staggers to the roadside, sits down, tears gliding down his cheeks).* I want my real skin back. I need to see a doctor. They hate our kind. The elders said they will send Nwerong behind us.

SAVAGE

I love my new skin. It belongs to me. Why should another person struggle to control it or determine its look? It should be under my control. I have always wanted it to look fresh, with protruding buttocks and breasts, and to have blood down there. This is what sells on the streets of social media. I have over ten million followers on my Facebook page. I make a lot of money from that. Facebook pays me.

LIVINUS

Have you forgotten that *Nwerong* had banned us from Kibaaka land?

SAVAGE

We won the case in Court. The law is for everybody. We have the protection of the law, don't worry. Barrister Johnson is a human rights' activist. She will fight our battle.

LIVINUS

I thought the Court said *Nwerong* and the Traditional Council did not follow due process.

SAVAGE

(Blushes). I'm big enough to decide for myself, *mehn*. If the dudes *wanna* do something stupid, I'm *gonna* fly back to America *mehn*! They can't cage me, you know. I'll see you later, *mehn*. *(He turns to walk away)*.

KATIKA

(Remembering what Gheeh just said). "We will send *Nwerong* behind the riders." *(Musing)*. What kind of life is this? I wear diapers like a baby. Flies follow me everywhere I go. My father disowned me. Nobody wants me. They cover their nostrils when they see me. They refuse to shake hands with us. They refuse to share the same space with us. Children get confused when they want to address us. Whenever they begin with 'aunty', there is always a friend nearby who corrects with 'uncle', and at the end, they all laugh in mockery and run away. Women who, as victims of discrimination and oppression should sympathise with us, have become our most severe critics and aggressors, telling their children not to greet us. They even refuse to sell cooking oil and food items to us. We can only send Dzekewong, the only understanding friend we have, to buy for us, but he is soon getting tired of our errands. Everything about him

is money. Mobs pull us out of cars and beat us… How do I live my entire life rejected, insulted, avoided, and booed? Why did I do this to myself? I need to see a doctor. I don't want *nyash* again.

LIVINUS

(Musing). I need to find a way to travel to America where I can live my life the way I want. I need to travel to Douala to hustle for money for my papers… But where will I stay when I get to the city? Will my sister and her husband open their door to let me in? Or will they, like Mama Manka and other people of Kibaaka, turn me out and warn their kids to avoid any contact with me? *(Turns to Katika, his hand clamped over his nostrils)*. I am leaving you. *(He walks away)*.

ACT 3

Scene IV

IN THE FON'S PRIVATE SITTING ROOM

MANKA
(Sets food on the table). Your Highness, the table is ready. I prepared your favourite meal, fufu, vegetables and *Ka'ti Ka'ti*. *(Picks a slice of Ka'ti ka'ti with a fork and takes to Your Highness)* This chicken tastes delicious. I know you will like it.

YOUR HIGHNESS
You would have thought of my food when you spent days naked in the streets. I have become an afterthought…
    Heavy footsteps attract the attention of Your Highness and wife to the door. A voice is suddenly heard croaking outside).

MEDZEFEN
(Barges in with a furrowed face). Manka, as you don decide for become man pikin, my own be say, if mother of my children, Biy Wiiba, carry bare body follow you go sleep for road again, *(laughs threateningly)*, hmmmm, I go *comot* cutlass make *Ngomna* hear we *(turns and staggers away).*

YOUR HIGHNESS
Manka, you seem to enjoy the humiliation I am getting even from tassel smokers and palm wine tappers because of you and Bongkisheri.

MANKA
Your Highness, I have a meeting to attend…

YOUR HIGHNESS
Shut up! *(Manka shrugs).* Do you realise that I've been extremely tolerant with you…? I have spent lonely nights in bed while you sleep in the other room or parade the streets bare body. All your activities have been at the expense of my throne and domestic duties as husband, duties that you well know I cherish

so much. Manka, when I allowed you to go and represent Bongkisheri at the Beijing Women's Conference, I thought I was sending you to go and learn how to become a better housewife. But what have I got in return? You now lead a group of mad women with whom you sit in the streets like a hatchery of hens; they now ask for equal rights and want to put on thinking caps because they have been misled into thinking that taking care of the affairs of this land is the same as haggling at Kibaaka market. *(Shakes his head).* If it is the madness you contracted from Bongkisheri and Beijing that has misled you into thinking you can own land in *Kibaaka*, then programme the burial of Bongkisheri...! *(Heavy approaching footsteps, followed by insistent knocks at the door, oblige Your Highness and wife to cock their heads. The knock becomes persistent and louder than before-bang, bang, bang...)*

YOUR HIGHNESS

Your hands are not hard enough. Why don't you use a hammer? Look for a hammer and break the door with at once... *(Turns to his wife)* Manka, another Ba Medzefen is at the door, looking for his wife... *(The door opens slowly and Bame barges in, dragging Kila, followed by Fomu).*

MANKA

Bame, why are you dragging your sister like a goat?

BAME

She greeted the bad boys.
(Manka and Your Highness shift attention to Kila's chest which is tied round with a bandage).

MANKA

We will talk about that later. *(Points to the bandage around Kila's breasts).* Kila, what's the bandage doing around your chest? What happened? Are you hurt?

BAME

She always "irons" her breasts and ties the cloth around her chest before she wears her uniform.

MANKA

"Irons" her breasts? *(Bame nods).* Jesus Christ! *(Manka drops her chin, stares at Kila's chest, open-mouthed, wide-eyed).*

BAME

I met her in the kitchen, heating the surface of the orange on the flames of the gas cooker and "ironing" her breasts.

MANKA

Why do you iron your breasts?

KILA

(Touching her sticking-out budding breasts). There are oranges on my chest. I don't like the oranges.

MANKA

Who told you that by ironing and binding breasts you can retard their growth? Who taught you that?

KILA

Jaidzeka.

YOUR HIGHNESS

This is a consequence of neglecting your children to lead Bongkisheri women in a stupid protest.

MANKA

Kila, don't iron your breasts again. *(Kila nods).* Don't tie a cloth around your chest again. The breasts on your chest are a sign that you are becoming a woman. I will talk to Jaidzeka.

FOMU

Mum, Mum, Kila greeted Livinus…

YOUR HIGHNESS

(Thunders). She did what?

KILA

Your Highness, I am sorry. I will never greet them again.

YOUR HIGHNESS

Go down on your knees, immediately! *(Kila kneels).* Kila, don't go near people like Livinus, Savage, and Katika! They will teach you bad behaviour; avoid them! *(Kila nods).*

KILA
Your Highness, Bame and Fomu greeted Aunty Regular.

MANKA
Regular is your Aunty. Who says you shouldn't greet her? *(Kila points to Your Highness and Manka looks at him, surprised).*

YOUR HIGHNESS
Is it not Regular that has taught you how to become a man? Manka, who does not know Regular? Who does not know that her expertise in wrenching fruits of the womb is unrivalled? Is there any difference between Regular and the climbers? Have you ever heard the cry of a baby in her house? Is she living with her husband? Is that the category of woman my children should associate with? Manka, I don't want my children anywhere around a woman like Regular. You heard me!

MANKA
Your Highness, can she go and change now? *(Your Highness walks out).* Kila, go to your room and remove the cloth from your chest. Dress properly before you join your brothers on the table. When you finish eating, join me behind. There's work to do. I also need to educate you on self-hygiene *(Manka and Kila exit).*

ACT 3

Scene V

MANKA AND HER CHILDREN AT THE REAR OF HER APARTMENT

MANKA
Kila, hold the armpit areas of your uniform together, like this *(indicates)*. Rub soap all over the surfaces... Keep the soap away. Now, begin to rub the dress with the palms of your two hands *(bends forward to assist)*. That is how to wash your school uniform. You must make sure you wash the armpit areas and the edges... Rinse your dress and spread it out on the rope.

MANKA
Fomu, what have you done since you came back from school?

FOMU
I washed the dishes and the pots and fed the fowls.

MANKA
Where's Bame? *(Calling)* Ba-ame, Ba-ame...,

BAME
(Comes running). Mum, I am here.

MANKA
What have you done since you returned from school?

BAME
Mum, I washed your car and mopped the floors. I also arranged our books on the table. Our teacher gave us homework.

KILA/FOMU
(Simultaneously). I also have homework.

MANKA
Let's go in. *(The move to the study).*

In the Reading Room

MANKA
Remove your books from your school bags and put them on the table. Let me see what you have been doing. *(The children place their books on the table. Manka opens and flips through the pages as she speaks).* I hope you have been doing your homework while I was away. *(Fomu and Bame nod).* Kila, you didn't complete your maths and physics assignments.

KILA
I hate Mathematics and Physics.

MANKA
Why?

KILA
I am a girl. Maths is for boys. Physics is for boys. I will not pass in Maths and Physics when I write the GCE. I want to study English Language and history and become a journalist like the woman who is always on the television screen and saying… This is Fonyuy Hilary, reporting live from Kibaakaba National Station, ha ha ha ha ha.

MANKA
Stop joking. Who told you that Mathematics is for boys only? Who told you that Physics is for boys only? Tell me.

KILA
Our Mathematics teacher.

MANKA
(Shakes her head). I need to talk to your teacher. He shouldn't use such discouraging statements during his lessons. Kila, you can do well in maths and physics *(Kila nods).* Anybody can do well in maths or physics if they work hard. What you need is the right orientation at the right time. I scored 'A' Grades in mathematics, physics, Literature, English Language and History when I wrote

the General Certificate of Education Examinations at the Ordinary Levels, although I studied Mass Communication in the University. But I am a woman. You can be anything you want to be if you work hard. *(The children nod)*. We will finish your homework later, follow me. *(She leaves and they follow)*.

IN MANKA'S APARTMENT

(Manka and the children are seated in her apartment)

MANKA

We need to continue where we ended last time. Kila, there are parts of your body which neither a man nor another woman should touch. These include your breasts, your lips, and the place where your legs meet *(touches her groins)*, your *mbembe*. Not even your uncle, cousin, brother, female friends, male friends, or whoever should touch you there. If that happens, inform me immediately. You can also inform your Highness, or your brothers. The same applies to you Bame and Fomu *(they nod)*. There are certain things that are done only by people who are married to each other. Sleeping with a man or a woman is one of them. If somebody tells you to open your legs or the place where excrement comes out of your body, don't accept, shout for help. Stay away from that person. They will destroy you if you accept to do it. Tell the person you will report him or her to your parents, have you heard me? *(They nod)*. Stay away from people like Savage, Katika, and Livinus. Bame, Fomu, you can leave us now *(They exit the room)*.

MANKA

Kila, do you know the name of this thing? It is a sanitary pad. It is used by ladies and girls when blood starts flowing from this place *(touches the passage where urine passes from the body)*. The blood that flows from a woman's laps at particular periods of the month is a sign that she is now a woman, it is sign that she can become pregnant and bear a child if she sleeps with a man. You can also carry disease, fall sick and die if you sleep with a man. I want to show you how to use a sanitary pad when you experience menstrual flow. Hold the pad where your legs meet, here *(places a pad between her legs, gives another pad to Kila and asks her to do same, and she does)*. Arrange it to feel comfortable... Correct. Now, pull up your panty to cover it..., go on..., excellent. Now, repeat the process..., good. The role of the pad is to absorb blood from soiling your legs and what you are wearing. You need to change it every four or five hours when you start bleeding. *(Kila nods. Manka looks at her watch).* Heh! We will continue another time. I have a meeting to attend in about thirty minutes. I should be on my way now.

MANKA
(Looks at her wristwatch). That's all for today. I have a meeting to attend in about thirty minutes.

Outside the Palace Courtyard

MANKA
Bame, Fomu, the Mechanic will be coming to check my car. There's a leakage somewhere. Make sure you follow up and inform Your Highness when he comes. I will use public transport *(She hurriedly leaves).*

ACT 4

Scene I

IN FRONT OF ABILITY'S COMPOUND

ABILITY

(Musing). Shufai Laika and Ndzewiyi were sent to plead with Honourable to convince the women to end the protest and embrace dialogue. No, *(wags his finger in protest),* that would not happen. There should be no peace in this land! The protest must continue. I am already an ex-convict and can no longer work in the Public Service. The protest is the only opportunity to make money and become relevant like the likes of Honourable and Your Highness. I was appointed to coordinate the Vigilante Group, to pay their salaries and to buy security outfits, because of the protest. Your Highness hired me to influence the elections because of the protest. Conflict is business. My job ends when the protest ends. No! I need to fuel the conflict. I will do anything to frustrate every move to kill the protest. I need money to get a wife and live like a man. What do I do now? *(Taps his head).* I need to find out if Manka has accepted to surrender the land to Your Highness… I need to set up Manka and Honourable *(Nods).* I can use Regular to destroy Your Highness and his marriage. I must go to the palace now.

ACT 4

Scene II

AT THE TABLE

ABILITY
(Walks in, claps hands three times, cupped hands to his mouth and greets). Mbeeeh.

YOUR HIGHNESS
Ability, have you come?

ABILITY
Mbeeeh. *(Turns to Manka who has also lifted her head to greet).* Our wife, I can see you are taking good care of Your Highness.

MANKA
That's my duty, *Ba* Ability, have you come? You came at the right time. Food is ready. Join us, please.

ABILITY
Mother of Children, thank you. My intestines were already grumbling and protesting. This food will calm them down. Wrap up some of the food; I will take it home so that my son and my intestines will not have any reason to start grumbling in the evening *(laughs),* ki, ki, ki, ki, ki, ki.

YOUR HIGHNESS
(Smiling). Ba Ability, you can tickle a corpse.

MANKA
(Manka goes out, after a short while she returns with food wrapped in fresh plantain leaves and places on the table before Ability). Ba Ability, this is enough to take you for two days.

ABILITY
Our wife, you are the best gift Kibaaka ever had, ki ki ki ki ki.

MANKA
It is well, Ba Ability. *(She serves the food and turns to Your Highness)*. Your Highness, I have served your food and juice. Do you still need anything?

YOUR HIGHNESS
Get my palm wine from the fridge and bring.

MANKA
I just checked, Your Highness, it is finished. I will inform your tapper to bring us palm wine. I have two meetings to attend in the Town Hall today. The Governor invited the women to a meeting. *(Ability quickly sticks out his neck)*. I might not return home early. I have given directives to Bame to get your food heated and served on time. I should be on my way now. *(Pauses, and after a while she turns and walks out)*.

ABILITY
(After about three minutes, he tiptoes quietly to the door, sticks up his neck, peers across the yard and returns to his seat). Ehherrh, Your Highness, has Manka accepted to return the land to you?... Did she even tell you the person that sold land to her?

YOUR HIGHNESS
Ability, you know her. She never answers any question directly. Each time you ask her a question, she wants to reason you out of the question.

ABILITY
Your Highness, your word is law and not a wish.

YOUR HIGHNESS
It looks like she's been drugged with human rights.

ABILITY
I know what to do. Your Highness, the Town Hall meeting with the Governor and the second one with the women should be about the women's protest. I need to be there, yes, I need to know what their plans are if we must grab that land.

YOUR HIGHNESS
Did they invite you to that meeting?

ABILITY
Your Highness, you cannot steal from the house you know nothing about. There must be an insider. I need to infiltrate them to be able to plan counter-strategies that will help you become the landowner.

YOUR HIGHNESS
Ability, you are really the right person to lead the Information Gathering wing of the Council of Elders *(Smiles)*.

ABILITY
Your Highness, I need money for this job. You can't do this kind of undercover work alone. I need to pay the people I work with.

YOUR HIGHNESS
(Leans back, closes his eyes, after a while, he opens them and asks). How much are we talking about?

ABILITY
I normally charge a heavy amount of money for risky jobs, but due to my love for the Royal Family, and because I don't want *Nwerong* to grab the throne and give to Ndzebarah, I am ready to accept 200,000frs. I will not disclose what I want to do now until the job is done.

YOUR HIGHNESS
(Withdraws and returns after a couple of minutes with a brown envelope. He tilts his head, peers across the door and gives the envelope to Ability with directives). Do anything you can to help me get that land, but don't hurt anybody.

ABILITY
I have never failed an examination. *(Ability opens the envelope, counts the bank notes, smiles and gets up to leave).*

YOUR HIGHNESS
Did you succeed to give the money to Dzekem? *(Ability opens his eyes and mouth wide)* ... I am talking about the money you collected to bribe the voters...

ABILITY

Ooh! Orrh! Your Highness, things like that are not done in a hurry. I need to work on the mindset of the women first. Allow everything to me. I don't even want us to involve people like Fola, Dzekewong, and Gheeh. You can't trust them with secrets.

YOUR HIGHNESS

I thought as much.

ABILITY

Your Highness, I will be on my way now. I will get back to you soon. *(Walks out, Your Highness leans back, staring vacantly).*

At Bongkisheri Center

(Meeting between the Women and Barrister Johnson).

MANKA

Bongkisheri!

WOMEN

(Chorus). Power to the woman. Collective strength is victory.

MANKA

Thank you so much and thank you for coming at short notice. We have two issues to discuss. I need to brief you on my meeting with the Elders and we need to start planning the activities for the International Women's Day. As you all know, we suspended the women's strike, understanding that the Elders had pledged their readiness to resolve our grievances, specifically our demand for land rights. I was surprised when Shufai Laika and Your Highness still told me that land belongs to the man.

WOMEN

Heeeei!

MANKA

The Elders insisted that I transfer ownership of the land to Your Highness, and also suspend Bongkisheri activities on the land. Shufai Laika said it was the orders of Nwerong… *(The women open their eyes and mouths wide, look at each other, turn away their heads and then, twist their lips, throwing their hands open in gestures of surprise).*

BINLA

What do we do now?

BARRISTER JOHNSON:

The strike must resume after the celebration of Women's Day.

WOMEN

Yeeeeeees.

MANKA

Bongkisheri!

WOMEN

(Chorus). Power to the woman. Collective strength is victory.

BARRISTER JOHNSON

We will not rest until we win the land ownership battle!

BIY WIIBA

Bongkisheri, we just heard that the matter is now in the hands of Nwerong. We are only women. We cannot go anywhere with this kind of fight. This is Kibaaka.

BARRISTER JOHNSON

The law will fight our battles. Government has removed the lock on our lips. Women are no longer land tenants. We can now become landowners *(Manka and Binla nod).*

BIY WIIBA

Have you heard such a thing happening in other lands? *(A few women throw their hands apart).* Barrister Johnson, the woman is only a branch and not the tree trunk.

(Barrister Johnson and Manka look at each other, and then, at the women).

BARRISTER JOHNSON

Dear women, do not be afraid. Government knows that we are doing what we are doing. I am behind you. I am your strength. Mrs Ghamogha, you need to follow me to my office after this meeting. I need to prepare a letter of observation, a call to order, which you will deliver to Your Highness. *(Biy Wiiba opens her mouth and eyes wide, crosses her hands on her chest and stares at Barrister Johnson).* Preparations for the International Women's Day can continue while Mrs Ghamogha follows me to my office.

MANKA

Thank you Barrister Johnson. May I suggest that you come with me and hand the letter to Your Highness, yourself? That should be after the meeting with the Governor.

BARRISTER JOHNSON

That's fine by me.

BIY WIIBA

I have a suggestion. We need to make our meetings brief *(Beri, and a few other women nod in support).* The father of my children beats me like a child each time I return home late *(Barrister Johnson opens her mouth wide).* I was severely beaten with the branch of a tree when I returned from the protest. I have to be on my way now before he discovers that I attended Bongkisheri meeting again.

BERI

I received beatings too.

BARRISTER JOHNSON

Domestic violence will not stop until you start speaking up. Come and inform me each time your husband beats you. *(The women nod, some reluctantly. Barrister Johnson stares at Biy Wiiba as she hurriedly tears through the door and shakes her head).* Mrs Ghamogha, please follow me to my office now. *(They leave while the meeting continues).*

Thirty Minutes Later

(Manka stumbles on Ability across the yard, squatting behind a car, on

her way to a store to buy an envelope).

MANKA
Ba Ability, what are you doing here? *(Stares at Ability, open mouthed).*

ABILITY
(Ability lifts his head, looks around, and turns to Manka).

MANKA
I hope there is no problem.

ABILITY
Manka, can I trust you with a secret?

MANKA
Secret! *(Opens her mouth).*

ABILITY
Yes…,

MANKA
I don't understand.

ABILITY
If you tell Your Highness or anybody what I am about to tell you, I will be fined by the Traditional Council but it is you that will suffer the most because you will miss many things you should know and take discreet decisions to protect your land.

MANKA
Ba Ability, whatever you tell me will remain between us.

ABILITY
Good. Your Highness is planning to use Nwerong to seize your land. Nwerong has the power to send you on exile for buying land in Kibaaka. You are a nice woman and your group is doing a lot for Kibaaka women. You don't deserve to suffer. That is why I decided to tell you what to expect.

MANKA
Ba Ability, thank you so much. So, what can I do now to keep my land, and to also avoid this exile sentence?

ABILITY
What do you yourself think you should do?

MANKA
(Drops her head, pauses for a while and then, lifts up her head). The protest will continue after our elections and celebrations coming up next week. That's what the women leaders just decided. We are also counting on Barrister Johnson.

ABILITY
Smart woman. *Erher.* Manka, do not only rely on the protest. Honourable is now a strong member of the Traditional Council with his recent promotion to the rank of Subchief. He is now also a powerful member of the Nwerong cult. That's him *(points)* across the yard. Meet him now. Inform him about the plans to seize your land with the complicity of Nwerong. Your Highness listens to him; Shufai Laika listens to him. Everybody listens to him because of his position and money. There are only two things that can win a battle against Nwerong: political power and influence. Honourable has both.

MANKA
(Nods). Ba Ability, I hope the men could have your mindset. Thank you so much. Let me go and meet Honourable now.

ABILITY
Manka, I will follow up and feed you with more information. What I need is your silent collaboration and nothing will happen to your land. You can go now. *(Manka goes to meet Honourable across the yard).*

Manka and Honourable

> *(Ability squats behind a parked car from where he constantly sticks up his neck and peers at Manka and Honourable discussing across the yard).*

MANKA
Honourable, Your Highness wants to seize my land with the complicity of

Nwerong.

HONOURABLE
To the best of my knowledge, Nwerong hasn't met since the protest started.

MANKA
I was told that the Traditional Council has ordered me to suspend all Bong-kisheri activities on the land. Please, help me. That land is the future of my children. It will become family property if the land title carries the name of my husband. He has other wives and children.

HONOURABLE
I can see tears in your eyes. *(Pulls out a tissue from his pocket and wipes tears gliding down Manka's cheeks, an action that attracts Ability who instantly cocks his head).*

ABILITY
(Hangs his mouth open, opens his eyes wide, nods his head repeatedly and says), Your Highness must hear this.

HONOURABLE
Have you informed my wife?

MANKA
Yes, I left her drafting the letter of observation.

HONOURABLE
The law is the only weapon you will use to win this battle. These people are too attached to their ways. They can do anything to defend their ignorance. The law will fight your battles.

MANKA
(Tries to remember what Ability just told her). "Nwerong has the power to send you on exile for buying land in Kibaaka). Honourable, can the law fight another law?

HONOURABLE
Go and meet my wife. She knows what to do. Don't be afraid. We will fight

for you but do not let the Elders know that we discussed this matter. *(Manka nods)*. Mrs Ghamogha, we are supposed to have a meeting with the Governor. He just called to say we should delay the meeting. He's attending to State matters. Are you aware?

MANKA

I left my phone in Barrister's office. In any case, which gives me time to do other things before he arrives. Thank you so much Honourable. *(Honourable smiles, Manka turns and walks away).*

(A Few Minutes Later)

(Ability storms the sitting room of the palace, panting and sweating).

YOUR HIGHNESS

Ability, is something chasing you?

ABILITY

Y-y-your Highness, Your Highness, what I am about to tell you will shock you. *(Your Highness opens his mouth)*. I saw Honourable touching your wife's cheeks in a gentle and loving way!

YOUR HIGHNESS

What do you mean?

ABILITY

What shocked me more was their collaborative visual encounter and also the way she allowed Honourable's fingers to creep freely over her face as if her face was a drawing board.

YOUR HIGHNESS

What are you talking about?

ABILITY

I am a man and I know when action is innocent and when it is guilty. I didn't like their visual collaboration. I didn't like the way Honourable's eyes and fingers kept tiptoeing all over Manka's face. I can read postures. When it comes to matters of the heart, the woman positions herself and the man locates her.

Who even knows how far that visual encroachment will take them if nothing is done on time to stop it!

YOUR HIGHNESS
Stop it, now! I will not sit here and watch you speak about my wife in that disrespectful manner! Manka can be everything else except being unfaithful!

ABILITY
Your Highness, I can swear before the shrine of Rifem that I saw what I just said. I am even sure that this has gone on for long.

YOUR HIGHNESS
Is that what you really want me to believe?

ABILITY
Your Highness, please, think like a man. This man has been insulting you in coded language, well dressed language. You might not understand but some of us do. What do you think Honourable was talking about during the council when he said *(tries hard to remember)*: "If you refuse to harvest the ripe pumpkin plant growing along the shoulder of the road because its seed came from the droppings of a flying bird, a stranger passing along the road will harvest the abandoned plant? His family will eat the precious meal…"? Tell me, who are the trio that represents this triangle? Who is that precious plant? Who is the one that refuses to harvest? Who is the harvester? *(Your Highness cocks his head, his mouth agape, Ability nods).* Why do you think Honourable only randomly detonated verbal explosives against anybody who dared to point out the excesses of Manka and her group? It also seems to me that you have suddenly forgotten the strong defence Honourable mounted in her favour in order to dismantle the strong evidence we brought against her and Bongkisheri. Do you think such a defence was offered for free? Your Highness, was it not in your presence that Honourable flung insults at me in defence of your wife and her group? Tell me, what could be Honourable's interest in Bongkisheri? Is his wife one of those desperate and illiterate women of Kibaaka who needs help from your wife's group? No! Don't you think Bongkisheri only offers Honourable and Manka the opportunity to meet behind your back after meetings as they did today? Didn't you observe the way Honourable cunningly enlisted the support of Shufai Laika, bragging openly how a stranger would harvest the rejected pumpkin? He needed somebody to nod when he argued in favour of

Manka? He even deployed strategies to overthrow my arguments in favour of banning Bongkisheri, imposing taxes on the NGO, and on strangers. He successfully speculated and resisted my attacks on the women's protest. Your Highness, do you think it was for nothing that Honourable struggled to crush every argument from me in favour of using Nwerong and the Traditional Council to get back the land to you in order to help you avoid the wrath of tradition? Open your eyes. Tell me, who stands to gain if you are dethroned? Let me tell you. Honourable is in favour of land ownership rights for women. Do you know why? If Manka keeps her land, you will be dethroned and completely weakened. Any opposition to the liaison he has with Manka will be eradicated. Any opposition to his land-grabbing agenda in Yerr-Bukang where he suddenly became Subchief will be eradicated. Your Highness, do you think Honourable is performing all these services to your wife for free? Honourable is fighting you. Ask me how. Who else has fought his way up to become the Subchief with his own traditional boundary in Kibaaka? *(Your Highness opens his mouth and cocks his head).* Who else is grabbing and selling land in Yerr-Bukang village with impunity? Who among us can do that and get away with it without incurring the wrath of the SDO and the Governor of Kibaaka? What else can you fight Honourable with if your power as Fon of Kibaaka is taken away from you, Errrh? *(Stares at Your Highness for a while and then continues).* Your Highness, you need to wake up.

YOUR HIGHNESS
(Breaths heavily, hangs his mouth open, confused). Two rams drinking from one pot at the same time, it cannot be! Ability, do you mean to say Wirkitum has dared to climb the tree that the home leopard has climbed? I will confront them with this abomination.

ABILITY
Not so soon…,

YOUR HIGHNESS
(Louder). Should I wait until I become a foster father before I can act?

ABILITY
Your Highness, Honourable is the law and can take legal action against us if we raise an alarm with no physical evidence. Remember that I worked in the Information Gathering Department of the Military before I was dismissed. So,

I know what I am talking about. I suggest we go gradually. Leave everything to me, for now. I will watch them more closely and give you information and when it is time to act, you will act on evidence. If you confront her now, they may become more careful and evade our watchfulness. Behave as if nothing has happened. We may ruin the efforts to destroy Bongkisheri and recover the land if we let the cat out of the bag now. Even if you send her packing as some men would do in this kind of situation, she would go with the land title and her money and you would remain the loser. *(Your Highness nods)*. Yes. You would lose the land, the throne, and the money she makes. I know what I am talking about.

YOUR HIGHNESS
You are a good adviser. *(Puckers his face)*. But, if it turns out to be true, these two Come-no-Gos will get it hot for this!

ABILITY
Gbam. Your Highness, there are many ways to punish them. I can set Honourable up and cause an alarm that will leave Government with no choice than to transfer him to those mountainous areas where slim roads cut through hanging hills. And when Barrister Johnson leaves, there will be nobody to fight for Bongkisheri and Manka.

YOUR HIGHNESS
What will I do without you, Ability? *(Ability smiles)*. Now, how will that be done?

ABILITY
A single petition will dethrone and demolish Honourable. *(Your Highness nods)*. My pen stings. Honourable is not just the Parliamentarian of Kibaaka. He is also the Director General of Taxation in Kibaaka. A simple petition is enough to bulldoze him out of *Kibaaka*. I know one Journalist, Abdullahi Godlove. He writes and publishes libels for money. All we need is to pay him well and he will publish our story. I will write a petition against Honourable citing all his investments including those his high cars, the cattle ranch, his houses and hotels across the country. I will then pay the Journalist to publish it. Once that information goes out, Government will send their auditing team after him. Ki ki ki ki ki. Either he becomes a tenant in Kondengui or his name will be top on the transfer list. I can also set him up and conduct *Nwerong* to strip off his

title. I can serve as a good substitute for the continuation of his traditional term of office as Subchief, and also Third in Command in the Council of Elders *(Your Highness shakes his head)*. Your Highness, leave everything to me. Just pretend as if there is nothing when Manka returns. Don't do anything that can frustrate my plans. I am doing everything in your interest and I need your collaboration to succeed. It is you that needs the land, to keep the throne, and not me. Your Highness, I need money, about 200,000frs to cook up a story against Honourable and pay a journalist to publish it.

YOUR HIGHNESS
Can I really hold my tongue when she returns?

ABILITY
Silence is a strategy.

YOUR HIGHNESS
(Stares fixedly at the wall as he speaks). Sending out a libel against Honourable is a good idea. It will serve as a lesson that nobody eats from the dish where I eat. I will get the money. I am expecting my salary in the days ahead.

ABILITY
What are friends for? Your Highness, there's another thing. Today's all women's meeting was summoned by the queen to plan a resumption of their protest march.

YOUR HIGHNESS
Do women want to take over the world? *(Shakes his head)*. Manka has exceeded bounds. Our people say if you play with a puppy it shows your nakedness to the world. *(Stares vacantly across the room)*. Ability, how can a man hear that his wife is cheating on him and still hold back his fist? What do I do to this terrible woman that I call wife?

ABILITY
Your Highness, there are many things you can do to clip her wings. She needs serious beatings immediately she returns. Do it to regain your bedroom dignity. A man must be a man. *(Your Highness locks eyes with Ability)*. Yes. But don't mention the affair with Honourable for now *(Your Highness nods)*.

YOUR HIGHNESS
Our people say, it is no bravery to beat a woman, but it is sometimes a necessity.

ABILITY
Your Highness, consider reporting her to Nwerong if you still like the throne.

YOUR HIGHNESS
I have been thinking in that direction. But my fear is that Nwerong might send her on exile.

ABILITY
Then, marry Dzekem…,

YOUR HIGHNESS
Ngiri! Did you say marry…! *(Stares at Ability open-mouthed).*

ABILITY
(Agrees). Mbeerrh…!

YOUR HIGHNESS
I will do no such thing. Ability! Do you know what you are talking about? By the way, how would marrying Dzekem help me to get the land?

ABILITY
The thing you carry between your legs is a disciplinarian. A woman is another woman's medicine. The most stubborn woman becomes humble and submissive like a lion in a woman's cooking pot when her husband marries another woman. Your Highness, I have taught you how to use your authority as a man. I have taught you how to use your authority as the Fon. *(Your Highness stares vacantly across the room).*

YOUR HIGHNESS
Ability, I am not interested in any woman. My mind is fixed on two things now, the land and Honourable.

ABILITY
Your Highness, what about just faking familiarity with Dzekem? *(Nods his head as he speaks).* Just fake it. It is just a strategy to make Manka jealous. When a

woman feels threatened by the presence of another woman around her husband, she stops nagging and listens to the husband. Just pretend to care about Dzekem. Our people say we do not keep our eggs in one basket. We need to keep changing strategies as we work. This is simply called, moving from plan A to Plan B and shifting your paradigms. When I worked for Government as Information Gathering Officer, we used to smell our enemies seven hills away and take them unawares. Manka is a big social problem and cannot be solved with a single method or formula. We will handle Honourable later, the same way.

YOUR HIGHNESS
You are a strategist. You are truly a think tank. I need to listen to you.

ABILITY
Your Highness, I will resign working for you if I fail. All I want is for Your Highness to authorise me to come over with Dzekem. She is young and beautiful. Her presence in the palace will stir suspicion and jealousy in Manka. She will feel threatened and insecure and will definitely prefer to give you the land than to lose you to Dzekem. No woman wants to lose her position as the favourite wife to another woman. She would do anything to remain the most preferred. As our people say, a woman would not be a woman if she were not jealous.

YOUR HIGHNESS
(Your Highness nods consent). Ability, you are right, but don't raise any hopes of a relationship with Dzekem. And don't let anybody know our game plan. Just tell her Your Highness wants to have a word with her discretely. I may just ask her a few questions about the protest, or anything, when she comes.

ABILITY
That's what this game is all about, strategy, *(laughs)*, ki ki ki ki ki. If Manka happens to bump into Dzekem and Your Highness, Dzekem should get up abruptly, and leave. The abruptness is part of the strategy. It will create more room for suspicion.

YOUR HIGHNESS
(Nods). Ability, you have to hurry before she comes back.

ABILITY
I will be right back. *(Walks out).*

(An Hour Later)

(Enter Ability and Dzekem).

DINKA
(Stretches his hand to greet Ability, smiling, but Ability ignores). Ability, Ability, ha ha ha ha, wuna come well oorrh. *(Looks at the curls dangling down from Dzekem's head like intestines and comments).* Abili, na ya woman bi dis? Hei! You get eyes ohhhh. Ya woman fine pass, I swear, ha, ha, ha, ha. Madame, come good ohhh…

ABILITY
Will you shut up! Shut up! *(Dinka quickly raises his shoulders and squashes his lips with his fingers).* Now, go inside and inform Your Highness that we are here to see him.

DINKA
(Rushes in and bends forward before the Fon, with his hands cupped to his mouth). Your Highness, Ba Ability and *wan* woman deh outside. Dem say dem wan see you.

YOUR HIGHNESS
Tell them to come right inside.

(At the doorsteps)

DINKA
Ba Abili, Your Highness say make wuna come right inside.
(As Ability and Dzekem walk in, Dzekem stares open-mouthed and wide-eyed at the gold bulb holders hanging heavily from the ceiling. She shifts her eyes to the beautiful high back leather chair and then to the beautifully tiled walls).

ABILITY
(Cups his hands to his mouth and heaps praises on the Fon). Bvere'eh, Nchang

nchang! *The only being with eight hundred eyes!*

YOUR HIGHNESS
Ability, have you come?

DZEKEM
(Stands a few steps before Your Highness, bending forward).

YOUR HIGHNESS
(Sits half-smiling and half-sad, throughout). Dzekem, you may sit down.

DZEKEM
(Timidly lowers her buttocks on the chair, and stares at her feet, her head hanging heavily over her shoulder).

YOUR HIGHNESS
(To Dzekem). This palace is not only for the Elders. *(Ability continuously shifts his looks from Your Highness to Dzekem and back, smiling and nodding his head jerkily, as Your Highness struggles to sustain an uncoordinated chat).* Young people can also find time to come around and share their worries with the Fon... Huh? *(Dzekem cups hands to her mouth).* The Fon is for everybody. So, you can always come to me and report wrongdoing..., or whenever you have issues that you think I can intervene and address..., you can also encourage other youths to do same ..., not so?

DZEKEM
(In a shy and subdued voice). Mbeeeh.

YOUR HIGHNESS
I learned that...
    (The door opens slowly and Manka walks in. She opens her mouth and eyes wide and looks at Dzekem, sitting close to Your Highness).

DZEKEM
(Gets up and bends forward). Good afternoon, Ma...

MANKA
Dzekem, I just left you at the meeting. You didn't tell me you will be coming

to see me. I hope all is well? *(Hangs her mouth open).*

DZEKEM
(Turns and casts a glance at Ability, and then at the Fon, looking confused). Yes, Ma.

MANKA
(She looks at the Fon, shifts her stare to Ability and Dzekem in that order, and then, turns to the Fon). What's happening here…? Are the children, okay? *(Calls).* Ba--me, Fomu, Kila…!

KILA
(A voice is heard off the room). Yes, Mum. We are coming. *(Kila rushes in).* Mum, I am here.

MANKA
Where are your brothers? *(Bame and Fomu walk in). Manka takes a deep breath and tells the children to leave).* You may now leave. *(The children look at each other, turn and walk out. Manka turns to Ability).* Ba Ability, I hope all is well?

ABILITY
(Stammers). Ah-ah, emmm…, Our wife, yes…, *(Gets up).* Your Highness, I will be on my way now…,

DZEKEM
(Shifts her look from Ability to Your Highness, and then, back to Ability as she stands open-mouthed). G-g-good bye Your Highness, goodbye, Ma.

MANKA
(Stares at Ability and Dzekem walking hurriedly through the door, before turning to Your Highness). Is everything okay…? Why did they walk out so abruptly immediately I walked in?
> *(Without responding, Your Highness gets up and walks across the door, leaving his wife staring open-mouthed. She throws her hands apart looking confused and her handbag drops on the floor, mutters something to herself, turns and walks out).*

MANKA

(To Your Highness). If it is what I am thinking, then, I will inform Barrister Johnson for appropriate action. *(She turns and walks away).*

ACT 4

Scene III

Manka's Kitchen

MANKA

(*Thinking aloud*). Why would Ba Ability and Dzekem suddenly get up and leave immediately I walk in? Why! And why would Dzekem just follow without a word? She even looked confused. What's happening…? In any case, I will find out from….
(*Biy Wiiba tiptoes into the kitchen*).

MANKA

Mami Biy, what are you doing here, at nighttime…?

BIY WIIBA

(*In a muted voice*). Your Highness is tired of eating fufu and *njama-njama* every day.

MANKA

I don't understand.

BIY WIIBA

Your Highness is making plans to marry Dzekem… (*Manka leans back, open-mouthed, wide-eyed*). Yes.

MANKA

He is not a fan of women. Are you sure of what you just said?

BIY WIIBA

That is what Ability told the father of my children. You must not tell anybody. If it goes out, the Elders will drag me before Nwerong for leaking palace secrets. They don't even know that I overheard them.

MANKA

(*Lowers her buttocks to the floor and stares vacantly*). "Your Highness, why did they walk out so abruptly immediately I walked in? Is everything okay…?" (*Shakes her head*).

BIY WIIBA

Ability also said that Your Highness told him that immediately he marries Dzekem and transfers all attention to her, you will stop being the man and give him your land. (*Manka's eyes well-up with tears*). They even agreed to keep it a secret from you and the villagers, at least for now. (*Manka wipes tears drizzling down her cheeks with the edge of her cloth*).

MANKA

If Dzekem can do this to me… (*Shakes her head*).

BIY WIIBA

Manka, that is not all *oohh*. As I took the road to come and tell you what I heard Ba Ability telling the father of my children, I saw some men approaching. Their faces were covered with long stockings leaving only their eyes. I was afraid of their looks and so I hid behind a nearby tree. But I heard what they said about your land as they walked past by.

MANKA

What did you hear?

BIY WIIBA

One of them whose voice resembled that of Dzekewong said you will not recognise Bongkisheri hall when next you visit your land.

MANKA

(*Stares blankly across the door for a while and speaks*). If they destroy anything on my land, I will inform the Police.

BIY WIIBA

The big man in the Police office is from this land. No stranger can win a war against the son of the soil. Let me leave you now. (*Biy Wiiba sneaks out*).

MANKA

(Remembering her late mother's words to her and her sister, Regular, recorded on her phone). "Seeds of my womb, I don't have anything to give you but my words are food. This is the end of the road for me. The voices I hear now are seven hills away from me. I am about to begin my last journey. Manka, I do not regret because I know you are the trunk of the family tree. Continue to be the mother hen whose wings are spread over its chicks when the hawk hovers overhead. But there is something I also want you to know. The big book the Whiteman has put in your head is a good thing because it has opened your eyes. But that book is the root of your problems. Your ways are different from the ways of Kibaaka people. The Graffi man and his ways are like a man and his shadow. Graffi people and their ways are like the branches that suck from the breast of the tree trunk. They will do anything to keep the trunk alive. Regular, be the fence around your sister, Manka. I want you and Manka to keep together like a bunch of plantains. Our people say a single broomstick easily breaks, but a bundle of broomsticks will not be easily broken. I can now go in peace". *(Opens her eyes and muses).* My husband wants to marry another woman as blackmail to seize my land just because his people say land belongs to the man. He has the backing of his people. What do I do to keep my land…? What can I do to stop him marrying Dzekem! I don't want to lose him to another woman. What can I do? *(Turns and lies on her side, breathing heavily, cheeks soaked in tears. She tugs off her sweat-drenched hugging gown from the collar and drops it on the floor, sits upright, and supports her chin on her hand).* Should I do a new land title carrying my husband's name to save my marriage? That land automatically becomes family property when it carries his name and my stepchildren will feel entitled by birth right. My children will be cheated of what belongs to them; they will be forced to share their inheritance with strangers. How do I get my husband to understand that his polygamous status is the reason I am afraid to transfer ownership of my land to him? *(Prowls on the floor).* The protest must continue. I need the advice of Barrister Johnson.

ACT 4

Scene IV

(The Next Day)

(Enters Ability)

ABILITY
Now that my traps are set, what next? *(Taps his head in a thinking gesture)*. I need to go to the palace to find out how Manka is reacting to the shock, to plan counter-strategies.

(Thirty Minutes Later)

(Your Highness is seated on his high-back stool, pensive, when Ability sneaks in).

YOUR HIGHNESS
Ability, have you come?

ABILITY
(Cups hands to his mouth and hums). Hmmmmm.

YOUR HIGHNESS
Is there anything I should know?

ABILITY
(Tiptoes to the door, stretches his neck across the door, looks in the right and then, in the left direction, and returns to his seat). What was her reaction when Dzekem and I walked out immediately she walked in?

YOUR HIGHNESS
(Trying hard to remember). She said: If it is what I am thinking, then, I will inform Barrister Johnson for appropriate action." Manka has become something else. She left my house in the morning again without my consent.

ABILITY
She left the house… I heard loud screams across the town. Is it possible that the women are back in the streets?

YOUR HIGHNESS
I gave Manka my heart! This is what I get in return. I'm afraid, things are getting out of hand.

ABILITY
I will warn every man never to repose trust in a woman, lest she controls him and wrecks his destiny. The experience of the first man teaches us that women are evil beings who disrupt men's plans to satisfy their greed. The worst thing that can happen to a man is to allow himself to be controlled by a woman. The worst thing that can happen to a man is to be carried away by her shifting looks, what stupid and blind men call beauty. The logical end is always that he loses control to her and allows himself to be governed by her. When such a fool tends to desecrate manhood by taking orders from a woman, he calls this madness love. Such a man is like one under the influence of palm wine. Such a man will share his own secrets with the woman and a man who shares secrets with a woman will soon take orders from her. Such a man is only a fool and a blind bat, a toy in the hands of the manipulative and frivolous creature. He is not worthy to be a village elder and should never even be admitted into the presence of men. If by some chance he finds himself among men, he should remain as silent as his fellow women when men speak. Your Highness, it is not late to recover what you have lost and what you are about to lose. The thing a man carries between his thighs is a disciplinarian. Your slap is a disciplinarian. I have thought you how to use your authority and redeem your dignity. I need to find out what the women are planning to do. I will be on my way now. *(Turns and walks out leaving Your Highness in deep thoughts).*

(Thirty Minutes Later)

Manka and Barrister Johnson

BARRISTER JOHNSON
(Stares at Manka). Your eyes are red and swollen. What happened? *(Manka wipes tears drizzling down her cheeks with her handkerchief).* Are you okay? How is your family doing? Is everything fine?

MANKA

Your Highness is planning to marry Dzekem. *(Breaks into tears)*. Hi heuh, hi heuh hi, heuh…

BARRISTER JOHNSON

Is that what he told you?

MANKA

I bumped into Dzekem and Your Highness in my sitting room yesterday. She got up and left immediately I walked in. I don't really know what to make of it…, emm…, I am not sure of anything right now. I'm just confused.

BARRISTER JOHNSON

Why do you think someone would randomly come to your house, sit near your husband, and just get up and walk out immediately you walk in?

MANKA

That's exactly my worry.

BARRISTER JOHNSON

I don't think Dzekem would be bold enough to come to your house, knowing she is intimate with your husband; but her actions do not seem to be innocent.

MANKA

Definitely. The proximity of Dzekem to my husband and her leaving immediately I walked in fuelled my doubt. *(Barrister Johnson nods)*. I asked Your Highness why Dzekem felt uncomfortable immediately I walked in and he walked out on me, without saying a word.

BARRISTER JOHNSON

Really? *(Stares at Manka open-mouthed)*.

MANKA

Yes *(Wipes tears from her cheeks)*.

BARRISTER JOHNSON

(Pauses). Oops! I am really curious about the issue of marriage plans between the suspects. Without casting doubts on what you said, what were the other

indicators that she felt uncomfortable, and why would you think that means that they plan to get married?

MANKA

Immediately I walked into the sitting room, she stood up from her seat with her head tilted, looked at me with fright, and then at Your Highness; shifted her eyes to Ability, and walked out in a hurry.

BARRISTER JOHNSON

(Rolls her eyes as she screams). Wh-at! *(They stare at each other for a while)*. This is unbelievable coming from a Bongkisheri woman! This is strange! Dzekem could do that! And she is a member of Bongkisheri! I need to invite her to my office and get her own version of the story… But why would Your Highness want to marry another woman, considering the complaints about jealousy, fights, quarrels, ehhrr insecurity, discrimination, threats to life, conflicts over property ownership, and sharing formular which women from polygamous homes bring to the palace, the Traditional Council, and sometimes to my chambers so often?

MANKA

That's exactly my worry. My husband has been putting pressure on me to transfer ownership of my land to him. But I told him that the children he inherited from his late father would feel entitled to the land I bought for my children once it carries his name. That they may start fighting for their own share as happens in other polygamous homes. He wasn't happy when I raised these issues. He now wants to marry Dzekem to get me jealous. His plan is to transfer his love and attention to Dzekem once they are married, hoping that would get me jealous and oblige me to surrender the land to him. That's what somebody told me in confidence.

BARRISTER JOHNSON

Polygamy does not make sense to those who still have sense. *(Shakes her head)*. Give an African power and money, the next thing he does is marry many wives, create a queue of baby-mamas, make children with their wives as well as outside wedlock, drink, complain, criticise, hate, turn his manhood into a fertile ground for diseases, make enemies with people from different religions, political parties, and tribe *(shakes her head)*. Wait…, wait, Mrs Ghamogha, what type of marriage did you and your husband choose?

MANKA
Monogamy.

BARRISTER JOHNSON
(*Smiles*). Your Highness cannot take another wife again unless the first marriage is dissolved through divorce.

MANKA
The children conceived on the leopard skin belong to the Fon and are entitled to his properties, even if he inherited them. That is what tradition says. My husband has other wives and children he inherited from the late Fon of Kibaaka who was his father. That's why I need to protect what is mine.

BARRISTER JOHNSON
You are his only lawfully wedded wife in that marriage. Whatever the case, Dzekem needs to be called to order. (*Manka nods*). Now that you are here, we will go together so that I can personally deliver the Call to Order letter to your husband as you suggested yesterday. I printed it before you came in (*Stretches her hand, collects the letter from her table and gets up*). Let's go. (*Suddenly exclaims looking at Manka's dress*). Oops! You wore your dress inside-out! See…, the inner surface is outer!

MANKA
(*Looks at her dress open-mouthed*). I didn't notice it. I will change when we get home. (*They walk out*).

Outside Barrister Johnson's Chambers

(*Ability sticks out his neck from behind flowers, and stares across the yard. Binla, Foka, Biiywong, Beri, and others surge across the yard holding shovels, diggers, young trees, and cutlasses and stop in front of Johnson and Manka who stare at them open-mouthed*).

BINLA
(*Points in the direction of Bongkisheri meeting venue, panting heavily*). Cows, g-goats, heah, heah… Alhadji Musa's cows and goats have entered our farm again… (*Manka stares at Binla open-mouthed, wide-eyed*). Yes,

MANKA

Jesus Christ!

BINLA

Right now, they are still there. *(The women nod while the pale looking Biiywong lowers her buttocks to the ground).* Our maize, our onions, our pepper, the large cabbages we saw last week are destroyed…

MANKA

Again!

BINLA

Yes. *(Manka shakes her head).* If you go behind the market and look across the neighbourhood, you will think you are watching matted ants.

BIIYWONG

The portion of the farm where we scattered excreta *(Barrister Johnson leans back open-mouthed)* and planted cabbage, onions, and pepper, *(shakes her head)* … nothing remains; only naked ridges. The crops are all shaved.

BARRISTER JOHNSON

You scoop human waste from pit toilets and take to the farms?

MANKA

She is talking about fowl droppings.

BARRISTER JOHNSON

Okay. I understand.

MANKA

The women invested much, cultivating that land. When we raised and sold our last batch of chickens, we erected a different fence for the new set. We planted onions, cabbage, and pepper seedlings on the droppings. The plants did so well. The last time I checked, they were fully developed, almost ready for harvesting. From their healthy sizes, Binla and I estimated that we would harvest some fifty bags of onions, twenty bags of pepper, and over thirty bags of cabbage from the farm. Unfortunately, *(Clicks her tongue).* Mcheeep. *(To the women).* How did you know I was here?

BINLA

As it was the turn of the women of Abakwa neighbourhood to plant trees around the farm, we decided to go there early. As we approached the farm, we saw cows and goats eating our maize, onions and pepper, and trampling on plants. We decided to come and see you so that we can together inform the Fon. On our way to the palace, we met Ability and he told us that he saw you entering Barrister Johnson's office.

BERI

The Fon must hear this! *(The women nod).* Let us go to the palace and inform the Fon.

BINLA

How many times have we reported Alhadji Musa to the Fon and the Elders and nothing is done? Is it the first time his cows have destroyed our crops? The last time we took the matter to the SDO, the man said he had given strict directives to the Council to impound stray animals. We didn't hear from them thereafter. Who does not know that Alhadji Musa prefers to go and bribe the SDO with cows to get his impounded cows released than to pay for destroying our crops?

BARRISTER JOHNSON

Is that what is happening, yet nobody informed me?

BIIYWONG

(Drags her words). H-h-he has been doing that.

MANKA

(Looks at Johnson). You need to help us.

BARRISTER JOHNSON

Baba Alhadji Musa must pay for the damage this time... *(The women nod, smiling from jaw to jaw).* Mrs Ghamogha, you need to go to that land with the women, try to evaluate the damage and write a complaint on behalf of Bongkisheri and bring to me. *(Binla and Manka nod).* Don't forget to include evidence of the destruction of crops and plants, as well as your witnesses. Take pictures. *(Manka nods).* You may give the report to Mrs Ghamogha to take a look at it before it is brought to me. I will handle it later. *(Manka nods and the women disperse. Turns to Manka).* We are going somewhere now. Hop in my car.

ABILITY
I must rush to the palace and inform Your Highness about what I saw.

(*Thirty Minutes Later*)

(*The main access road to the palace from the junction is fringed with well-trimmed trees on both sides. Ability is walking up to the Palace when he looks across the vicinity and sees a car approaching*).

ABILITY
(*Bends over, wipes his eyes, peers across the neighbourhood again, and says*). That should be Barrister Johnson. She should be coming to drop off her friend, Manka, in the palace.
(*He quickly tears through the hedge of trees and sits on his heels. After a while, the car pulls up slowly into the courtyard of the Palace, hoots and stops, attracting the attention of Your Highness who is walking back and forth. Ability tiptoes further up the path, bends forward, and peers from behind the trees. Barrister Johnson and Manka step out of the car and stop in front of Your Highness. Manka bends forward while Johnson remains standing*).

BARRISTER JOHNSON
(*Stretches her right hand to the Fon for a handshake*). Hi Chief, I am Barrister Johnson. (*Manka leans back, open-mouthed*). How are you doing?

MANKA
Barrister Johnson, I am sorry, I forgot to tell you. We do not shake hands with the Fon. You just have to wait for him to greet you first.

BARRISTER JOHNSON
Euh, really! (*Manka nods*). I'm sorry, Chief, I didn't know about that. (*Stretches the letter to Your Highness*).

DINKA
(*Rushes forward*). Drop dat letter for *grang*, Big Madame. I go collect *givam* for Fon. You be woman. Woman no di touch hand for Fon.

MANKA
(Nods, collects the letter and drops on the ground, in front of Dinka). You can't give it to the Fon directly. *(Dinka picks up the letter, hands it to Your Highness and drifts back).*

YOUR HIGHNESS
(Unfolds the letter and begins to read while Ability cocks his head and bends the flap of his ear, trying to listen).

Subject: Call to Order
Your Royal Highness.

The attention of Barrister Johnson and Co Chambers has been drawn to attempts by Your Highness and the Elders, to seize a stretch of land at Kibaaka Up-Station, belonging to Mrs Ghamogha, and to a decision, by the same people, prohibiting the use, and access to the said land. We hereby note that your action, like the prohibition, is illegal, and should with immediate effect be retracted to avoid legal attention.

Signed
Barrister Johnson

YOUR HIGHNESS
(Stares at Manka open-mouthed, wide-eyed, then, turns to Barrister Johnson, shakes his head and lifts up his finger). Barrister Johnson or whatever they call you, our people say our god does not bite but will do so when you push him to the wall. For your information, I am not always this generous with enemies of our land. This is the last time I will see you and my wife together!
(Both ladies hang their mouths open as they look at each other without a word).

BARRISTER JOHNSON
Can I say some…,

YOUR HIGHNESS
(Points to the road leading away from the Palace with his staff and looks at Barrister Johnson). You don't test the depth of the river with your foot! Leave my palace now! *(Thunders).* Are you deaf?
(Barrister Johnson and Mrs Ghamogha shrug simultaneously while

Ability tosses his head with a smile).

BARRISTER JOHNSON
It's okay, I will leave. *(She turns and gets into her car and drives off).*

MANKA
Your Highness, what was the meaning of that? How could you tell her to go away like that? That was too disrespectful.

YOUR HIGHNESS
Has it come to this? Manka, who gave you the audacity to think you can gang up with the so-called Barrister Johnson to threaten me? Who deceived you, her husband? And she has the guts to think she can frighten me, Your Highness, with this piece of trash. Who should call who to order? I'm asking you. Are you still in your right frame of mind? Is something wrong with you? *(Remembers what Ability said to him).* "Your Highness, so, this is what you have become, letting a woman make decisions for you?... The worst thing that can happen to a man is to allow himself to be controlled by a woman… He is not worthy to be a village elder and should never even be admitted into the presence of men. If by some chance he finds himself among men, he should remain as silent as his fellow women when men speak. Your Highness, it is not late to recover what you have lost and what you are about to lose. The thing a man carries between his thighs is a disciplinarian. Your slap is a disciplinarian." *(His chest is rising and falling as he flings the letter at his wife's face, and rants).* I need to kill the man in you, today. *(Ability nods in a goading gesture and cocks his head as he peers across the yard through a tiny space between the leaves).* Manka, you have crossed the boundary line! Keep stirring up trouble for this land. Let me tell you, when the time comes, your Barrister Johnson will not help you. *(Shakes his head).* It is only a foolish woman who goes under the rain having only one wrapper. She calls herself Johnson, a man's name, and she has no child to show for her sex. How will one know her sex? Has she not been the one marching on the streets with men dressed as women, or may I say women dangling the penis between their legs? *(Manka shrugs).* Will you deny that she is like the likes of *Savage, Livinus, Katika,* and others like them? How do I know what is between her legs if I have never heard the cry of a baby in her house? All your associates have a problem with their sex. Your own sister, Regular, is known as "the man" all around town; here you are, playing the man with me at home and with tradition over land ownership. Keep associating with men in

women's dress and appearance, you are all members of a confused sex. A gang of stubborn creatures that deliberately deny their own sex. No man with balls, not to talk of a man of my standing, will tolerate what you are doing. Does this your legal patron of mad women, Barrister Johnson or whoever you call her, even knows what you do behind her back? Does she know that her own so-called husband is negotiating a child from you? *(Manka leans back, wide eyes and open-mouthed).* Wasn't it just yesterday that your secret boyfriend, the so-called Honourable Wirkitum, was spotted robbing his fingers on your jaws with your consent and collaboration? Deny it, if you dare!

MANKA
I refuse to be insulted.

YOUR HIGHNESS
(Ability keeps nodding and smiling, moving his hand rapidly forth and back in an inciting gesture). You have the effrontery to bring this sexless being to threaten me. You refuse to give me the land! You allowed a Come-no-Go to touch what belongs to me! Listen very well. Your excesses will soon force me to withdraw the privilege you enjoy as the only legal wife of the Paramount Fon of Kibaaka.

MANKA
How do you mean?

YOUR HIGHNESS
When a pig refuses to eat from a dish, cast its food on the floor.

ABILITY
(With a smile, Ability nods his head repeatedly).

YOUR HIGHNESS
Get ready to watch a woman who will love and respect me walk into my heart!

MANKA
I refuse to be numbered!

YOUR HIGHNESS
I am a man. I can marry as many wives as I want!

MANKA

So, it is true?

ABILITY

(Smiling from his hide-out). My traps are doing an excellent job.

MANKA

Well, life is a choice. You can choose to live your life the way you want it. Unfortunately, you cannot choose to avoid the consequences of wrong decisions.

YOUR HIGHNESS

Your place is already taken in my heart.

MANKA

If you choose to be counting wives and problems while your mates like Honourable are celebrating achievements, then, get ready to shoulder the heavy responsibilities that come with polygamy…

YOUR HIGHNESS

(Slaps Manka on the face). Paah, paah, paah. You dare confirm it? *(A rainfall of slaps on her face again)*. Pah, pah, pah, pah…, *(Like the catalyst in the Royal fight that he is, Ability peers through the leaves, kicking out his legs in a goading gesture, as if to say, go on, beat her)*.

MANKA

(Screams aloud). You slap me?

YOUR HIGHNESS

I will do it again and again if you dare mention Honourable in my presence! *(Her continuous screams attract Bame, Fomu, and Kila. Jaidzeka and her mother Rush out from their apartment, and stand across the palace courtyard, watching, lifting their legs and kicking out, smiling, and nodding their heads in stirring gestures, as Your Highness unleashes a series of punches on his wife's forehead, knocking her to the ground. Fomu, Bame, and Kila struggle to stand in the middle of Your Highness and their mother who has staggered to her feet, crying, urging their father to stop the beating. The wild screams seem also to attract the approaching Biy Wiiba and Binla who rush to the scene, look at the Fon, turn and look at each other, and then, throw their hands apart).*

MANKA
Bongkisheri will fight my battles. The law will fight my battles. *(Binla nods while the open-mouthed Biy Wiiba swiftly plants the palm of her right hand onto Manka's lips to prevent her from talking back at the Fon).*

YOUR HIGHNESS
Which law? Does the law fight another law? If you drag the Fon to court, you have dragged tradition to court. Your law recognizes traditional law. There's nothing you can do.
(Your Highness turns and walks back inside).

BIY WIIBA
Manka, you are a woman. You don't talk back when the father of your children is talking. Kibaaka must not hear that this kind of thing happened. The children are watching.

YOUR HIGHNESS
(Thinking aloud). What will people say when they hear that the Fon of Kibaaka has beaten his wife? I shouldn't have done that in public... But Ability said she is sleeping with Honourable.

(Outside the Courtyard of the Palace)

MANKA
(Cleans blood gliding down her cheeks with the edge of her dress and turns to her children). Stop crying. I will be fine. Go back inside. *(The children pull away hesitantly, dragging their feet across the yard, while throwing glances at their mother).*

BIY WIIBA
(Looks at the blood on Manka's swollen face and asks). Manka, what happened?

MANKA
(Stares vacantly across the yard as memories of the Fon's reaction to the letter of observation, and of the accusations of infidelity, float before her face). "Manka, who gave you the audacity to think you can gang up with the so-called Barrister

Johnson to threaten me? Who deceived you, her husband? Who should call who to order? Wasn't it just yesterday that your secret boyfriend, the so-called Honourable Wirkitum, was spotted robbing his fingers on your jaws with your consent and collaboration?" *(She wipes her face, closes her eyes and tries hard to remember Honourable's reaction the moment she went to complain about the plans to seize her land).*

MANKA

I was told that the Traditional Council has ordered me to suspend all Bong-kisheri activities on the land. Please help me. That land is the future of my children. It will become family property if the land title carries the name of my husband. He has other wives and children.

HONOURABLE

I can see tears in your eyes. *(Pulls out a tissue from his pocket and wipes tears gliding down Manka's cheeks)."*

(Manka opens her eyes and muses).

MANKA

(Thinking aloud). Someone has poisoned his mind. Honourable actually wiped tears from my eyes, but that action was innocent. Someone who saw it must have told him.

BINLA

(To Manka). Be strong, Ma.

BIY WIIBA

I know how you feel. I also received beatings. Three days before today, there were cuts all over my body. I was urinating blood, having been beaten with a pounding stick by the father of my children for marching bare body. This whole thing about our rights and equal opportunities will run us all into problems. There is nothing we can do about it.

MANKA

The law will fight this battle for me *(Binla repeatedly nods in a goading manner that attracts Biy Wiiba).*

BIY WIIBA

(Opens her mouth and eyes wide, stares at Binla, and then at Manka).

MANKA

I must seek legal redress. I must go to court.

BIY WIIBA

Go to court? *Hei!* Manka, some solutions are problems. Kibaaka people and your in-laws must not hear this kind of talk. They will turn their backs on you. Do you want to be banned from gatherings?

BINLA

How do we stop the men from beating us if we cannot speak up?

BIY WIIBA

You are a woman. There are better ways. We can use the woman's way to win bedroom battles. Just cook the meal he likes best and serve him with fresh palm wine to accompany the food. He will not lift his hand on you again. That is the only way to prevent the father of your children from beating you. That is what my mother told me.

MANKA

(Thinking). Biy Wiiba's method is the method of most women, but such a method is a recipe for oppression. Why would any woman adopt such a method which means living in constant fear? Besides, if I adopt her method, I will lose the land I am fighting for. No, I must seek legal redress… But…, if I take my husband to court, will the women still stand by me? Will they not consider it taboo? How will they take it if they hear that I took my husband to court?… Will they not call me names and hate me? How will the people of Kibaaka react if they hear that I took their Fon to court? *(Shakes her head as she wipes the blood gliding down her cheeks).* God! Can a woman really speak?

BIY WIIBA

Manka, I know how you feel, but we must not do everything Barrister Johnson tells us to do. Our ways are different from the new ways.

BINLA

(Looks at her wristwatch). Presi, we came to see you so that we can go to our

farm to evaluate the damage, and to also remind you that the women are already waiting for you to start the meeting.

MANKA

Jesus Christ! I almost forgot we have two important assignments to do today. We will go straight to the farm now and check the crops before joining the women. We will not spend much time there. I will go inside now and clean up, and change.

BIY WIIBA

(Binla and Biy Wiiba suddenly bend forward as Dinka tears across the courtyard, holding a Peace Plant on one hand and grabbing a fresh leaf between his lips).

MANKA

Is that not Dinka! What's that he's holding, and where's he going to? *(Opens her mouth to call Dinka across the yard).* Din…

BIY WIIBA

(Quickly clamps her palm over Manka's lips and cautions her). Don't say a word. *(Binla nods).* Just bend forward. You cannot talk to the messenger of the Palace when you see the leaf gripped between his lips. Just shift aside and bend down. Only a man can talk to him. *(Binla nods. Manka walks into the house).*

IN THE SITTING ROOM

(Manka walks in dressed to go out. A blood-stained bandage is wrapped around her forehead).

YOUR HIGHNESS

Manka, since you have decided to test the depth of the river with your feet, I have decided to inform Nwerong that you have bought land in your name. I have just sent Dinka to Shufai Laika with a message for Nwerong. Get ready to hear from Nwerong soon! You will not only surrender the land to me; you will pay heavy fines and if you are unfortunate, you will be banished, sent on exile. That is the punishment for any woman who wants to become a man in Kibaaka. I have another message for you. If my investigation confirms that you and Honourable are seeing each other, I will pluck off your eyes and cut off your ears before sending you to the grave. As for what I will do to Honourable, I will not say it now.

MANKA
(Drifts back, turns and stretches her head across the door, looks around, returns and tries to speak twisting her face in pains). Thelma…,

YOUR HIGHNESS
Ngiri! Did you just call me by my name?

MANKA
Yes, I did. Thelma, listen to me, I can take any insult but not accusations of adultery. I guess you or whoever, framed up the story to avoid explaining to me what Dzekem came to do in my house. Well, you owe me an explanation.

YOUR HIGHNESS
I owe you an explanation! *(Shakes his head open-mouthed and speaks).* I am now the one to give you explanations! Manka, before you go back to your gathering of hens turned cocks, I want to remind you of one fact that you cannot reverse: I paid bride price on your head and not the other way round. Once you have sold your fish at the Kibaaka market you cannot expect to have them back and keep the money. I am going to show you that I am the man in this union.
(Manka turns and walks out of the room, texting a message to Barrister Johnson as she walks towards her car. The message pops up on the screen of her telephone, and she reads).

MANKA
(Reads). Dear Barrister Johnson, Your Highness wants to involve Nwerong in the land matter. I suggest we do a new Land Title carrying the name of any of my sons. I need to present that paper to Nwerong to avoid their exile sentence and heavy fines. What do you think?

BARRISTER JOHNSON
(Texting). Yes, but it takes a long time to get the Certificate of Change of Name which must be signed by the Minister of Lands. Don't worry. We will seek legal redress. I am busy now. We will discuss the issue later. I will see you soon.

MANKA

Mama Biy, Binla, get into the car. We're late. *(She drives off).*

At Bongkisheri Farmland

(Enter Masked Boys (Dzekewong, Tomla, Viban and Tombir).Manka, Biy Wiiba, and Binla hunch over ridges, counting the damaged ridges and plants, and jotting down notes when a group of masked boys suddenly creep towards them from behind, shout orders, kicking them to the ground).

VIBAN

(Kicks Biy Wiiba on her side and descends on her). No look my face! Open leg them!

TOMLA

Cover your eye! *(Kicks Manka in her buttocks sending her to the ground where she lies flat on her stomach, screaming in pain, struggling to kick out).*

WOMEN

Somebody he-eelp…somebody heeeeelp….

TOMLA

Close dat your mouth and cooperate! Open your two leg dem, quick, quick! If I hear one word from *wuna* mouth again, dem go bury all *wuna* today. *(Like Viban and Tombir, he kicks her legs apart, pulls down his trousers, descends on the subdued victim and begins to claw into her legs).* If I see you or any woman for dis farm again, you go open foot carry me again.

MANKA

(Listens to the voice and muses). The voice sounds familiar. So, this is about the land!

TOMLA

(Gets up and asks his friend to take over). Kewong *(Dzekewong quickly holds his lips squashed as if to say do not mention my name),* come chop na. You no de hungry?

DZEKEWONG

Dem no be talk say make we chop. Dem be only talk say make we lookot the farm and beat them if dem enter farm again.

> (After a while, they get up and run into a nearby farm leaving the women wiggling on the ground like wounded worms).

MANKA

(Tilts her head, rolls her half-closed eyes across the yard, and speaks in a hushed voice). They are gone.

BIY WIIBA

(Panting). Let's hurry and leave this place before anybody finds out.

MANKA

(Panting). My laps are hurting. He held my neck down and forced his way in. I am invaded again.

BIY WIIBA

It must not be mentioned anywhere. Nobody should hear about it. Not even your husband!

MANKA

Why?

BIY WIIBA

This is Kibaaka. What will people say when they hear that you slept with another man? They will use it to insult us. Where will I hide my shame? No! They will use it against us some day. If the father of my children hears that I slept with another man, we will never join again.

BINLA

It is true. They will cut grass and branches of trees to raise a bed with on the scene. That is what they do where such a thing happens. They raise a grass-bed on the scene and hoist the woman's bra or shredded pant on the bed. Nobody will marry me if they hear about it.

MANKA

We need to report the matter to the Police.

BINLA

It should not go out. The people of Kibaaka do not distinguish between forceful and wilful sex. They will blame us; they will say we wore revealing dresses.

MANKA

Are these really Bongkisheri voices? Has Bongkisheri been working to unlock or seal the lips? Are we still afraid to speak out when the lock on our lips has been broken? Shall we still foster our own suppression by keeping our oppression secret? My kind, you speak not for yourselves, you say just what our sex believes. *(Shakes her head).* We need to be treated immediately to avoid possible infections. *(Binla nods approval, wiggling in pain).*

BIY WIIBA

I will go and consult where nobody knows me. My sister is married to a Ndungu man, they live in Bakissam. I will go there for a visit and then, visit a doctor.

MANKA

We will consult in Bakissam. But we must inform the Police. Allow everything to me. I will write the complaint. I will also inform Barrister Johnson to assist us in this fight. No woman should suffer invasion again! *(Binla nods approval).* Let us leave this place before they come back. You heard what they said. *(They get up, dusts their arms, legs, dresses, and stagger to the car).*

ACT 4

Scene V

ABILITY AND REGULAR

(Ability walks up the path with quick heavy steps and bumps into a huge, dark, broad-shouldered muscular woman with round eyes. She is wearing a low-shoulder blouse that reveals sprinkles of hair on her chest, the tattoo of a key on her chest, and parts of her breasts).

REGULAR

Abili, is something chasing you?

ABILITY

Regu, I have looked for you everywhere.

REGULAR

I hope there's no problem.

ABILITY

If you do not want to write your sister's obituary, then, tell her to leave the palace when she is still in one piece.

REGULAR

I don't understand.

ABILITY

Are you telling me that nobody has informed you?

REGULAR

About what? *(Stares at Ability wide-mouthed, her chest rising and falling).* I hope nothing has happened to my sister?

ABILITY

Thank God Manka was rescued alive after the brutal punches and kicks Your

Highness served her.

REGULAR
What happened?

ABILITY
She bought land. The chaos that that act has created are far reaching. She might even be expelled from Kibaaka.

REGULAR
Ghamogha will hate my reaction.

ABILITY
Who does not know Regular? Who does not know that you are the only woman who can win a battle with in-laws. Regular, do something. As I was approaching the palace, I heard a voice crying in pain *(imitating):* "wa-ai, waai, hooi, hooi, somebody he-e-lp, somebody he-e-lp". I thought either Bongkisheri women have gone to report that Alhadji Musa's cows destroyed their crops, or the villagers have caught Fola sleeping with somebody's wife again and have dragged him before the Fon. Regular, you could think you were watching John Cena, Roman Reigns, or Patrick Nganou, knocking down and kicking a subdued opponent.

REGULAR
That marriage is dead and needs a coffin!

ABILITY
Rengreng! Who does not know that Regular is the only woman who will liberate women from domestic violence?

REGULAR
I am going to the palace now!

ABILITY
Don't tell anybody what I am about to tell you. If you do, Your Highness will hide many secrets from me which your sister needs to know and do what she can possibly do to remain the owner of her land. He may even drag me before Nwerong for taking palace matters to the public.

                           REGULAR
I will die with any secret that protects my sister's land.

                            ABILITY
Good. Your Highness is making plans to marry Dzekem to make your sister feel jealous. He thinks that when another woman comes into his life, Manka would feel threatened and surrender her land to him in order to gain back her privileged place in his heart. There's nothing he plans to do and does not seek my opinion on it. The throne is at stake. The Fon would do anything to grab your sister's land in order to keep the throne.

                           REGULAR
Not when I am alive!

                            ABILITY
Nwerong will dethrone Your Highness for allowing a woman to buy land in her name. And Your Highness is not ready to lose the throne and become a nobody. That is why he can even sacrifice his love for Manka to get that land.

                           REGULAR
She once told me in confidence that that land belongs to her three children. I will join forces with Bongkisheri to help my sister.

                            ABILITY
There's one obstacle Bongkisheri will face in the land battle. Your Highness has the support of the Traditional Council.

                           REGULAR
(Remembers what her late mother told them before passing on). "Regular, be the fence around your sister, Manka. I want you and Manka to stay together like a bunch of plantains. Our people say that a single broomstick is easily broken but a bundle of broomsticks will never be broken." *(Opens her eyes and speaks).* I am ready to do anything to protect my sister, and to help her keep her land. What do I do? I need you to help me get my sister and her land out of that marriage. I need you to help me.

                            ABILITY
I will help you but not openly. Whatever we do should remain a secret. I don't

want the Fon to report me to Nwerong. *(Regular nods consent). Herr,* Regu, I am doing all this because of the love I have for you ohhh. You know I have always loved you and you know I knew you before Fola and that old man called Verdzekov used their financial muscles to snatch you.

REGULAR
If I get what I want, you will get what you want.

ABILITY
I have never failed an examination.

REGULAR
I need to find my sister now. *(Turns and leaves).*

ABILITY
Let me see how the Fon will continue to enjoy his marriage.

ACT 5

Scene I

AT THE BONGKISHERI WOMEN'S CENTRE

(Manka, Binla, and Biy Wiiba walk into the hall, attracting all eyes as they sit on a raised surface alongside Barrister Johnson and Biiywong, facing the crowd. The dust on their twisted dresses and arms, the blood-stained bandage around Manka's forehead and her swollen red eyes attract different reactions across the hall. The women lean back, open-mouthed, wide-eyed, stare at Manka and the two women, turn and look at each other, shift their stares back to Manka, and then, throw their hands apart in surprised and questioning gestures. With a fixed stare at Manka's bruised face, some of the members of the EXCO ask questions).

BARRISTER JOHNSON
W-w-w-what happened…?

BIIYWONG
(Her hands and lips tremble as she speaks). P-p-president, were you people attacked by dogs? *(Hangs her mouth open).*

MANKA
(Twists her face, bites her lips, like someone in pains, lifts her mouth to Barrister Johnson's ear and whispers). I'll explain later. *(Turns to the women and greets in their usual slogan).* Bongkisheri!

WOMEN
(Lift up their clenched fists and respond). Power to the women. Collective strength is victory. The woman's turn. It is good to be happy.

MANKA
Thank you so much. Barrister Johnson, Fellow women, good afternoon and thank you for your concern. There's nothing to worry about. It is well. *(Stares at Biiywong's trembling hands).* Biiywong, we are really happy to have you with

us today. This should be a sign that you are feeling much better. I wasn't really expecting to see you in the morning. We learned you were very sick again and we planned to delegate women as usual to visit you with a small envelope for your drugs. Mami Biy, Binla and I will be coming on behalf of Bongkisheri. *(The women nod approval).*

BIIYWONG

T-t-t-thank you s-s-so much. *(Turns and faces Manka, smiling).* I want to t-thank our P-president so much. She-she has been sending me f-f-food and m-money. Manka is-is t-t-the reason I am still alive. She has been doing a lot for Ntumfon and I hope she will continue even w-w-when I am no more breathing.

MANKA

Fellow women, *(opens and closes her mouth and eyes, struggling to speak).* Well, I have a slight headache. I will be brief. We have four issues on our agenda: the Elections, Cookery demonstrations as part of activities ahead of the International Women's Day; the destruction of our crops, feedback from my meeting with the Elders, and the way forward. I will not be present during cookery demonstrations and other discussions. As you all know, the Governor pleaded with the women to call off the protest, promising that the Traditional Council was ready for a fruitful dialogue with the women. We also agreed to call our own meeting to assess the progress made so far in addressing our demand to lift the contentious ban. *(The women nod with heightened curiosity).* Although we were not invited to any formal meeting with the Elders as such, the Elders' Council did meet and sent a representative, Shufai Laika, to inform me that land belongs to the man…

BIIYWONG

W-why did they ask us to suspend the protest then?

WOMEN

(The women throw their hands apart). Ohoorr!

MANKA

Fellow women, the protest will resume next week.

WOMEN
(Spirited applause tears across the hall). Feyi.

BARRISTER JOHNSON
(Nods to the decision with a smile). Good decision.

MANKA
Bongkisheri EXCO will fix a new date for the sit-down protest and inform all of us…

WOMEN
Feyi.

MANKA
(Barrister Johnson whispers something in her ear. She turns to address the women). Barrister Johnson just suggested that given the present conditions which include the destruction of our crops, the threats to take away my land, and to ban Bongkisheri, we should postpone the elections until further notice…

WOMEN
(Cuts in). Rengreng…

MANKA
We have taken note. The next item on our agenda is cookery demonstrations. During our last meeting, we assigned the women of Bukang-Yerr branch of Bongkisheri to do a demonstration on fried rice and the marking of toghu, as part of our activities toward the International Women's Day celebrations. The person assigned to lead the lessons is Mama Habiba. Mama Habiba, get ready with your team please.

HABIBA
Tenk you *Piresiden*, we are ready. *(She steps forward and beckons the women of her branch to join her).* Join me here oohhhh. *(Habiba and other women move to one corner and start arranging their items).*

MANKA
Fellow women, as I said earlier, I am not feeling fine. I need to go to the hospital now. I will now leave you to continue with the demonstrations. *(Turns*

to Barrister Johnson and speaks in a muted voice). Barrister Johnson, I'll like to have a word with you across the yard, please.

BARRISTER JOHNSON
No problem. *(They two women walk out).*

ACROSS THE COURTYARD OF BONGKISHERI WOMEN'S CENTRE

BARRISTER JOHNSON
You look shabby and tired with bloodstains all over your body. What happened?

MANKA
Mami Biy Wiiba, Binla and I were *emmmr* invaded by masked men at the Women's farmland, the extension below the Community Forest.

BARRISTER JOHNSON
What do you mean by "invaded"? Was there any penetration? *(Manka nods).* W-w-w-what? *(Manka nods, wipes tears gliding down her cheeks).*

BARRISTER JOHNSON
(A long silence). I am sorry about what happened to you. Do you have any suspects in mind?

MANKA
One of them said: "If I see you or any woman for dis farm again, you go open foot carry me again." Another one mentioned "Kewong." I suspect that Dzekewong was there but he didn't touch us.

BARRISTER JOHNSON
So, this is about land.

MANKA
I think so.

BARRISTER JOHNSON
I know what to do. The three of you involved should write a complaint and bring to me. Make sure you ask for a medical report from the Doctor. *(Manka nods).* I am sorry again. I will see you later. Come with your medical report.

(They separate).

(Five Minutes Later)

MANKA AND REGULAR

(Manka is driving out of the meeting premises when she sights Regular on an approaching motorbike flagging her car. She pulls up to the shoulder of the road and parks. Regular jumps down from the bike, squeezes money into the hand of the rider and crosses the road to meet her sister, leaning over her car).

MANKA

Regular, why are you sweating like this? I hope there's no problem.

REGULAR

If death is actually punishment for wrongdoing, what is Ghamogha still doing here on earth?

MANKA

What are you talking about?

REGULAR

(Shakes her head, pointing to the bruises and the bloodstained bandage around Manka's face). Your eyes are swollen as if you were stung by bees. Look at your gown, twisted, dusty *(Yanks specks of grass from Manka's hair).* Manka, I learned your husband did this to you, just to frighten you and seize your land.

MANKA

That is the price my kind pays for speaking out.

REGULAR

Is that the price you want to pay too? Are you not the one who has been encouraging women to speak out when their rights are abused?

MANKA

He is a man. He has the backing of the Elders.

REGULAR
(Thunders). I am going to teach your so-called husband and Elders that I, Regular, did not earn the title, "the man", for nothing.

MANKA
Regu, misunderstandings between husband and wife do not require external intrusion.

REGULAR
Manka, I know you're dying in silence. You need to heal. Divorce is the only drug that can liberate you and your land from the prison called marriage.

MANKA
Divorce?

REGULAR
Don't you see that marriage takes a woman hostage? Do you need somebody to tell you that you have been kidnapped twice? Manka, walk away with what is left of you.

MANKA
Regular, I am a married woman. The father of my children paid bride price on my head.

REGULAR
Yes, I know the so-called bride price is what has given your husband total rights over you and your senses. Manka, how much was it? Crumbs, isn't it? I have enough money in my account. Let's refund the bride price tomorrow and then, you can walk out of the prison called marriage and keep your land.

MANKA
Regular, I don't know what to do but that's not the way to go about it.

REGULAR
You have been fighting for women. You mean you can't fight for yourself? Manka, you risk losing everything you desperately want to be, including your land if you continue worshipping marriage and domestic tyrants! *(Manka is silent)*. Manka, our mother asked me to look after you and I am sure she would

not be happy with me if I continue to fold my arms; sit quietly and watch that butcher you call a husband slaughter you. No, no. I will fight your battle. Leave everything to me and wait for results. Your so-called husband needs to feel your absence since he refused to appreciate and value your presence. I will help you go out there and rent a house.

MANKA

It has not come to that.

REGULAR

Roadside talk says the Fon is planning to marry Dzekem. Is it when his matrimonial hive is swelling with hostages like you that you will realise that marriage is a prison?

MANKA

I understand your concern, but it's a normal thing for couples to disagree. I can't leave my husband. What about people calling me a single and free woman? Have you thought about that?

REGULAR

Do you prefer to die in the name of wanting to be "Mrs"? What is wrong with some of these women! Should a woman die for her marriage to survive? Must one risk her life to be called 'Mrs' at all cost? What are you doing in a toxic marriage? You have a job; you have money. You have connections. You can knock doors that the so-called husband and elders are afraid to look at. Money can do things. Marriage is for lazy women. A woman needs her own space. That's the only way you will be free and happy. That's the only way to protect your land from land grabbers.

MANKA

What about my children? *(Squeezes her face in pain as she speaks)*. When a woman leaves a marriage, she has decided that her children will be raised either by separate parents or by a stranger. I cannot take a decision that will satisfy me alone and penalize my kids.

REGULAR

The results will be the same if your husband kills you. The same children will be brought up by Ghamogha alone or by his next wife. Don't you think the children will be better off with you alive than when you are dead? What stops you from walking out of this toxic marriage with your children?

MANKA
Have you bothered to find out if that is what I want? What will people say when they hear that I abandoned the father of my children, or stole his children away?

REGULAR
Did you bother about what people will say when you bought land? Are you not the one who advised me that single life should not mean homelessness and I went ahead to buy my own parcel of land through Ability where I am building in somebody else's name? Many women are secretly doing it. By the way, has any man ever bothered about what you want or do not want? Forget about what people will say. You are the one receiving the pain and the punches. Your mission is not to please anybody but to do what makes you happy and free. Is that difficult to understand? Leave those children with their father, then.

MANKA
It is not a good idea to walk away from marriage when kids are involved. *(Holds her forehead with her hand, twists her body in pain as she speaks).* I don't think it is proper for a woman to abandon the responsibility of bringing up her children, not even to another woman. That's what I am saying. Are you sure my children will get proper upbringing growing up with another woman who will definitely see them as a threat to her own children's inheritance? Regular, which of Ability's children is in the classroom? Which of them speaks English? Have you seen Ntumfon these days? Where's Ability's daughter? Why is Ntumfon and his sister not in the classroom? My sister, marriage survives on patience and tolerance.

REGULAR
Get ready to tolerate violence and lose your land. Get ready to watch your husband exploit your patience and tolerance for life.

MANKA
Bongkisheri is working hard to stop that.

REGULAR
Where was Bongkisheri when your husband was smacking and pouncing

you? Look at your face!

MANKA
If you want your marriage to survive, you must learn to tolerate and endure.

REGULAR
Get ready for more beatings in your marriage of endurance. Get ready to lose your land in your marriage of tolerance.

MANKA
I did not marry an Angel. We still love each other.

REGULAR
Your husband has a strange way of loving. What is he doing with Dzekem when you still love each other? Tell me! You are in love with yourself. When Dzekem moves into your house and replaces you in your husband's heart and bed, you will agree with me that you were really in love with a dream. *(Manka rubs her hand on the blood-stained bandage, writhing in pain).* Manka, you are my only surviving sister. I don't want to lose you. I will not be able to handle the pain of losing you. *(Wipes tears from her cheeks).*

MANKA
I appreciate your concern, but the Fon is still my husband. I cannot destroy what I am expected to repair. We married for better, for worse.

REGULAR
Can't you see that this slogan was coined by men to justify endurance, tolerance and domestic violence? Don't you realize that the "better" side of marriage is for the man and the "worse" for the woman? Does 'for better, for worse' exclude your own happiness? Does it not validate violence against women? Is not a broken marriage better than a broken face?

MANKA
Every woman needs a man. Regular, I am tired of people calling you a barren farm. Our mother will not be happy if you leave this world the way you came. Your name needs to stay alive when you leave this world. You need a man. You need a roof over your head. You need a family. You need to be a mother.

REGULAR
You can be a mother without being a wife, or a wife without being a mother.

MANKA
And what will you tell your child or children when they grow up and start asking you where they came from?

REGULAR
I knew it would come to this when I learned that Fada Anton and his Christians recently made you the President of the Catholic Women's Association and co-opted you in his marriage-counselling committee. Forget about what Fada Anton tells you every Sunday; marriage is not an achievement.

MANKA
My husband is the reason I am a wife and a mother.

REGULAR
Why do you always struggle to yoke "wife" and "mother"? You can be a mother without being a wife. And you can be a wife without being a mother. Do not forget that you can be happy and fulfilled as a single woman. A single life is a life of felicity.

MANKA
Stop deceiving yourself. No woman is single by choice. No woman is happy being single.

REGULAR
Manka, are you a servant or a partner in marriage?

MANKA
Regu, I have made my choice.

REGULAR
You want to justify your stay in bondage. You are determined to carry your "Mrs" title to the grave. *(Shakes her head)*. Manka, if it is a charm working on you, I will not rest until I liberate you from it and from that butcher and land thief you call husband!

MANKA
My husband is not a thief. You need to respect him.

REGULAR
If we are talking about the same person, say "our husband" or, are you still in your monogamous dream? I have always wondered whether the same man that gave birth to me gave birth to you! Do you really care about your own happiness? Is there something you cannot provide for yourself? Are you like some of these Kibaaka women whose husbands are their financial saviours?... I am sure that land grabber has given you charms.

MANKA
You cannot continue to insult my husband that way! Besides, he is the Fon.

REGULAR
I worship achievements and money, not titles.

MANKA
Regular! *(Stares at Regular, open-mouthed)* ..., You are not familiar with the matrimonial scene; you can't advise.

REGULAR
I did not come here to be insulted…
(Screams and desperate yelps for help suddenly begin to waft across the yard, attracting their attention. They look at each other open-mouthed, and turn toward the direction of the noise, throwing hands apart).

VOICE
Somebody he-elp, somebody he-e-e-e-e-e-lp…

MANKA
What's happening over there? Get into the car. Let's go back there and find out what's happening. *(Turns her car and drives back to the courtyard with her sister. Biiywong lies straight across the door with eyes wide open and white while the women are screaming as they struggle to fan air into her mouth).* What happened to her?

BINLA
She slumped.

MANKA
(Places her ear on Biiywong's chest, looks at her white eyes and shakes her head). Lift her to my car please. We need to rush her to the hospital. *(Regular and Binla lift her to the car across the yard).* Someone should go and call Fada Anton to come to the hospital and pray for her.

(Thirty Minutes later)

(The women are gathered in front of the Doctor's consultation Room, sticking out their necks).

MANKA
Beri, go and inform the parents of Biiywong that she slumped and we rushed her to the hospital. We need her family members around. *(Beri withdraws as Binla and the woman who went to see Fada Anton return).*

WOMAN
Fada Anton says the Catechist will come and pray for her. He complained that Biiywong has not been paying her tithes and marking her Card…
  (The door opens and the Doctor walks out of the consultation room and stands facing the curious women).

MANKA
(Without wasting time, Manka steps forward, her lips and hands trembling, and asks). Doctor, how's she?

DOCTOR
She suffered a cardiac arrest. I am sorry, she didn't make it…
  (The whole place is thrown into confusion and lamentation with smacking of buttocks, crying, screaming, and exclamations. Some simply cross their raised hands over their heads).

MANKA
(Crosses her raised hands over her head, her mouth wide. She steps behind and makes a call to inform Biiywong's uncle).

BIY WIIBA
How do we break this kind of news to her mother?

YULEM
(Stamps her feet hard on the ground). Hooi, ebeeei, hililililili, chei! Biiywong, why have you done this to me? Why? Who will bring me garden eggs and okra pods again? Wuyee….
(Manka and members of the EXCO drift back, speak in teary voices and return to talk to the women).

MANKA
(In a trembling voice). Dear women, we have lost one of our members. She was a nice woman. *(The women nod in consent).* As usual, Bongkisheri women should be at her parents' compound every day until she is buried. Tomorrow, the Financial Secretary and I will go and withdraw three hundred thousand frs CFA from Kibaaka Credit Union. I suggest we hand the money to Biiywong's parents.

BIY WIIBA
Bongkisheri Bylaws say in the event of the death of a member, the condolence envelope shall be handed to her husband. We should give the money to Ability.

BINLA
We cannot give the condolence envelope to Ability. Biiywong was living with her parents when she died. She died a single woman.

BIY WIIBA
Ability paid bride price on Biiywong. Her people did not return the bride price when she left her husband. She cannot be buried in her father's compound. Ability was still her husband at the time of her death. Her corpse belongs to Ability. Her body will be buried in Ability's compound. That is what the ways of our land say.

MANKA
Really? *(Biy Wiiba nods).*

BINLA
Ability abandoned Biiywong and her son even when she fell sick. Her parents

have been moving her from one herbalist to another without any assistance from Ability and his people. His daughter is in the city, sleeping around. Ability does not deserve the money and the body of Biiywong. He cannot bury the wife he abandoned with two children. *(Some women nod in approval).*

BIY WIIBA
Our people say that we do not sell a goat and hold the rope.

MANKA
Biiywong was a Christian. I thought she should be buried at the church cemetery.

BIY WIIBA
When a woman dies, only her husband has the right to decide where her body would be buried.

YULEM
Let us give the money to the father of Biiywong. I am sure he will bury his daughter in the Catholic Church cemetery. Biiywong was a Christian. She used to wash the church every Saturday and farm Fada's garden until she fell sick. *(Points to the Catechist, who approaches and steps forward).*

MANKA
Catechist, she didn't make it.

PA JACOV
Her uncle already informed us before I left Fada Anton.

MANKA
We were discussing her burial before you came. We have a condolence envelope to assist the family with but we need to know where she will be buried.

PA JACOV
She owes tithes and other church contributions. She cannot be buried where faithful souls are unless her contributions are paid. That is what Fada Anton said.

BIY WIIBA
That money must be given to Ability to avoid the anger of the gods.

MANKA
I have listened to you all. Bongkisheri Bylaws say we should give the condolence envelope to the spouse or the next-of-kin of the deceased. Considering the circumstances of her death, I suggest we give half of the money to Biiywong's parents to cover the expenses they incurred while she was sick, and part to Ability to organize her burial.

WOMEN
I support, I support, I support, I support…
> *(The women nod in approval except Biy Wiiba who keeps shaking her head in protest).*

PA JACOV
I suggest we use part of the money to pay her church contributions so that she can be buried like a Christian. God will transfer her soul from small fire to Heaven if she is buried in the Christian tradition.

MANKA
What puzzles me is that the church has never evaluated the work I hear she continuously did on Fada's farm but is more interested in her unpaid church contributions. I think her children need that money more than the Church. *(The women nod in agreement)*. Biiywong left with her son, Ntumfon, and her daughter. She once told me her son was living with her at her parents' compound and later went to live with his father. Her daughter is a babysitter in the city. We need to help Ntumfon. Bongkisheri will take over his education and upkeep.

WOMEN
(Chorus in a unanimous approval). Rengreng.

MANKA
We will all gather where mourning is taking place. I will see you all later. I need to consult my doctor now.

> *(They disperse in different directions).*

(Two Days Later)

Funeral at Ability's Compound

(The men, seated on chairs around Ability, in his sitting room are drinking palm wine, beer, eating, and making stories. Ability's son, Ntumfon, aged about ten, sits on the floor, constantly wiping tears gliding down his cheeks, with the back of his hands. His dwarf toes are interwoven with sprinklings of nodes. They look like ginger, smeared with sticky mud. His hair is tangled, looking like matted ants. His finger and toenails look like the talons of a duck. He has on a torn shirt over threadbare shorts, revealing his tiny male member sleeping on his thigh like an earthworm that did not fully develop before birth. Once in a while, a woman falters out of the plantain farm or side road, staggers into the compound with hands crossed over her head. She would fall down and roll across the courtyard, gets up, drags her feet heavily and noisily, taps her buttocks, dances erratically in sympathetic emotional display, biting and curling her lips at intervals, lamenting, screaming, crying, recalling the good things Biiywong did, how generous she was, pointing randomly at surfaces before proceeding to join the other women seated and sobbing on wet leaves lined across the floor in the 'ngai' or family hall. Billows of hairy grey smoke spiral through the perforated sheets of zinc up the smoke-filled hall. Inside and behind the hall, women are cooking on stone firesides; receiving gifts of food items from villagers and family members; serving cooked food in leaves and in baskets. Villagers drift in groups across the yard, eating fufu and vegetables from leaves. Some are dipping fingers and scooping and swallowing chunks of pounded yams well-moulded into lumps with a tiny crater in the middle. In the middle of the compound, some men are raising a canopy and arranging chairs in sections for visitors. Another crowd of villagers stands at the rear of the compound, staring with admiration at the heads of the gravediggers, all young men, jutting from the deep grave where they are stamping their feet in unison to the rhythm of the drums. As the onlookers watch the burial, they unconsciously move their heads to the beat of the energetic dance, moving their heads forward and then shifting and turning back and forth. A long line of family members of both Biiywong and Ability and other sympathisers dance gracefully around the grave, holding fowls, crates of soft and alcoholic drinks, a basket of boiled groundnuts,

and heavy packages from which they constantly remove sachets of hard drinks and fling to the cheerful gravediggers and to the members of the Holy Trinity Salem Choir led by Ba Jacov, all dancing close to the grave).

GHEEH
(Shakes his head as he stares at Ability jumping up to catch the sachets of whisky drinks thrown to onlookers, choir dancers, and the gravediggers).

DZEKEWONG
(Jumps out of the grave and drags a fowl from the grip of Pa Jacov, protesting). Which work church de do here? Na we be grave diggers. Make church shift before I vex start fight!

PA JACOV
Dzekewong, you and your boys have collected nearly all the fowls and drinks. The choir has got only two crates of drinks. These items are not only for gravediggers…

ABILITY
Too much has been given! *(Ability grumbles, dragging two crates of drinks and three fowls from Dzekewong. His eyes fall on a bag).* Dzekewong, what is that blanket still doing here? What did I tell you to do when the choir members brought it? Didn't I ask you to keep it somewhere in my room so that my son will grow up and use it? *(Ability points to a big wrap placed near the drinks).*

DZEKEWONG
Pa Jacov, *ansa dat kweshon.*

PA JACOV
Ability, Trinity Choir brought that blanket so that the family can use it to bury Biiywong. She was a good woman with a good heart.

GHEEH
Ability, go back inside.

ABILITY
(Carries the blanket, two fowls and two crates of drinks back to his house before joining the Elders back in his sitting room).

GHEEH
Ability, take heart. You should not be seen moving around.

NTUMFON
(Repeatedly taking in short sudden breaths as he wipes tears gliding down his cheeks with the back of his hand). hi, hi, he, he, he, hiiii, hiii…

ABILITY
(Opens a bottle of beer with his teeth, turns it directly into his mouth, gulping with loud gurgles. He then turns and speaks to his son in Lamnso). Ntumfon, men do not cry. Crying is for women. Wipe your tears. I begged you and your sister to stay with me, but you chose to follow your mother. See how she has brought you up to behave like a woman. I learned your sister is in the city. Go and take food and stop crying like a woman. *(Ntumfon gets up and beats away dust from the buttocks of his shredded shorts as he walks out with his head bent over his shoulder).*

SHUFAI LAIKA
Ability, Ntumfon is still a child. I remember that he was born during the year of hunger, the same year my grandson was born. Take it easy on him. He is feeling the pain of losing a mother. It is normal for him to cry. But, Ability, why does he look so shabby and uncared for? Our people say that the elder who eats all his food leaving nothing for the young will carry his own load home.

ABILITY
Tell that to my late wife.

NTUMFON
(Returns with a flat plantain leaf loaded with five loaves of fufu, vegetable sauce with two slices of meat and begins to eat).

SHUFAI LAIKA
(Turns to Ntumfon). Su wo yeeh boayikir. *(Shufai Laika asks him to wash his hands before eating. Ntumfon rushes outside, washes his hands and returns to his seat. As Ntumfon eats fast struggling to tear meat from a big bone between his palms, Ability shakes his head, staring pitifully at the veins stretching along his sunken neck and forehead like tiny farm ridges).*

ABILITY
(Staggers to his feet).

NDZEWIYI
Ability, tell me what you want, I will go and get it for you.

ABILITY
Don't worry. *(He goes out and returns after a few minutes with a deep plastic bowl which he places at the door for condolence contributions and then returns to his seat. Shufai Laika, Gheeh, Verdzekov, Pa Jacov, Ndzewiyi, Medzefen, and the other men look at each other in silence, shifts their eyes to Ability and then away, shaking their heads, twisting their lips. Once in a while, people coming in, including those already seated, would drop some coins or bank notes to the bowl. The last people to walk in are Honourable and his wife, Barrister Johnson. Honourable counts fifty thousand francs directly into the bowl, dropping one note after the other, attracting a smile from Ability and a curious stare from the open-mouthed Dzekewong who is following from behind and carrying a beautifully carved wooden stool. Meanwhile, Honourable's wife drops a sealed brown envelope into the bowl. Dzekewong places Honourable's stool near Shufai Laika and shifts away. Another seat is placed close to Honourable for his wife.*

HONOURABLE
(Turns and exchanges smiles with Shufai Laika). Hi mehn.

YOUNG MAN
(Bends forward before Honourable and wife, holding a tray containing a dish, two bottles of Guinness, and a jar of palm wine, smiling as he speaks). Gud aftanon Honourable, aftanon Bigi Madame. Honourable, dis fud and bia and pamwain na for you and Madame. De pam wain sweet sotee. Tisham; you go confirm. Na me tap de pam wain.

HONOURABLE
Thank you so much. We had some food and drinks before coming here. We will eat your food and drink the beer and the sweet palm wine next time *(Barrister Johnson nods in assent while the smiling young man quickly walks out with the drinks. Dzekewong rushes after him).*

SHUFAI LAIKA

(*Watches Dzekewong with a smile as he fights to grab the food across the door*).

BARRISTER JOHNSON

Mr Ability, take heart and accept our sincere condolences.

ABILITY

Thank you, Barrister.

BARRISTER JOHNSON

(*Gets up and beckons to her husband who also gets up. She dips a hand into her handbag, pulls it up and squeezes some money into Ntumfon's eager hands, gazing at the young man's bushy hairs and dishevelled attire as she speaks*). Heh Mehn, use this to shave your hair and get yourself some new clothes, right?

NTUMFON

(*Smiles bending over his head as he speaks*). Beriwo. Berifeyi. (*Quickly hides the money in his pocket stealing a glance at his father who has lifted his head to look at his son's hand*).

SHUFAI LAIKA

(*Translates what Ntumfon has said into English*). He says thank you. He is very grateful. That's Ability's son.

BARRISTER JOHNSON

Really! (*Asks Ntumfon*) What class are you, young man? (*Ntumfon smiles silently while Ability drops his head, looking at his feet*).

SHUFAI LAIKA

Ntumfon, *a du mwa'ah?* (Do you attend school?)

NTUMFON

(*Shaking his head in protest*). Haya. (No)

BARRISTER JOHNSON

Ask him if he speaks English.

SHUFAI LAIKA

A sungnin lam bara'ah? (Do you understand or speak the White man's language?)

NTUMFON

Haya, ai di hear one, one *(Smiles shyly as he says he understands only a little).*

BARRISTER JOHNSON

Bongkisheri will take over the responsibility of his education. I will arrange for that. Inform his father to meet Mrs Ghamogha. She will get a school for the young man, and do the rest. *(The villagers and Ability smile at Barrister Johnson, nodding their heads in respect and joy).*

SHUFAI LAIKA

(Turns to Ntumfon) Bongkisheri yii wai wo lav mnwa aa du ye'ei mnwa bara. (Bongkisheri women's group will sponsor you in school to learn. That is what she has said).

NTUMFON

Weeeeeeeiiy, tank you Big Madam. Big *tank* you.

BARRISTER JOHNSON

We will be on our way now.
(Barrister Johnson joins the Elders, smiling as she holds her husband's hand and they walk out, exchanging pleasantries at the door with the Mayor who is accompanied by a young man carrying four crates of drinks).

ABILITY

(Thinking aloud while staring at his feet). My people say when two elephants fight, it is the grass that suffers. Look at my son; the only thing that makes me feel like a man. He cannot speak even pidgin English. He is wearing rags. Look at his ribs and bones protruding from his chest. He looks as if he bathed in mud before coming here… It is not good for children to be raised by separate parents. I brought this big shame to myself. I wish I had not been sleeping around with different women and telling my wife to do whatever she wished. I regret bringing in a second wife.

Some minutes later, Ability collects the bowl full of money from the door, and drifts behind the house).

ACT 5

Scene II

AT THE TRADITIONAL COUNCIL

TOWN CRIER

(Hits the gong at the Road Junction). Nkeng, nkeng, nkeng. People of *Kibaaka* land, people of *Kibaaka* land, all roads lead to the palace today. All roads lead to the palace today. *Nwerong* has spoken.

OUTSIDE THE PALACE HALL

(Regular and Binla stand at the courtyard, holding up banners and placards with the following inscriptions: "The Woman's Voice Matters; Women's Rights Matter; The woman's Turn; Give Back our Land Rights; The Lock on My Lips is Removed; Power to the Woman; Collective Strength is Victory". *The protest invites angry reactions as the Vigilante boys suddenly run up the path, holding branches of fresh leaves and long bamboos, chasing and thrashing the protesters who run into the hall).*

(Five Minutes Later)

AT THE PALACE HALL

(Facing the crowd, Your Highness is sitting on a high-backed stool, tattooed with different cultural figures. He is wearing a heavy long toghu gown with red, green and yellow shades, strewn with cowries at the edges and neckline. On his head sits an imposing leopard skin cap with a red feather and a wet leaf stuck to it. A three-layer necklace of beads, well-blended with cowries and studded with a mixture of orange, white, and black colours go around his neck and descends slightly to his chest to form what looks like a tiny settlement of bees. Your Highness looks in his gorgeous traditional regalia like a plantain trunk clustering with suckers and jackets of leaves. In what looks like a hierarchical arrangement, the

Shufais and heavy weight titled men sit on short wooden stools in deferring rungs, beginning from the right, with Shufai Laika. The Shufais are wearing thread-bare raffia fibre caps, and heavy toghu gowns marked with zigzag designs of laced threads of diverse shades of green, red, yellow, wine, and orange. Hanging slantways across the chests of titled men are scabbards made from animal skins. In the centre of the raised area is a round-bottomed clay pot with a long neck, sitting on a thickly plaited thatch grass stand. Sewn onto the neck of the clay pot are cowries. A small drum with a rope twice circling its neck stands near the pot. A few steps below the raised section meant for titled men, the villagers sit. The women and children stand at the rear from where they constantly stretch up their necks like goats tethered to stakes to glean the proceedings. The men are drinking palm wine from horns and calabash cups. In what looks like a display of cultural power and authority, the titled men with red feathers quivering on their caps step forward one after another, clap their hands thrice, cup their hands to their chins in the typical Nso customary manner of greeting a Fon or Paramount ruler of the land, and hum like bees, before returning to their seats).

YOUR HIGHNESS

Sons and daughters of the womb of Kibaaka land, I greet you.

ELDERS

(Cup hands to their mouths as they respond). Mbeerhh.

YOUR HIGHNESS

An owl does not perch on the rooftop at daytime to hoot for nothing. We are here to hear the land dispute case between Manka and the people of Kibaaka. Shufai Laika may proceed.

SHUFAI LAIKA

(Cups his hands to his mouth facing Your Highness). Eyes and ears of the land, the sun that shines in darkness (*Your Highness nods and he turns to the Elders*). Teeth of the elephant, Roots of Kibaaka land, Eyes and ears of the gods, cult of traditional giants, I greet you.

ELDERS

(Hum). Mmmmm.

SHUFAI LAIKA
(Looks around with a questioning stare). Honourable Shufai Wirkitum is not here. Is he still breathing?

GHEEH
We have not heard women crying since the sun showed its face.
(A car hoots repeatedly off the courtyard. Dzekewong tears through the door carrying a high-backed stool which he places next to Shufai Laika before shifting away).

WIRKITUM
(With his lips and face scowling, Ability stares at Wirkitum's plaited hair that looks like cornrows and shakes his head). Hi folks, I'm sorry for coming late.

SHUFAI LAIKA
Honourable, *Nwerong* does not wait for anybody.

ELDERS
Rengreng.

WIRKITUM
You're right, *mehn*. It's not in my habit to come late for meetings. Something held me back. The Financial Audit Commission came to my office this morning with a petition letter signed by the Elders of Kibaaka *(the Elders lean back, open-mouthed)* accusing me of corruption and embezzlement of public funds and requesting for my immediate transfer to Kurawa *(Ability hushes a smile. The Elders, with opened mouths and eyes, look at each other, and then turn and stare at Wirkitum again, throwing their hands open in questioning gestures).* The petition claimed that I stole and diverted money meant for constituency projects into my private business citing my three hotels, my cattle ranch, and other possessions as proof of the allegations. Yeah, it also said my compound looks like a car-stand ... So, my office was temporarily sealed this morning until investigations are concluded. *(Unnoticed, Ability shades his eyes with horizontally window-like fingers, smiling as Honourable repeatedly wipes beads of sweat gliding down his face).*

GHEEH
Honourable, just carry five cows to the Big Man. Oil his lips and all your sins

will be forgiven.

ABILITY

Rengreng.

SHUFAI LAIKA

Sons of the soil, you heard what Honourable just said. Did we write any petition against our brother, Honourable?

ELDERS

(Responding negatively). Ngang!

SHUFAI LAIKA

Honourable, we are sorry about what happened. We want you to understand that what the petition said does not represent our collective views about your person. That claim was not made by the Traditional Village Council. Our hands are clean. *(Jacov and Alhaji Musa repeatedly nod in agreement).* You will get justice if your hands are clean. *(The Elders nod).* Elders and people of our land, now that the majority of the Elders of the Traditional Council are here, we can start. Manka may step forward.

(In a stooping posture, Manka walks to the front, and stands before the Elders, bending forward).

SHUFAI LAIKA

(Coughs, looks around, and turns to face the Elders). Kibaaka is a well-ordered society where men are men and women are women. But the women of Kibaaka have been trying to dictate to us how we should run the affairs of this land. Do we leave them to rule us?

ELDERS

Ngang!

SHUFAI LAIKA

An abomination has happened! A woman has bought land in Kibaaka.

VILLAGERS

Ngiri! (The villagers scream wide-eyed and open-mouthed, raising and crossing their hands over their heads; some fling their hands apart, shaking their heads in gestures of shock).

GHEEH
Whose daughter is she?

VERDZEKOV
Where does she come from?

ABILITY
Who raised her?

MEDZEFEN
Is she from here?

ABILITY
Is her father a son of the soil or a plaited rope?

FOLA
And who is the woman in question?

SHUFAI LAIKA
Manka.

VILLAGERS
Hei!

GHEEH
The weevil that eats the palm tree lives inside the palm. Sons of the soil, this mess is committed by an inner core member. Did I not warn the Fon against marrying a Come-no-Go? But what did he tell me? She is a second generation of Come-no-Go and so she has Kibaaka blood in her. I told him a snake is a snake, no matter its age, but he would not listen. I told him that a half-blood is a half-blood, but he would not listen. Manka, didn't your father teach you how to behave like a woman?

SHUFAI LAIKA
Manka, is it true that you bought land in your name?

MANKA
My fathers, the law has removed the lock on my lips.

VILLAGERS
(*In a chorus*). Ngiri! (*The open-mouthed and wide-eyed Elders look at each other and then at Manka. They turn their heads away, one after another, lifting and dropping their shoulders, throwing their hands apart*).

SHUFAI LAIKA
Nobody sings out of tune. Manka, who sold land to you?

MANKA
Our fathers, the law has untied the rope with which the woman was tethered to the kitchen. The woman is no longer in the cage of tradition.
(*As the Elders shake their heads, throwing their hands open in gestures of disbelief and shock, Gheeh steps forward, wipes his eyes, stares briefly at Manka and returns to his seat*).

ABILITY
This is a declaration of war against tradition! She has attacked and insulted every facet of tradition. There's nothing left.

YOUR HIGHNESS
That is my wife! Ask her a simple question and she will take you to heaven, hell, and back, but will never answer the question. What she tells you is not what you ask her but what she wants you to hear or understand.

GHEEH
Where is this woman taking her power from?

ABILITY
Bongkisheri!

SHUFAI LAIKA
(*Turns to the Elders*). Fathers of fathers, cult of traditional giants, eyes and ears of the gods, the trunk on which the branches suckle, can the roots sit on treetops?

ELDERS

Ngang! (No).

SHUFAI LAIKA

Can the mouth bite the finger that feeds it?

ELDERS

Ngang!

SHUFAI LAIKA

Nobody drags a rope with tradition. *(The Elders nod in consent).* Manka, who sold land to you? *(Manka is silent).*

VERDZEKOV

Manka, release the name of the person who sold land to you now otherwise we will conclude that you have actually taken up arms against tradition.

MANKA

Elders of our land, what tradition is fighting is not me; what tradition is fighting is development. *(Sustained murmurs are heard across the hall).*

SHUFAI LAIKA

Roles are assigned and not assumed. Land belongs to the man. Crops belong to the woman. Manka, has somebody ever told you that?

MANKA

Our fathers, the law has granted land ownership rights to the woman.

YOUR HIGHNESS

(Intrudes). Watch your tongue woman! You are not here in my bedroom. This is Nwerong speaking.

ABILITY

Manka, whose law do you respect?

MANKA

Our fathers, I do what is right. At home, I am a wife, outside of home, I am many other things. *(The Elders shake their heads).*

GHEEH
I can now see what our Fon has been going through in the hands of this woman *(Shaking his head).*

DZEKEWONG
Dis is de rison I refuse to marry a woman who knows big book. My fada used to tell me dat a woman who knows big book does not respect de fada of his children at all. *Na yii dis di happen.*

ABILITY
We will give you another chance to insult us. Manka, that land must bear the name of a man. This is Kibaaka. We cannot change tradition. Are you a man? *(Both Regular and Manka stare at Ability, open-mouthed, wide-eyed).*

MANKA
(Sits on her hinds wriggling her waist like a wounded worm). Elders of our land, kindly exercise restraint where tradition rules with excesses.

VERDZEKOV
(Cuts in shouting). This is an insult, woman!

ABILITY
Nwerong has never been this generous with a kitchen rebel. *(Regular stares at Ability open-mouthed, and then turns away).*

SHUFAI LAIKA
Ability, calm down. The farmer directs the growth of a plant or stem by bending or pruning until it starts to grow better. If you use force, you will break the plant. Take it easy on her. This court is also a classroom. You do not beat a child for breaking the water calabash and send her outside into the rains. Who will fetch water for your household? *(The elders nod, and he turns to Manka).* Our wife, land belongs to the man. The woman can farm the land and harvest the crops. She cannot become the landowner. You have to give that land to your husband and avoid the sting of tradition.

MANKA
Our fathers, the women suspended the protest because we were told that the Traditional Council was willing to listen to us, and to find solutions to our

grievances. We will go back to the streets and resume the protest if that land is taken away from me.

BONGKISHERI WOMEN
(*shouting in unison as Regular and Binla lift up placards and wave peace plants*). Give back our land. There shall be no peace without land rights!

ELDERS
(*In silence, they stare at Manka, and then at each other, shift their stares to Regular and Binla, raise and drop their shoulders, and turn their faces away*).

GHEEH
Elders of our land! Did she just threaten us? He-eei!

ABILITY
Our people say that the man who wants to start a war should gather enough bullets so that he will not be killed in his own war when his own weapons are finished.

ELDERS
Rengreng.

ABILITY
Manka, you are a woman. Tradition decides what you can do and what you cannot do depending on what you have between your legs.

ELDERS
Rengreng.

MANKA
Our fathers, why is tradition still an enemy of the new ways?

SHUFAI LAIKA
We do not quarrel with tradition. We do not drag a rope with tradition. (*The Elders nod consent*).

MANKA
Our fathers, kindly soften the heart of tradition.

GHEEH

Our people say that the disgrace and the shame of the madman's nakedness does not go to the madman; it goes to his family. People will laugh at us and at our Fon and call us women when they hear that a woman has bought land in Kibaaka.

ELDERS

Rengreng.

SHUFAI LAIKA

Our wife, *Nwerong* will remove the beads around the Fon's neck and the leopard skin around his waist if you remain the landowner. That is what Tata Gheeh is saying. That land must bear the name of the man. Give it to your husband.

ELDERS

Rengreng. Wongbei! Dzebei!

MANKA

Our fathers, the land you say I should give to my husband is the reason women can now take care of themselves and put food on the table and also contribute financially to the education of their children. Over fifty Bongkisheri women, including single mothers, have been lifted out of poverty as a result of the empowerment and training programmes we provide free of charge. Bongkisheri has taught women many skills. *(The women stick out their heads from the rear, smiling and making affirmative noises as she speaks).* We organise monthly trainings for women on marking toghu and African wears, cookery, baking, food processing, sewing, fashion design, and making beads and bags. We have also distributed sewing machines and equipment, including funding assistance and scholarships to many women and girls studying sciences and technology. We assisted Meluf Hospital with medical equipment worth fifteen million frs CFA. We created the Community Forest and bore holes in some settlements. We financed extension and constructed toilets in the women's section of the Kibaaka Royal Palace. We constructed toilets and a water facility in Bukang-Yerr Village. The women used my land as collateral security to obtain loans for these projects and to get funding from Government and big groups. These achievements would not have been possible if we did not have land for our projects. Our fathers, where did I go wrong in helping to build Kibaaka?

SHUFAI LAIKA

Our wife, we appreciate the work Bongkisheri is doing. But our choices and personal interests cannot override tradition. You committed an abomination by buying land in your name. Your projects will not stop because the land you use now bears the Fon's name. Nwerong is willing to forgive and cleanse you if you will listen to us. Your Highness is the custodian of the tradition and customs of Kibaaka land. He will be removed and replaced if any Land Title in his traditional territory bears the name of a woman. He is like a babysitter who can be held accountable if anything happens to the baby. Give that land to Your Highness to avoid a war with tradition. Nobody takes up arms against tradition. Nobody has ever won a war against his people, and as you know, the voice of the people is the voice of the gods. This is not me speaking.

GHEEH

Nwerong has spoken! *(The Elders nod approval).*

MANKA

Our fathers, I am married to the Fon. The Fon belongs to nobody; he belongs to everybody. My mother told me that the Royal family is like a tree with many branches sucking from the breasts of the same trunk. I am not the only wife of my husband, although I am his only legally married wife. He has other wives. When his father died, he inherited the throne. He also inherited his late father's wives and the children conceived on the leopard skin as tradition demands. Now, if I transfer the ownership of my land to my husband, he automatically becomes the legal owner of my land. The land will definitely become the property of the entire Royal family because Kibaaka tradition says what belongs to the Fon, belongs to all the children conceived on the leopard skin. My fathers, can my children still claim exclusive inheritance rights to the land I single-handedly acquired for them when it bears the name of the Fon without the risk of being dragged into ownership battles with the other children conceived on the leopard skin? Will their half-brothers not claim inheritance and ownership rights over my children's land on grounds that the Fon is also their father? *(Regular, Binla, and other women smile).*

ELDERS

(Opening their teeth like roasted goats. Many of the Elders drop their heads, staring at their feet. Shufai Laika stares vacantly across the hall).

SHUFAI LAIKA

(Takes a deep breath and lifts his head). Our wife, we have heard you. Your major worry is the likely ownership battles between your children and the other children with whom they share the same father but different mothers if the land you bought happens to bear the name of the Fon. We have a solution to your question. The gods blessed your family with male children, Bame and Fomu. Nwerong says you have to do the new Land Title in the name of one of your sons. *(The Elders nod their heads in gestures of satisfaction).*

MANKA

Our fathers, Your Highness and I have three children; Bame, Fomu, and Kila. If I do the Land Title in the name of one of my sons, I will simply be transferring the problem I have with you as men to my own children. Such a paper gives a single son exclusive ownership right over the land that should belong to the three of them. *(The Elders shrug).* Tomorrow, Fomu or Bame will use the same argument against my daughter, principally, that land belongs to the man and not the woman. I cannot guarantee that Kila will be given her own share of the land when Your Highness and I are no longer around. We all know the story of the tortoise and the birds who were invited to a feast in Heaven, and the tortoise took the name "All of You". People grow up and change. Our people say we give birth to a child and not to the child's character. Besides, there is also the possibility of any of my sons becoming the crown Prince and eventually the Fon of Kibaaka land. We will likely come back to this same ownership battle if I give ownership of the land to one of my sons and he happens to become the Fon later. My fathers, you can now understand why that land must bear my name.

SHUFAI LAIKA

(After a long silence, he withdraws and returns with a mirror and puts it on the ground, saying). Manka, take it. Look in the mirror and tell Kibaaka whether you saw a man or a woman.

MANKA

Our fathers, I do not know if I should look with my eyes or with my mind. However, when I use my eyes, I see a woman. But when I use my mind, I see something beyond a woman. *(The Elders shrug).*

SHUFAI LAIKA
Woman, look in the mirror and tell Kibaaka whether you saw calabashes on your chest or beard on your chin. *(Manka is silent)*.

YOUR HIGHNESS
Manka, are you a man or a woman?

MANKA
I became a woman the day words became my creator. Words carved me like a piece of wood and sectioned me up. Words pitched me on stage like a stake planted in the farm to direct the growth of creeping plants. Words made me a guest in the house. Words gave me a name and tethered me to domestic hatchery like a bird roped to a cage to restrict its movement. Words gave me roles. I became a woman when I was conceived in words and carved in words. *(The elders hang their mouths open)*. I live in the world of words where I am nothing but a stranger in my homeland. I call myself the brainchild of words. Take me out of words and you will discover that I am other things that words and carvers refuse to acknowledge. Look beyond my linguistic ancestry and you will find in me another life and role. My fathers, it is wrong to use breasts and beard as criteria for human abilities for that would mean that where the eyes cannot reach does not exist. *(The elders throw their hands apart, looking at each other in turns). Shufai Laika beckons a few Elders forward. They discuss in muted voices, and then return to their seats.*

(Ten Minutes Later)

SHUFAI LAIKA
We do not drag a rope with the things that hold us together. Manka, this is Kibaaka. Land is for men. The harvests belong to the woman. We did not create tradition. We grew up and met it. Live in what has been built. *(The Elders nod in approval). Shufai stretches his hand to Your Highness as he speaks)*. Teeth of the Elephant, Eyes and Ears of the land, this is 100 000frs. Collect it. *(Your Highness collects the money)*. Give the money to Manka.... *(Your Highness drops the money on the ground, staring at Manka)*. Our wife, collect the money. What that means is that Your Highness has bought the land from you.

ELDERS

Rengreng!

MANKA

(Manka is silent).

SHUFAI LAIKA

Our wife, you cannot take a gun and shoot your own foot. Your Highness will be washed in public. He will become naked if that land bears the name of a woman. *(The Elders nod in approval).*

MANKA

Our Fathers, listen to the cry of the woman.

SHUFAI LAIKA

(Turns and glides the drum over). Ability, come forward. Play the *manjong* rhythm for the elders to get up and dance.

Ability pulls the rope fastened to two drums and ties it around his waist. He bends over the drums, closes his eyes partially with a lingering smile on his lips and begins to hit the drums alternately with his hands and a club, generating deep regular repeated sounds, thuds, beats, signals, and half-intermittent erratic pounds that pulsate well with the song while he sings. With the exception of Wirkitum whose irregular dance moves do not seem to blend with the pulsating melody of drumbeats, the elders file across the floor, singing the chorus, clapping their hands and clanging machetes in the air, dancing gracefully, moving the upper parts of their bodies, arms, and legs back and forth to the rhythm of the song in unison.

ABILITY

Ooooh-hoo'orr (2x)

ELDERS

Aaah hoooo

ABILITY

(Beats the drum). Ntam, ntam, ntam ntum; Ntam, ntam, ntam ntam, ntam…

SHUFAI LAIKA
You may now sit down. *(The elders return to their seats)*. Manka, you just watched the elders dance. If you were to dance with the elders, would you change the dancing steps, or dance in harmony to the melody of *manjong*?

MANKA
I don't know whether what I have just watched is a stage performance or life. My fathers, permit me to ask a few questions. Can a woman speak? Is a woman different from an actor on stage? Is the woman's life not scripted and programmed the same way the stake is planted in the farm to direct the growth of a creeping pumpkin stem? Is her life not just a stage where she performs roles prescribed by traditional tyrants? *(Ability leaps across the floor but is held in restrain by the Elders)*. Can a woman compose her own song and choose her dance steps? Can she beat her own drum and dance to the rhythm of her own song? Could the composers have asked for another melody? Could the drummer have played another rhythm? Haven't I been programmed to live my life on stage and be guided like a creeping stem, given a nod or frowned at by my carvers the same way the stake is planted in the farm to direct the growth of a stem? *(The elders shake their heads; Manka wipes tears gliding down her cheek with the back of her hand as she bends forward)*. Haven't I lived my entire life on stage acting programmed roles the same way the dancers danced to the manjong song, simply because I became a woman? Is everybody not masking? Are we really who we are when the mask is on? Can I write my own script and choose my own role? Can one write another person's story without distortion? Is life not just a performance? Can the actor step out of the programmed role? Can the actor disobey the stage director? Are we really who we are when we are on stage, acting the cultural script?
   (While Honourable smiles, the elders twist their lips, turning and staring at each other with wide-open eyes and mouths, and shaking their heads).

YOUR HIGHNESS
(Rages). Nobody sings out of tune! You heard me!

SHUFAI LAIKA
Manka, how did your husband marry you? Can you remember and share with us how you became our wife?

MANKA

Our fathers, Your Highness was the prince when he and his uncle came to ask for my hand in marriage. His uncle told my father that they saw a ripe fruit in our compound and came to harvest it. My father accepted them but told them that he was like a stake that is planted in the farm to direct the growth of plants. He directed them to see my mother's people before seeing him. He also indicated a list of things they would buy for my mother's people. When they returned for the introduction, my father had died. My uncle told them that he was like a babysitter and arranged to take them to Bafut, to see my mother's people. The day was fixed and we travelled to Bafut. The prince and his people gave raffia wine, palm oil, five crates of beer, a blanket, a hoe, cowries, and an envelope, which I later learned contained two hundred thousand francs CFA, to my mother's family. The head of the family, Pa Ngwa, poured raffia wine into a cup and gave it to me. Following his directives, I drank from the cup and gave the rest to the prince; he too drank. The prince was presented to me as my husband. Pa Ngwa joined our hands together and said we should go and multiply. That was what happened.

SHUFAI LAIKA

Manka, you just confirmed that the family of the Fon, your husband, paid your bride price. You belong to him with everything you have. That is the meaning of bride price. Property does not own property. Give the land to the Fon. The throne is at stake.

ELDERS

Rengreng.

MANKA

Our fathers, that land must bear my name for reasons I explained already.

GHEEH

How can you belong to someone and something belongs to you?

ELDERS

Ohooorrr! (The elders throw their hands open with lips twisted in questioning gestures).

MANKA
Fathers of our land, I don't wish to sound rude, but we need to grow to the truth. We need to start seeing the woman as a complementary partner in marriage. And if that is not done, our children will come back to this court with more land ownership battles. *(The Elders twist their lips and faces).*

YOUR HIGHNESS
Manka I allowed you to keep vomiting abominations and insulting us than I would normally tolerate because a part of me feels for you.

VERDZEKOV
(Stares at Manka briefly, shakes his head and laments). It is true that the weevil that eats the raffia tree lives within it.

FOLA
I have never seen this kind of thing before.

ABILITY
How did we get to this?

GHEEH
I am afraid we will wake up one day to find ourselves taking orders from women.

ABILITY
(Cuts in). Exactly my point. Manka should be sent on exile for ten years as a warning to potential violators of the law! *(Wirkitum and Shufai Laika shake their heads in protest, some elders nod to the ban while some look confused).*

ABILITY
I used to think that tradition has normal and loyal fans but from what is happening here now, I am convinced that the dragnet of tradition traps only midges and protects elephants. It is now clear that we only pay lip service to tradition. Shufai Laika and his other accomplices keep swinging into the politician's mood when they should take decisions. Have we revised the rules?

ELDERS
Ngang!

ABILITY
Why is Manka so different from similar others we have sent on exile in this same hall? *(The Elders turn and look at the Fon)*. Is it the first time Nwerong would banish someone for committing an abomination in the land? Are we saying that the law is for midges and not elephants? *Huh!* I do not like this *Bafia* dance, this back-and-forth movement. This practice of double standards must stop! *(Gheeh, Fola and Verdzekov nod their agreement).*

SHUFAI LAIKA
Elders of our land, the shit that is sticking to our finger is from our anus. Our people say that when a stubborn child is beaten and thrown out of the house, the door should be locked with a bamboo stem and not with a padlock. *(The women and some of the elders nod in agreement).* Manka, we are not concluding your case now because you still have questions to answer. Before we proceed, if you change your mind while we are still here and accept to transfer ownership of the land to your husband, our Fon, inform us. We will still cleanse you. *(The elders nod).* Elders, we need to go outside and talk. The hearing is carried forward till further notice. *(Shufai Laika and the elders walk out, drift behind and begin to discuss in hushed voices).*

(Thirty minutes later)

(The hearing resumes)

SHUFAI LAIKA
The land dispute case between Manka and the people resumes. But, before we return to the land ownership question, we have a question to ask Manka. Manka, you led bare-body women, the Come-no-Gos, and the climbers and human riders in a protest march right to the heart of the land which is also the seat of tradition. The bare-body march you instigated bears every visible sign of rebellion and disrespect for the things that hold us together. Our wives are becoming ungovernable as a result of your activities. *(The Elders nod).* People are beginning to think that Bongkisheri is nursing a secret and dangerous agenda to overthrow tradition. Are you guilty or not?

MANKA
Our fathers, we want to be seen as partners, not competitors.

SHUFAI LAIKA
Manka, can you tell us why Bongkisheri women are still mixing with climbers and human riders like Savage, Katika, and Livinus that Nwerong had long sent on exile.

MANKA
Our fathers, I knew Savage, Katika, and Livinus before they became climbers and human riders *(Villagers look at Manka and then, at each other in questioning gestures).*

SHUFAI LAIKA
Manka, Nwerong sent the climbers and human riders on exile but the court brought them back, claiming that we did not follow the law. Are you on the side of Government or Nwerong as far as this matter is concerned?

MANKA
My fathers, I talk with climbers but I identify with men and women. *(The Elders sit back, stare at each other, shake their heads with lips twisted, and then, turn to stare at Manka again).* I identify with my kind, that is what I mean.

WIRKITUM
Heh Niggers, what's wrong in choosing to become a gay or a cross-dresser? They are not criminals, *mehn.* Savage, Livinus, and Katika are not children. They are big enough to decide who they want to become.

SHUFAI LAIKA
(Rages)! Let them go and be what they want to become where human riding is allowed! This is Kibaaka! *(The elders nod).*

WIRKITUM
Life is a choice, *mehn.* I feel it is insulting and kind of violates the rights of the gay, trying to stop people from associating with them.

SHUFAI LAIKA
Their ways are different. We don't trust them around our children.

WIRKITUM
You can tolerate people you don't trust, *mehn. Yep.* We need to learn to live

together with people who have opposing views.

YOUR HIGHNESS
(Cuts in). Not when the disease is spreading across the land and infecting our children. *(There is an uproar across the hall with everybody nodding their heads in agreement)*.

WIRKITUM
We need to stop hate speech and learn to live together, *mehn*.

YOUR HIGHNESS
(Thunders). This is Kibaaka! It is a blessing to be born a man. You cannot dangle a tuber of power between your legs and choose to ride your kind like a horse rider! *(The Elders nod)*. No! No! If your own father or mother chose to ride their kind like the yam stem channelled across the furrow or ridge on the farm to direct the growth of creeping plants, would you have existed? *(The villagers throw their hands open in questioning gestures)*. Every head of the household wants to see his family grow and stretch like a river. *(The elders nod)*. Who will give us male children to fight our wars if we allow a man to marry a man and a woman to marry a woman? Who will defend our land against enemies? Didn't our fathers say that everybody admires and respects the one that has a big family? *(The elders nod their heads in agreement)*.

WIRKITUM
Life is a choice, dude. Nobody has the monopoly of choice. You are proud of who you are; they are proud of who they are. Remember, you lost the court case when you tried to ban them from Kibaaka.

ABILITY
We did not follow due process. That's what the Judge said. Now that we know the right thing to do, we will go back to court with them *(The villagers nod)*.

SHUFAI LAIKA
We will return to the man-marry-man issue at the right time. Let's move forward. Manka, you have another question to answer. Why did you take a bedroom battle to the streets? You and your women were on your way to the palace before we stopped you. Why did you decide to take the protest to the palace?

MANKA

Our fathers, we went to the palace to say that the solution to our problem is the cause of our problem.

ABILITY

Stop it now! We are tired of your smoke screen. Elders of our land, this woman truly thinks she is smarter than all of us here. For how long shall we sit down and watch her pretentiously assume and use her pitiable victim position to insult us? For how long? She is not deaf. She heard our question, but instead of answering it, she chooses to play the victim as she has done all along. Someone has got to stop this madness....

FOLA

(Interrupts, pointing fingers to the ground). Now!

ELDERS

Rengreng.

YOUR HIGHNESS

That is my wife. Any question asked to her is always either an opportunity to sermonize on land rights doctrine or to insult us.

SHUFAI LAIKA

Any more questions for our wife?

ABILITY

Manka, you and Bongkisheri are responsible for my broken marriage. *(Manka hangs her mouth open).* You told my wife that polygamy is a killer disease. You also advised the women to lock their laps to any man who has more than one wife.

ELDERS

Ngiri.

ABILITY

The advice you gave my wife is the reason she left me when she realised that I was making plans to marry another woman.

SHUFAI LAIKA
Manka, you heard Ability. Are you guilty or not?

MANKA
My fathers, I am also a Relationship and Marriage Counsellor. I cannot destroy what I work so hard to build and mend.

SHUFAI LAIKA
Mother of children, Ability feels that your advice is responsible for his broken marriage. How do you react to that accusation?

MANKA
Our fathers, during every counselling session, I receive the following complaints from married women and single mothers: "I am only a woman, I don't have the power to stop my husband from marrying another wife or running after disposable or one-use women who may be infected. My husband is seeing another woman. The father of my son or daughter abandoned me for another woman the day I informed him that I was carrying his child. My son or daughter grew up without knowing his or her father. I raised my child alone but now, the man who got me pregnant and rejected the pregnancy wants his name on the child's birth certificate; he even wants to take his child. John, Derick, Franklin, or Desmond, claims he didn't father my son or daughter just to avoid giving me child support. My husband or my fiancée has a child with another woman. My husband wants to marry another woman. My ex was infected before he met me, he was taking drugs without informing me. I only discovered that he was HIV positive when I saw drugs hidden under the bed. I only discovered that he was already infected when I went for prenatal consultation and was tested HIV positive. He didn't get angry or shout at me when I told him what the doctor said. How can I deal with a cheating husband?" Most of the cheaters cheat with partners who are sleeping with other men or women, and this becomes a chain infection. Our fathers, your wives and daughters look up to me for solutions in the area of Marriage and Relationship Counselling. However, I have never advised any woman to abandon her marriage. I only tell them that it is dangerous to share a man with another woman the same way it is dangerous for a man to share his wife with another man. I just want them to understand that if one person in a relationship is infected, the other partners and their attachments would also be infected. Our fathers, I hope you now understand why I tell Bongkisheri women that polygamy is like a

cooking pot where diseases are prepared and shared around. *(Wirkitum and Shufai Laika nod their heads, smiling).*

ABILITY

Manka, do you realize you just confessed to destroying my marriage? *(Shakes his head).* Truly, household heads must be careful each time they smell the presence of Manka around their backyards.

ELDERS

Rengreng.

ABILITY

Manka, can you deny the role you and your women group played in tearing my marriage apart when my wife attacked and fought the lady I wanted to marry and then gathered her clothes and left my house on the same pretext that polygamy is a killer disease?

MANKA

Ba Ability, we need to draw a line between advice and advocacy. *(Dzekewong, Gheeh, and Medzefen stare at Manka open-mouthed, looking lost).*

SHUFAI LAIKA

Dzekewong, Gheeh, Medzefen, advocacy means encouraging or accepting to live with a man who already has a wife or wives.

YOUR HIGHNESS

Manka, in the case of Ability, do you think your counselling and advice destroyed his marriage or repaired it?

ELDERS

Ohorrr!

MANKA

Our fathers, I educate people. I talk to the women on the good and bad sides of the different forms of marriages. I use the same experiences they share with me to present the situation as it is and then, allow them to make their choices.

DZEKEWONG
Dis woman get big sense. *(Dzekewong praises Manka, a statement that attracts anger and frowns from the Elders).*

ABILITY
What does this one actually stand for? *(Stares at Dzekewong with ridges across his forehead).*

VERDZEKOV
A man can marry as many women as he wants. It is his money. *(The Elders nod in approval).* This is Africa. You are inciting a war against the ways of our land when you condemn polygamy.

ABILITY
Tell her!

MANKA
Our fathers, certain ancestral customs are crimes. *(Honourable and Shufai Laika nod in agreement).* We need to teach the right thing by exposing the consequences of bad choices.

ELDERS
Ngiri!

ABILITY
Manka, did you just say our ways are crimes?

MANKA
Our fathers, when a man marries many wives or is seeing other women outside his marriage, his problems multiply. He runs many homes. He has many bills to settle. He has many mouths to feed. Some run away from the responsibility of providing for the child they brought into the world. Some abandon the upbringing of the child in the hands of the woman who might not even have the means. At the end of the day, the child is penalised. Many children grow up not knowing who fathered them. Such children live in pain when they suffer discrimination, rejection, lack of love, or lack of recognition. They are seen as a burden by their stepfathers. They are denied love. Society describes them as children conceived in the palm bush. They become a social problem because

there was no father figure in their life to guide them. They lack proper home training. Some end up in the streets and not in the classroom. Abandoned vehicles become their home. Some take up arms. Some do drugs to forget the hurt by being high. Believe me, a man who is seeing many women is likely to bring children to the world that he cannot care for; he is likely to harvest diseases and distribute to potential victims just because he feels vindicated by the ancestral custom that says a man can marry or buy as many wives as he wants because it is his money. Look at late Pa Njimum Lukong. It is alleged that he inherited his late elder brother's three wives, ignorant of the fact that his elder brother died of AIDS and that the brother infected his wives before dying. He died just two years after his elder brother. The whole village claimed the medicine man has declared that Pa Lukong was poisoned. But look at what has been happening. Where is his wife? His whole family has been dropping dead one after the other. Both his inherited wives and the ones he got married to are all dead. Is food poison contagious?

YOUR HIGHNESS AND ALL THE ELDERS
(Covering their bended heads with their hands and exclaiming) Ngiri! Ngiri! Ngiri!

ABILITY
Our wife, for the last time, control your mouth. Have women complained that they do not like polygamy?

ELDERS
(In chorus) Ohrrrrrrrrrrrrrrrr!

MANKA
(Sits on her hinds and supports her head with her left hand, twisting in pain). Our fathers, if you put a baby in a cage with goats, it will grow up and eat grass, walk on all fours, bleat like a goat, and sleep on its own urine, thinking that that is who she is and where she truly belongs as well as the right thing to do. That is the truth. Women who are in polygamous marriages are not there because they like it. The situation in many homes in Yerr-Bukang village speaks for itself. I was there with the women. Backyards of huts and homesteads are always littered with tiny mountains of excreta. One girl who looked as if she was between eighteen and twenty years, although she could not remember her age, told us with tears in her eyes that her father withdrew her from school in

Primary Six because he didn't have 1000frs CFA for her school fees; that he gave her to his friend who once saved his life during hunting. She had five children, none of them in school. Binla may like to share her own experience with us.

BINLA

(The Elders look at each other, and then at Binla, open-mouthed as she steps forward and begins to testify). I grew up without knowing my father. My mother was my father. Her first husband hated her and asked her to leave his house because she couldn't give him a male child. She started sleeping with other men in order to make money to raise the two daughters she had with her first husband. She told me she was also sleeping with Pa Fola. *(Fola drops his head staring at his feet).*

ELDERS

Heiiy!

BINLA

When she was pregnant with me, Pa Fola abandoned my mother and denied the pregnancy just to save his marriage. I was abandoned by the same person that brought me into the world right from the time I was still in the womb. I grew up without knowing my father. I went to school right to the High School and passed my examination with good results but I could not go to the university because my mother had no money. That was when I started feeling the absence of a father figure in my life. I forced my mother to tell me where I came from. I just wanted somebody to call me his daughter, to join my mother to tell me to do this or not to do that. *(Wipes tears gliding down her cheeks and continues).* Before my mother died, she told me that Pa Fola abandoned her the same day she informed him that he had impregnated her. She also said there was a possibility that either Ability, or Dzekewong, Taa Gheeh, Verdzekov, Alhaji Musa, and Pa Jacov could potentially be my blood father because she was sleeping with them… *(The people whose names are cited quickly drop their heads, looking at their feet as different expressions and emotions of shock erupt simultaneously across the hall).*

VILLAGERS

(Exclaiming in various ways). Ngiri! Mbarang! Holy Ghost Fire!

BINLA

If my father was there for me, I wouldn't have had two children before sixteen. My mathematics teacher used to call me: "babies making babies." I usually dodged his classes…

ABILITY

(Interrupts). Binla, listen very well. We are not in Kibaaka market here. The next time you accuse right-thinking men of this village on the basis of rumour you got from a lousy woman who could neither stay in marriage nor hold her itchy thighs together, you will receive the heaviest fine of your miserable life. *(The accused Elders nod in approval).* Do you hear me? Return to your seat. *(The Elders stare at Binla in anger as she drifts back to the rear and lowers her buttocks to the edge of a stool).* Well, our people say the elder who wraps himself in immoderation will end in disgrace.

VERDZEKOV

Who even asked Binla to speak? Binla, you must inform us that you have something to say and wait for approval before you step forward.

MANKA

(Gets up and bends over, adjusting the bloodstained bandage tied around her head). Our fathers, we all heard the testimony from Binla. Her experience is just one of the reasons the women are against polygamy, and prefer one man, one wife.

ABILITY

Nobody asked you to comment on her unreliable report. Is she not a member of the so-called Bongkisheri? We didn't expect anything better from her. Her report is just part of the play you planned to stage before this honourable court, with the intention of disgracing lustrous born and bred sons of the soil before their own wives. You think we don't know you prepared this quack story in the gathering of hens you call Bongkisheri?

ELDERS

Rengreng!

MANKA

(Twists her face as she speaks in pain). Our fathers, it is not a lie. Many of the

women in this hall keep complaining that they spend minutes, hours, nights, days, weeks and years thinking, regretting, disagreeing, quarrelling, competing for attention, fighting over ownership or over the sharing formula of property left behind by their polygamous husbands.

ALHAJI MUSA

Madame for *Alareni (looks briefly at the Fon and then away)*, I want to ask you *kweshon*. Are *husibands compilaining* that having many wives and many children is a big load on *dia* shoulder?

ELDERS

Ohorrrrr!

ABILITY

Manka, has any of these elders you are insulting complained that a big family is a burden to him?

MANKA

Our fathers, permit me to answer your question with a question.

YOUR HIGHNESS

There you go again! If you dare permit her, she will begin another sermon. Madame, you came here to answer questions and not to ask questions!

ELDERS

Rengreng!

WIRKITUM

Let's make this trial a fair one. She has the right to express herself. *(Ability twists his face)*. Mrs Ghamogha, speak if you have something to say in your defence.

MANKA

Thank you Honourable. Our fathers, we all heard what Binla had to go through because of her mother's failed polygamous marriage. If I may ask a related question, what are the consequences on society and the families when we fail to give our children a proper education and proper upbringing because we have many mouths to take care of with limited means? There are many, of course: they drop out from school like Binla; home training becomes ineffective; streets and abandoned vehicles provide accommodation for them; we push them into wrong choices; they start competing with mates from comfortable homes; the quest to make quick money pushes some into drugs, scamming, stealing, cults; some fall easily into the hands of human traffickers who promise them good jobs in foreign lands where some end up eating body waste and sleeping with dogs to survive. Our fathers, is there any polygamist who can deny his fair share of guilt in the crimes often committed by abandoned children?

ELDERS
Ngiri!

FOLA
She came prepared to insult us. So, these crimes do not exist in places where polygamy does not exist!

ABILITY
I hope this court is taking note of the insults this woman has been pouring on this honourable panel of judges. Manka, are you aware you are insulting the generous efforts of polygamists who have been strongly assisting Government in reducing unemployment by providing domestic employment?

DZEKEWONG
(Looking at Manka). Ansa de kweshon!

ABILITY
Manka, who else, apart from the polygamists whom you claim are lodging diseases in their male members, have brought unemployment to the low level at which it now stands?

ELDERS
Orrrhhoorrr!

MANKA
(Plants her palm on the bandage). Ba Ability, think of the children like Binla who cannot share a meal with their father because they have been abandoned to avoid paternity obligations. Think about the children who have never had the opportunity to call anybody father, and who cry everyday seeking to know where they came from because they were rejected before they were born.

Think about the women who live in hurt, in regret, in pain, suffering alone to raise the children or fighting and quarrelling every day because the bedroom timetable says it is another woman's turn.

ABILITY

Manka, who stands to benefit when a man marries many wives? Who is employed when a man marries many wives? Who lodges who? And who guards whom in that marriage? Who provides the roof over the woman's head? In short, who is the tenant that has free accommodation in marriage if not the woman? Look at your weight, is this how bulky and healthy you were when we married you to the crowned Prince? Ungrateful woman! Is this the reward polygamists deserve for lifting up single mothers and young girls from littering the streets?

YOUR HIGHNESS

She thought the people she will meet here are like me.

ABILITY

Manka, let me give you another chance to insult us further. There are more women than men in *Kibaaka*. If polygamy is abolished, as you have been preaching, where will the extra women take husbands from? *(The elders nod).*

MANKA

Our fathers, the training Bongkisheri provides is one that can help the woman to survive in any condition.

WIRKITUM

Congratulations Mrs Ghamogha. *(Turns to the elders whose noses sit high, and lips twisted).* Folks, didn't I tell you that it was important to give Mrs Ghamogha a chance to tell you what Bongkisheri is doing? What is killing us is ignorance… *(Ability hangs his mouth open, cocks his head and swallows hard, while the Elders shake their heads).* I believe there's a lot to benefit from Mrs Ghamogha and her group. *(Manka sits on her hinds again, pressing her hand against her head, her face twisted).*

MANKA

(Touching the bandage around her head as she speaks). Thank you, Honourable, for recognizing what Bongkisheri is doing in the interest of women and the

community. Each time we try to explain these things, we are confronted with name-calling and abuse.

ABILITY

Manka, what abomination did you commit again to earn abuse? *(The Elders nod).*

MANKA

I reported Your Highness to my Lawyer... *(The Elders lean back, staring at one another, open-mouthed, wide-eyed).*

GHEEH

You did what?

ABILITY

I said it! I saw it coming!

MANKA

My fathers, I was told Your Highness was planning to marry another woman. I was just trying to save my marriage.

SHUFAI LAIKA

To the best of our knowledge, Your Highness still has one legal wife, and the three he inherited from his late father. Who is the woman you are talking about?

MANKA

Dzekem... *(Different simultaneous reactions explode across the hall: Your Highness shrugs; the women and the men lean back, open-mouthed and wide-eyed, as they lift up their necks and stare at Dzekem who keeps shaking her head in protest).*

DZEKEM

My enemies want to tear me and my President apart! They will not succeed! The children of my enemies will not see the sun...

SHUFAI LAIKA

Keep quiet, woman! *(Turns to the Fon, saying).* Your Highness, is this the way you have chosen to inform your kinsmen about your marriage?

YOUR HIGHNESS
The thought has never crossed my mind.

SHUFAI LAIKA
Manka, where did you get the information that the Fon is planning to marry Dzekem? *(Manka is silent).*

VERDZEKOV
Speak or we will fine you for defamation!

MANKA
Mami Biy Wiiba told me she overheard Ba Ability *(Ability drops his head as the Fon stares at him open-mouthed)* telling the father of her children about the plan to marry Dzekem.

SHUFAI LAIKA
Biy Wiiba, come forward.

BIY WIIBA
(Staggers to the front, stands bending forward).

SHUFAI LAIKA
Biy, do you have any idea how your gossip affected the Fon and his marriage? I now know why Manka has been adamant. You poisoned her mind with gossip which could possibly influence her decision about accepting to give ownership of the land to Your Highness. You will not go unpunished.

ELDERS
Rengreng.

SHUFAI LAIKA
Biy Wiiba, during Manjong gathering, you will prepare njama-njama with dry fish and dry meat that can feed 100 mouths. *(Dzekewong smiles).* You will also come along with four large calabashes of palm wine and two black goats. Nwerong has spoken!

ELDERS
Rengreng!

SHUFAI LAIKA
You may now go back to your seat now. *(Biy Wiiba tiptoes in reverse)*. We don't have any other thing left apart from the verdict. People of our land, we will take the climbers and human riders to court in the days ahead.

VILLAGERS
(Unanimous). Rengreng!

SHUFAI LAIKA
We will tell Government that they are bad seeds that must not be allowed to germinate in this land because they will destroy our children. *(The villagers nod)*. Anybody or any group seen associating with them will also be banned or sent into exile.

VILLAGERS
Rengreng.

WIRKITUM
I totally disagree with you, *mehn*. The fellas we are talking about are humans. Life is a choice. We can't have the right to our choices and values which we practice freely and try to impose our ways on others!

VILLAGERS
Mbarang! (Scream as they stare fixedly at Honourable, open-mouthed and wide-eyed).

ABILITY
I am now convinced that the only reason this Come-no-Go *(pointing at Honourable Wirkitum with his left hand as he speaks)* is still keeping a woman under his roof is just to hide the fact that he is also a human rider! *(Honourable shrugs)*. Have you ever heard the cry of a baby under his roof? The answer is no. *(Wirkitum stares at Ability, his lips and face twisted)*.

YOUR HIGHNESS
What we need now is the answer to the main issue that brought us here. What do we do to get a new land title bearing my name?

ABILITY

(Stares at Wirkitum from the corner of his eyes as he speaks). Step number one, the Come-no-Go must go! Plaited ropes must go! Bongkisheri must be banned!

ELDERS

Rengreng.

WIRKITUM

Ebilidy, this is the last time I will sit and fold my hands and watch you call me Come-no-Go or human rider. Idiot!

ABILITY

An uprooted forest tree that begins a new life in the farmland where it is deposited by flood waters will never become a plant.

SHUFAI LAIKA

Ability, how many times will I tell you that Honourable Wirkitum is not a Come-no-Go?

ABILITY

Why is Shufai Laika always defending this Come-no-Go? Why? Kibaaka is unavoidably in danger of blood-pollution and extinction if we allow our land to be littered with *Come-no-Gos,* climbers, and human riders. What crime did I commit in fighting against destruction…? Have we thought about the fact that we may take the riders to court and Barrister Johnson twists the Human Rights law to extend their stay in Kibaaka again? And who pays the price? Our children, of course.

FOLA

Ability is right.

GHEEH

How do we handle the issue of human riders and Come-no-Gos without attracting the anger of the government? *(The Elders nod).*

ABILITY

Let's deal with the first problem. The *Come-no-Gos* will only stay in Kibaaka on one condition. They must pay Settlers' Tax and will have to renew their stay and titles every year. *(Fola nods)*.

SHUFAI LAIKA
Ability, we do not cut down branches from the family tree.

ABILITY
The crocodile lives in the water, but it is not a fish. A butterfly can shed off its skin, develop wings, and even fly *(moving his stretched-out hands sideways and forwards)* in the air like a bird; its true origin is still the creeping caterpillar.

SHUFAI LAIKA
Ability, are you still in your right senses?

ABILITY
The only person who has lost his senses is Shufai Laika. Yes. Is it because the Senior Divisional Officer recently created a new village with Wirkitum as the Chief that you have suddenly forgotten that he is a half-blood and a Come-no-Go?

WIRKITUM
Ebilidy, if you ever address me again as a Come-no-Go, I will come down to your level and you will go back to jail!

ABILITY
Wirkitum, did I mention the fact that your chieftaincy title was acquired from the senior title retailer through a fattening compromise involving goats and millions of CFA…? Listen very well. If Shufai Laika has joined the women and children to confuse your chieftaincy title for signs of origin, I am not part of that complicity to grant you citizenship. *(The elders roar with laughter while Ability continues to rant).*

WIRKITUM
Ebilidy, you'll pay for this!

ABILITY
The fact that the chieftaincy has clothed Mr. borrowed feathers *(points at Honourable)* in *Kibaaka* ancestral customary rights, and the fact that he has lived in Kibaaka for so long that children and women are beginning to forget

his true origin does not cancel the fact that Wirkitum is a plaited rope.

FOLA
Rengreng.

ABILITY
Wirkitum, listen very well, your title and long sojourn may have given you customary rights, but neither of them has given you birth rights. Do you know why? Kibaaka does not accept double citizenship. *(Some elders nod while Wirkitum shakes his head).*

WIRKITUM
Mr. Ex-convict, listen very well…

ABILITY
Wirkitum, let us be honest to ourselves. Can you even remember the road to your town in America? Can anybody recognize you in your own community today? Wirkitum, I think I should tell you in public what people like Fola and Gheeh and Dzekewong say behind your back *(The three drop their heads, staring at their feet. Looks around and continues).* Who amongst these elders does not know that on the other side of the river, illegal migrants or Come-no-Gos negotiate their stay? I am not advocating for the extinction of plaited ropes and Come-no-Gos! No! How can I? We can't sit quiet and fold our arms and watch endangered species, half-bloods and plaited ropes wither away when their very existence is an illustration of the legendary hospitality of Kibaaka and God's sense of variety in his creation. *(The elders erupt with laughter).* Mr. borrowed feathers, to show the extent of our generosity, on the last country Sunday of every year, all titled Come-no-Gos and plaited ropes shall renew their titles in an open ceremony before the entire clan.

ELDERS
(Hum approval, their forefingers pointing to the ground). Rengreng! Hei!

ABILITY
That way, we shall be able to know those whose stay has been prolonged and those whose titles have expired. Any titles renewed contrary to the above specifications shall not be recognised…

ELDERS
Rengreng! (As applauds and laughter continue across the hall, Honourable Wirkitum begins to pull off the beads around his neck, one after the other).

SHUFAI LAIKA
Honourable Shufai Wirkitum, don't do this, please, don't do this. Ability is not Nwerong….

WIRKITUM
Where were you when he insulted me and called me names? Where were you? And where was Nwerong? Hasn't he insulted and stripped me enough? *Huh?* Hasn't he referred to me all through in your presence as Mr. Wirkitum, borrowed feathers, human rider, climber, plaited rope, and Come-no-Go, instead of Honourable Shufai Wirkitum? Were you not present when Ability opened the floodgates of hell and rained uninterrupted insults at me to the amusement of all present? Were you not present when he kept asking me to return to my land or renew my title to live in Kibaaka without any signs of slowing down? And to think that Your Highness sat quiet as if nothing happened! What difference does it make now? No!

SHUFAI LAIKA
Do not remove the beads.

WIRKITUM
When marriage is broken, bride price is returned. *(Stretches his hands to give his beads, cowries, and the red feather he just pulled from his pocket to Shufai Laika).* Take it. *(Ability smiles).*

SHUFAI LAIKA
Honourable Shufai Wirkitum, Ability spoke for himself. We cannot tear the family apart. *(Pa Jacov, Ndzewiyi, Alhaji Musa and other elders nod their heads in corroboration).*

WIRKITUM
I have had enough and I have made my choice.

SHUFAI LAIKA

Not every choice is the right decision.

WIRKITUM

A wrong decision is better than a wrong marriage.

SHUFAI LAIKA

Nobody turns his back on his people.

ABILITY

His absence consoles me. Let him go.

SHUFAI LAIKA

Ability, you have continued to test the depth of the river with your feet. You have two market days to bring a goat, two cocks and a basket of kola nuts to the Traditional Village Council. Nwerong has spoken! *(Ability twists his face while Fola smiles. Pa Jacov, Verdzekov, Alhaji Musa, Ndzewiyi and others nod their heads at Shufai Laika along with goading gestures, attracting a relaxed look from Honourable. Shufai Laika turns to the Elders).* When a river is flowing, it gives birth to streams. The streams may flow back into the same river and it continues its journey as one body of water. We cannot separate three streams flowing in one river. We cannot cut off a stream from the river. What am I saying? Shufai Wirkitum is the child of two worlds. He is one of the branches of the Kibaaka family tree. He has our blood in his veins. He is three bloods in one body. He is the bridge between two worlds. *(Apart from Ability, Your Highness, and Fola, the elders nod their heads in corroboration, this time attracting a smile from Honourable).* He bears our name. He speaks our language. It is easier to mend a broken engagement but not a broken marriage. *(Turns to Honourable Shufai Wirkitum).* Son of the soil, return the beads and cowries to your neck. The beads and red feather Nwerong gave you were a sign of your position and place in the Kibaaka family tree. *(Turns to the Elders).* Have I spoken our minds?

ELDERS

Rengreng. (Ability frowns as Honourable sits down).

SHUFAI LAIKA

(Turns to Manka). Let us continue where we ended. Manka, if you have changed

your mind, inform us now. *(Manka is silent)*. The only way we can move forward is to deliver the judgement. Nwerong has the answers. *(The Elders nod in approval)*. People of our land, you may go out now and give the Council time to deliberate. You will return to the hall when you hear the sound of Manjong drums.

(Apart from members of the Nwerong cult, everybody walks out and drifts into smaller groups across the yard, throwing hands apart, with some turning from time to time and shooting accusing glances or pitiful stares at Manka who sits on the grass, surrounded by women, their hands supporting their chins, with some crossed over their heads. At the sound of Manjong drums beating from the hall, everybody starts to return to the hall. Ntum ntum ntum ntum ntum…)

(The hearing resumes after 30 Minutes)

(The guard hits the gong three times. Manka bends forward, wiping tears gliding down her cheeks with the back of her hand. The women stand up at the rear shivering in their group Kaba gowns like jackets of leaves on plantain suckers dancing to a passing wind).

SHUFAI LAIKA

Sons of the soil, the Fon has eight hundred eyes. We are the eyes of the Fon. The Fon is Kibaaka and Kibaaka is the Fon. We all have a duty to correct and to protect the Fon. Have I spoken our minds?

ELDERS

Rengreng!

SHUFAI LAIKA

A messenger does not own the message and cannot change the message. The parcel of land Manka bought in her name belongs to Your Highness. *(Your Highness lifts his staff of authority in the air and shakes it with a lingering smile on his face. The women cross their raised hands over their heads, Manka and Regular wipe tears gliding down their cheeks)*. Bongkisheri is banned. *(Screams of protest tear through the hall from the rear where the women are perching)*. Manka, on *wailun* market day, you will bring the following items to this hall: one hundred loaves of fufu corn, two pots of njama-njama soup prepared with

243

dry meat and tadpoles, three big calabashes of raffia wine, three big calabashes of corn beer, a basket of kola nuts and two goats. We will then cleanse you. We will take a court action against Livinus, Katika, and Savage in the days ahead. We will hire Lawyer Faya and he will do everything for us. *Nwerong has spoken. (The villagers nod repeatedly in satisfaction).*

(The hall erupts with different kinds of emotions as the Elders file out of the hall, Your Highness leading. Outside the hall, at the rear of the Palace courtyard, the women gather around Manka, their hands crossed over their heads).

ACT 5

Scene III

BARRISTER JOHNSON'S CHAMBERS

SECRETARY

(Bends her knees forward as she speaks). Ma, Mrs Ghamogha would like to see you. She's in the Secretariat.

BARRISTER JOHNSON

Tell her to come in.

SECRETARY

I will, Ma. *(The Secretary curtseys and walks out).*

MANKA

(Walks in, teary, and head bandaged, wiping tears from her cheeks with the back of her hand). G-g-good morning, Barrister.

BARRISTER JOHNSON

Good morning, Mrs Ghamogha. sit down please.

MANKA

(Stutters). I-I lost everything I have worked for. Nwerong gave ownership of my land to my husband and banned Bongkisheri.

BARRISTER JOHNSON

My husband told me everything. Wipe your tears. Nwerong is not the Law. I will meet them in court.

MANKA

(Stretches an envelope to Barrister Johnson. She pulls out two sheets of papers and flips through them). This is the complaint I asked you to write, and this one is the Medical Report… The Medical Report states that you suffered sexual assault but does not mention that the bandaged wound on your forehead

resulted from the assault, why?

MANKA

(She bends over the table and speaks in a hushed voice).
I was beaten by Your Highness. He wasn't happy that I refused to transfer ownership of my land to him.

BARRISTER JOHNSON

You need to do another medical report stating that the wound on your face resulted from domestic violence.

MANKA

He is the Fon. It can't be said in public that he laid his hands on me. Such things are not said in public. The Fon does not take the blame.

BARRISTER JOHNSON

(Bangs the table, creating a loud noise that causes Manka to shudder).
You can't be fighting for women's rights and yet you cannot speak up when your own rights are violated! Kibaaka is a State of law. You deserve justice. I will need a written complaint in which you state that your husband beat you, seized your land, and banned your group with the complicity of Nwerong. Gender violence has to stop! Your husband and Nwerong must appear in court to answer for their crimes!

MANKA

(Leans back open-mouthed and wide-eyed attracting a curious stare from Barrister Johnson. She then closes her eyes and begins to muse, unaware of being watched). What will the women say if they hear that I want to take my husband to Court? Will they still stand by me? How can a woman drag her husband to Court? How can I take the Fon and Nwerong to Court and still come back to live with the same people that created Nwerong? Will they not banish me from their land…?

BARRISTER JOHNSON

Mrs Ghamogha, do not be afraid. Nothing will happen to you and your land. Nothing will happen to Bongkisheri. The Law will fight your battles.

MANKA

(Nods). Thank you, Barrister Johnson. I will write the complaint. I need my land. I bought it for my children. I have worked so hard with the women for Bongkisheri to take root. We need our land and our group.

BARRISTER JOHNSON

We need change. *(Stretches a sheet of paper with a pen across the table).* Write the complaint on this sheet of paper. *(Steps out of the office into the secretariat and returns some minutes later; collects the statement from Manka and flips through nodding).* That's good, Mrs Ghamogha, there is something else I wanted to tell you. You are not the only one fighting battles. My husband and I are in serious trouble. Our bank accounts in the Kibaaka Central Bank have been frozen.

MANKA

Frozen? *(Barrister Johnson nods).* I am so sorry to hear this. Why would the bank do that?

BARRISTER JOHNSON

Our bank accounts are monitored and investigated because of allegations of embezzlement and money laundering. Someone we suspect to be Ability filed an anonymous and damaging petition against my husband. I have just directed my agent in Kibaaka Bank to transfer all the money from the accounts bearing the names of my domestic servant - Dzekewong, my secretary, and my husband and I into the Bongkisheri account since I have the account number of the group. In case there is any probe, you must maintain that the money belongs to the group and the source is donations, business, or fundraising activities. I can't tell you everything now. Do not discuss what I have told you with anybody.

MANKA

Sure. *(Muses as Johnson makes coffee).* I thought she was honest. Why would she move their money into Bongkisheri's account? Would that not implicate Bongkisheri? Why would she even open bank accounts in another person's name? People are not always what they seem. I don't know who to trust, if I can't trust Barrister Johnson.

BARRISTER JOHNSON

Would you take some coffee?

MANKA
Oh no, thank you.

BARRISTER JOHNSON
I can see a faraway look in your eyes.

MANKA
Yeah. It's about the money you want to transfer into Bongkisheri account. Is that not going to get the group implicated in some way?

BARRISTER JOHNSON
That's nothing to worry about. I will sort it out.

MANKA
That reminds me. Now that your bank accounts are monitored, I suggest you put the rest of the money we received for Bongkisheri Community Forest project into the group account… You remember the money came in Dollars and you suggested we keep it in your Dollar account pending when the currency exchange rate would be good before we could convert into CFA and put back in the group account.

BARRISTER JOHNSON
I acknowledge keeping Bongkisheri's money about $21,000.

MANKA
Barrister, you surely have forgotten the actual amount since it's been over five years now. If you don't mind a reminder, I think the money our toghu and forest projects earned was fifty thousand dollars and we were asked to open a dollar account to access the money.

BARRISTER JOHNSON
That's right. You conceived the project with your group and contacted me for advice on how to write a project to attract funding. I directed my secretary to build a website for Bongkisheri and she did it. I gave you legal advice and directives on project writing. I also recommended possible foreign and national organisations that are concerned with the Agric sector and climate change. You forwarded the project to Government and foreign donors and got funding from these agencies. Do you think my Consultancy rendered those services

for free? How do you think I make my money? Mrs Ghamogha, legal services are marketed. My legal fee is 40% of the total amount we receive for any group project. Calculate the sharing formula.

MANKA

(*Silent for a while and speaks*). I will explain to the women what you just said. (*Thinking*). She is not what I took her for. Last week she walked out of Fada Anton's office immediately I walked in. I overheard them talking about the sharing formula for the toghu business when I approached Fada Anton's door. (*Speaks*). Barrister Johnson, you have done a lot for us and I will always appreciate you for that. We will always appreciate if you let us know when your advice is free and when it is commercialized so that we should come to terms with that before starting off a project.

BARRISTER JOHNSON

That's right.

MANKA

Thank you so much, Barrister. I will be on my way now.

BARRISTER JOHNSON

Goodbye for now.

(One hour later)

IN MANKA'S APARTMENT

(Manka is lying on a sofa when Bush Faller knocks and walks in).

BUSH FALLER

(Bends over and hugs Manka before sitting beside her). Heh Auntie, good to meet you today. You look good but tired.

MANKA

My son, I am so happy to meet you after a long time. You are welcome. Kila said you were here to see me…

BUSH FALLER
Not just once, and each time, I was told, Mum is attending a meeting, she went to see Fada Anton, she went to see Barrister Johnson. You don't get tired? Ha ha ha ha ha ha.

MANKA
You are right, my son. I have been too busy. How is Dubai? And what job are you doing there?

BUSH FALLER
Just hustling. But I want to do the toghu business. I want to partner with Fada Anton. I met Jaika and she told me Fada Anton sells Bongkisheri toghu abroad and makes a lot of money from it.

MANKA
Yeah. Did you travel to London?

BUSH FALLER
No.

MANKA
Where did you meet Jaika? Or is she around too?

BUSH FALLER
She is in Dubai, hustling…

MANKA
Hustling? How? *(Stares at Bush Faller, open-mouthed).*

BUSH FALLER
She even told me that she wanted to return to Kibaaka.

MANKA
I don't understand. Jaika was sent to London, on scholarship. What's she doing in Dubai?

BUSH FALLER
She was initially working as a domestic servant for a woman. The lady was

wicked and gave her food only once a day. Her husband was also wicked. He was sleeping with Jaika. He would even beat her up to intimidate her not to tell his wife. She managed to escape. She shares a room with eight girls. Men are always going in and out of their room. She looks like a dying tree. She's even pregnant.

MANKA

Jesus Christ! Oh nooo. I need to see Fada Anton to find out what happened. If she is not in school, let her come back. Let me go to the kitchen and get something for you to eat while we discuss. *(She walks into the kitchen).*

(Two hours later)

IN THE SITTING ROOM.

(Dinka rushes in holding a Court Summons).

DINKA

(Stretches an envelope to Your Highness). Your Highness, na Massinger from Court bring dis book say make I give Chief. *(He bows and turns and walks out).*

YOUR HIGHNESS

(Tears open the envelope, flips through the Court Summons, and laments). After what happened at the Traditional Court, my wife still had the courage to drag me to Court! *(A long silence).* Well, I must be the man. *(Calling)* Dinka…, Dinka…, *(Dinka comes in running, and bows to Your Highness).* Go and tell Shufai Laika and Ability that I want to see them now, immediately! If you don't find Ability at home, check in the bars in his street. *(Dinka bows and jumps out running).*

(One hour later)

(In Your Highness' Sitting Room. Ability walks in, cups hands to his mouth. Your Highness silently gives the Court Summons to Ability who flips through it shaking his head).

ABILITY
This kind of thing has never happened before.

YOUR HIGHNESS
That is why I sent for you. I will be going to Court next week. As it appears, Barrister Johnson is my wife's lawyer. She is the one playing the drum and the women are dancing. You are a frequent visitor to courts and should know a good lawyer who can stand that lady in court.

ABILITY
Your Highness, Barrister Faya is a human rights activist, one of the best lawyers we have in Kibaaka. He was the one who fought for our release when Dzekewong, Fola, Gheeh, and I were arrested for destroying the juju and the water tank in Bukang-Yerh Village. He is a son of the soil. Our fathers say that the farmer gains boundary space by dragging the soil to his own piece of land. We call it in Kibaaka native language: "Self-first". Faya is the right person for this job. Your Highness, we need 1,000,000frs for legal fees. This is a difficult case…

YOUR HIGHNESS
One Million? *(Opens his mouth wide).*

ABILITY
(Cups hands to his mouth as he answers in the affirmative). Mbeeh.

YOUR HIGHNESS
How do you expect me to raise that kind of money?

ABILITY
Your Highness, you need that land to keep the throne and to avoid serving a jail term for domestic violence and land grabbing. Barrister Faya needs money. The money will be shared between Faya and the Judge who will handle your case in court. You are now on Government Payroll. Get a loan from your Bank if you still want to remain the Fon of this land.

YOUR HIGHNESS
(Leans back on his Royal Stool and closes his eyes. Opens his eyes, wipes sweat from his face and speaks). I will go to the bank now and apply for a loan. I will see you tomorrow.

(Ability cups hands to his mouth, hums and walks out).

ABILITY
Conflict is business. *(Smiles).*

ABILITY AND YOUR HIGHNESS

YOUR HIGHNESS
(Stretches a bloated brown envelope to Ability, saying). I want nothing but victory.

ABILITY
Barrister Faya has never lost a court case. *(Counts the money with a lingering smile on his face).* Your Highness, you have won the case already. Money is the language lawyers and judges understand. If there is wine or whisky in the Palace, bring it out so we can start the celebrations, ha ha ha ha ha. I am going straight to see Faya. I will be on my way now *(Walks out).*

AT A ROAD BEND

ABILITY
One million francs. Ha ha ha ha. 500,000frs for myself and 500,000frs for Barrister Faya. What next? Now that we have a common enemy, Regular must hear this. I need to inform her that the Fon has offered a bribe to Faya to influence the judgement in his favour. I should also bribe Regular to bear witness against the Fon in Court. She likes money. She would not want her sister to lose the land to the Fon. The Fon will keep appealing the case and I will keep making money. Ha ha ha ha ha. From Regular, I will meet Faya.

(Two hours later)

ABILITY
Barrister Faya, this is 500,000frs from the Fon. Barrister Johnson is Manka's lawyer. The Fon says he wants nothing but victory.

FAYA
(Counts the money with a beaming smile on his face). I have never lost a court case. Bring me more clients.

ABILITY
Consider it done as usual. What about my commission?

FAYA
(*Counts 30,000frs and gives to the smiling Ability. They shake hands, and snap fingers, nodding their heads repeatedly before separating*).

ACT 5

Scene IV

AT JOHNSON'S CONSULTANCY

(Barrister Faya Walks In)

FAYA
(Greets the Secretary). Hi, I'm Barrister Faya. I'd like to see Barrister Johnson.

SECRETARY
Good morning, Sir. I'll announce your presence, sir. *(Withdraws).*

(Enters the Secretary)

SECRETARY
Ma, there's someone at the reception to see you. He says his name is Barrister Faya.

BARRISTER JOHNSON
Tell him to come in.

SECRETARY
(Returns to the secretariat). You may go in, sir.

FAYA
(Walks in). Hi, Barrister Johnson. I am Barrister Faya.

BARRISTER JOHNSON
You're welcome to Johnson's Legal Consultancy, Sir. *(Points to a seat).* You may sit down.

FAYA
Thank you.

BARRISTER JOHNSON
How may I help you, sir?

FAYA
I'll go straight to the point. My Client, Your Highness, Fon Ghamogha, is scheduled to appear in Court next week to answer charges of alleged land grabbing and domestic violence levied against him by his wife, Mrs Ghamogha Manka. I am told Mrs Ghamogha is your client in the same case… My learned colleague, I want us to treat this issue as a family matter.

BARRISTER JOHNSON
I will do that on one condition. Tell the Fon to give back the land to the owner. He must restore every other thing he took away from his wife and her group.

FAYA
Barrister Johnson, Kibaaka people are very much attached to their tradition. What they believe is that land belongs to the man.

BARRISTER JOHNSON
That will be decided in Court.

FAYA
(Faya places a bulging envelope before Johnson, saying). This is 150,000frs for your fuel.

BARRISTER JOHNSON
I don't remember having rendered any legal services to you.

FAYA
Learned lady, the Fon cannot appear in Court. Only Nwerong can judge the Fon in public.

BARRISTER JOHNSON
Nobody is above the law.

FAYA
(Tops up the amount of money on the table). 175,000frs.

BARRISTER JOHNSON
Barristers are supposed to be people of good conscience.

FAYA
Barrister Johnson, this is a juicy negotiation. You and I are not civil servants. And you know how difficult it is to have a Registration Number to become a Civil Servant in Kibaaka. Be smart.

BARRISTER JOHNSON
(Stares fixedly at Faya's face). You are in the wrong place.

FAYA
200,000frs. Scratch my back. I scratch your back.

BARRISTER JOHNSON
They sent you to the wrong person…

FAYA
(Cuts in) To do the right thing.

BARRISTER JOHNSON
My conscience is not a commodity to be traded to the highest bidder.

FAYA
This discussion is about the fats and marrow of legal practice. We are ready to step up the amount to 225,000frs.

BARRISTER JOHNSON
(Louder) What happened to your professional ethics?

FAYA
(Twists his face as he speaks). Barrister Johnson, do you think the Elders and Nwerong will sit and fold their hands and watch you walk around freely if their Fon loses the land battle to the woman?

BARRISTER JOHNSON
Nwerong and the Fon are just the type of institutions I'm looking for.

FAYA
The Fon is a son of the soil.

BARRISTER JOHNSON
The law is not lenient to sons of the soil. Barrister Faya, I will resign as a Human Rights lawyer and activist if my client loses the land battle to the man. My strength is in my words!

FAYA
Do not be the stubborn fly that was buried with the corpse.

BARRISTER JOHNSON
Is that a threat?

FAYA
At the moment, take it as an advice.

BARRISTER JOHNSON
You have exactly ten seconds to leave my office, if not, I will call my Security for you! 1, 2, 3, 4 …,

FAYA
(Places his business card on her table, lifting up his hand). Call me if you change your mind. *(Walks out and hops into his car. He then returns the rejected money into his suitcase with a smile).* The more court hearings, the more money for legal fees and fuel allowance.

ACT 5

Scene V

AT THE COURT OF FIRST INSTANCE

(Everybody is seated).

JUDGE
Good morning, everyone.

AUDIENCE
Good morning, Your Honour.

JUDGE
I have before me, four complaints: Manka and the people of Kibaaka; the people of Kibaaka and the gay community; the women and Alhadji Musa; Manka, Biy Wiiba, and Binla against Dzekewong *(Dzekewong shrugs)*. That said, I will begin right away with Manka. Manka, you petitioned this Honourable Court to recover your parcel of land which you said your husband, Fon Ghamogha, seized from you with the complicity of the Elders and Nwerong, on grounds that you are a woman and a Come-no-Go.

MANKA
Yes, Your Honour.

JUDGE
Going forward, you claimed that your husband beat you in an attempt to compel you to transfer to him the ownership of the land you single-handedly bought for your children. Is that right?

MANKA
Yes, Your Honour.

JUDGE
In your words, your husband continued threatening and urging you to replace

259

your name on the land title with his?

MANKA

Yes, Your Honour.

JUDGE

Manka, you alleged that Nwerong and the Village Traditional Council have banned your group, Bongkisheri Women's Association and its activities, and has subjected you to intimidation and banishment on mere assumptions that Bongkisheri's doctrine of "No to polygamy" is responsible for the break-up in marriages? *(Manka nods repeatedly)*. You said the intimidation and threats of banishment have stalled the ongoing Bongkisheri empowerment projects on your land, and you want Nwerong to lift the injunction against ownership and access to your land. You are in court today not just to recover your land, but also demanding that women be allowed to own land in Kibaaka. Am I right?

MANKA

Yes, Your Honour.

JUDGE

A further part of your complaint states that Binla, Mami Biy Wiiba, and Manka suffered sexual assault *(Simultaneously, the villagers, Your Highness and the Elders lean back, open-mouthed, wild-eyed; Manka, Biy Wiiba and Binla drops their heads)*. You report identifies Dzekewong as one of the suspects. *(Manka nods approval, Dzekewong, Tomla, and Tombir shudder, Your Highness and the villagers look shocked)*.

VILLAGERS

Heeeei!

JUDGE

Order! The Vigilante Guards should not be allowed to leave the Court! *(Turns to Fon Ghamogha)*. Fon Ghamogha, your wife, Mrs Ghamogha, alleges that you beat her, seized her land and banned her group with the complicity of Nwerong and the Village Traditional Council. She also complained that Nwerong imposed fines on her for buying land and threatened her with banishment if she fails to do a new land title bearing your name. We want to hear your own side of the story. Did you seize your wife's land?

FON

Your Honour, land belongs to the man, my wife committed an abomination by buying land. We did what we did to protect her, the throne, and the family from the curse of the gods. *(The Elders smile).*

JUDGE

Fon Ghamogha, where is the land we are talking about located?

FON

It is located at Up-Station, directly below the Administrative Quarters.

JUDGE

Tell me about the dimensions of that land. *(The Fon stares at his feet).* Do you have any idea how much money was paid for the land?

FON

No, Your Honour.

JUDGE

Do you have any idea who sold the land to your wife?

FON

No, Your Honour.

JUDGE

Whose name is written on the Land Title and on the Sale Certificate?

FON

It is my wife's name.

JUDGE

Fon Ghamogha, your lack of information about anything related to the land in question is an acknowledgement that you are not the owner of the land.

FON

Your Honour, what belongs to a woman belongs to her husband, and I am her husband. *(The Elders smile).*

BARRISTER JOHNSON
There's no legal foundation for such a claim, Your Honour. This is a purely disarming patriarchal discourse that the Fon is using as a cultural weapon to rob my client of what rightfully belongs to her by the right of acquisition!

FAYA
Your Honour, customary law clearly stipulates that if the woman buys land in her name, her husband must refund the money to her and own the land. And if that is not done, the family will be visited with a curse.

BARRISTER JOHNSON
Your Honour, there is a difference between the law of the judiciary and traditional customs. We are in court and the only criterion for determining guilt, innocence, or ownership in this case is the law and not traditional customs.

JUDGE
Argument from counsel for the plaintiff, convincing.

FAYA
Your Honour, the law and customary law are binding in their areas and contexts of jurisdiction. The only context where traditional law would lose its relevance is when it becomes repugnant to natural justice.

JUDGE
Counsel for the defendant, that would be proven by the Court. *(Turns to the Fon).* Fon Ghamogha, how did you know about the land you said traditional law ceded its ownership to you?

FON
I stumbled on the land title, Your Honour. My wife hid it in my house.

JUDGE
Fon Ghamogha, you have no idea who sold the land to your wife. You don't know anything about the dimensions of the land. Your name does not appear on the Land Title and on the Sale Certificate. Is that right? *(The Fon nods corroboration).* How then did you become the owner of the land you seem to know nothing about?

BONGKISHERI WOMEN
Ohhorrr!

JUDGE
(Bang the table shouting). Order!

FAYA
Your Honour, land belongs to the man. My client's wife committed an abomination by buying land in her name.

JUDGE
Mrs Ghamogha Manka, did you know about the ancestral custom that says land belongs to the man at the time of buying the land?

BARRISTER JOHNSON
A cultural wrong is not a legal wrong, My Lord.

JUDGE
Your argument is legally acceptable. The legal basis for land ownership claims by the Fon has not been presented in this court.

FAYA
Your Honour, my client and his wife operate a joint bank account, I have evidence. *(The Court Registrar collects a sheet of paper from Faya and hands to the Judge. She flips through it).*

JUDGE
I need evidence that the money used to buy the land was withdrawn from the joint bank account of the couple. Fon Ghamogha, which day did your wife withdraw the money from your joint bank account to buy the said land, how much was it, and where is the evidence of withdrawal?

FON
I don't know, Your Honour.

JUDGE
What do you do for a living? I want to see your pay check. Do you have one?

FON
No, Your Honour. I am not a civil servant. It was only a few days ago that Government signed a decree to put First Class Chiefs on Government Payroll.

JUDGE
Do you do business?

FON
No, Your Honour.

JUDGE
Mrs Ghamogha, what do you do for a living?

MANKA
Your Honour, I am a teacher and a certified Marriage Counsellor. I also do business. The Women's group and I also mark and sell *toghu* and other African wears in Britain with the help of Reverend Fada Anton.

JUDGE
Can you tell this Honourable Court the source of the funds with which you acquired the land?

MANKA
Your Honour, the money came from four sources: my salary, my shares, the savings from my business, and the loan I obtained. I single-handedly raised the funds. I invested in shares in Bongkisheri. I obtained a loan of 10 million frs CFA from Bongkisheri Cooperative Society which I added to my other savings to buy the land.

JUDGE
When you bought the land, did you pay in cash or by check?

MANKA
I used check, Your Honour. I have here all the receipts in my name.

JUDGE
I would like to see them. Andrew, collect them. *(Manka stretches the receipts to the Court Registrar who gives them to the Judge. She flips through and turns*

to Manka).

JUDGE
Mrs Ghamogha, how much did you buy the land?

MANKA
I bought the land for 15,000,000 million frs CFA, Your Honour. I have the receipt and the Sale Certificate.

JUDGE
Let me see them. *(The Court Registrar collects the receipt, the Sale Certificate and the Land Title from Manka and hands to the Judge who examines them closely nodding as she reads from the sale certificate).* "A sales Agreement between Mrs. Manka Ghamogha, hereafter designated as "Buyer" and Honourable Wirkitum, hereafter designated as "Seller" …

YOUR HIGHNESS, ELDERS, VILLAGERS
(Exclaiming simultaneously in various ways and turning towards Wirkitum who now is looking boldly at the wall in a show of defiance). Errrh! Who? Wirkitum?

ABILITY
Orrrh! What did I tell you? What did I tell you? No matter how long a crocodile lives in the water, it will never be a fish. No one listened to me. Look now what it means to peddle citizenship. Until we get all the Wirkitums out of Kibaaka, we shall never know peace!

JUDGE
(Bangs her table with a club). Order! I won't tolerate any disorder in my court! Fon Ghamogha, I have here with me the Sale Certificate and receipts of the land bearing the name of your wife, Ghamogha Manka. None of the receipts carries your name. Now, explain to this Court why you want your wife's name replaced with your name on the land title when it is clear from the receipts and evidence presented so far that your wife single-handedly acquired the land.

FON
Your Honour, I paid her bride price.

BARRISTER JOHNSON
The payment of bride price does not withdraw the rights of the woman!

FAYA
Kibaaka is ruled by traditional customs, My Lord!

BARRISTER JOHNSON
Your Honour, Kibaaka is found in Kibaakaba and Kibaakaba is ruled by the law and not by ancestral customs!

FAYA
Your Honour, the Fon is a symbol of tradition, he is an institution! Judiciary law did not come to replace customary law!

BARRISTER JOHNSON
Your Honour, the Law is the law and nobody or institution is above the law!

FAYA
We need to put things in the right context, My Lord!

BARRISTER JOHNSON
Your Honour, the land in question was single-handedly acquired by my client and therefore belongs to her!

FAYA
Objection, Your Honour! Manka was not single when she acquired the land!

BARRISTER JOHNSON
Marriage is not assimilation, Your Honour.

JUDGE
Council for the Plaintiff, your argument is guided by the law.

FAYA
(Turns to the Fon). Your Highness, how did Manka become your wife?

FON
I have a Marriage Certificate.

JUDGE
Let me have it *(Faya collects the paper and gives to the Judge who peruses it and speaks)*. Counsel for the Defendant may proceed.

FAYA
Thank you, My Lord. Your Highness, is the family of Manka aware that you are married to their daughter?

FON
Yes, Barrister Faya. I paid bride price on her.

FAYA
My Lord, my client paid bride price on his wife. What that means in Kibaaka native customs is that what belongs to the wife belongs to her husband. Following Kibaaka traditional customs, My Lord, the land in question belongs to my client by virtue of his position as the husband…

BARRISTER JOHNSON
Objection my Lord!

JUDGE
Objection sustained.

FAYA
My Lord, the land Mrs Ghamogha Manka claims is hers, is located in Kibaaka, and according to Kibaaka traditional customs, land belongs to the man. We cannot change tradition.

BARRISTER JOHNSON
Nowhere in the Constitution of Kibaakaba is it stated that land belongs to the man.

FAYA
The Constitution of Kibaakaba recognizes and accords a special place to customary rights. Mrs Ghamogha should be charged with violation of Kibaaka traditional customs that confer land ownership rights to men only.

BARRISTER JOHNSON
Objection, Your Honour, there is no law in the justice system that denies the woman the right to own land!

JUDGE
Objection, sustained.

FAYA
My Lord, the Constitution of the Republic of Kibaakaba recognizes the place of ancestral customs. The same Constitution states that Paramount Rulers, Fons, and Chiefs are the auxiliary of the Administration. It may be of interest to my learned colleague to know that Customary Courts exist with Judges approved by the Constitution. My Lord, acting on the right conferred on it by the Constitution, the Traditional Council which is the Customary Court of Kibaaka land already passed judgement on this same land dispute in favour of my client. The code of law used on the land dispute trial was the customary law which the Constitution recognizes. Your Honour, my learned colleague is simply exhibiting gross ignorance of our Constitution.

BARRISTER JOHNSON
Objection, Your Honour. My learned colleague needs to be educated that what is customarily objectionable is not necessarily legally objectionable until proven so by the law. This also applies to the issue of women's rights to land ownership!

JUDGE
Objection sustained!

FAYA
My Lord, traditional customs say that land belongs to the man, while the Law says that land belongs to both the man and the woman. In that respect, the Law of the Judiciary cannot be the sole yardstick in a trial that involves two different systems of law! *(The Fon and the Elders nod in approval).*

JUDGE
Argument against convincing.

BARRISTER JOHNSON
Your Honour, my learned colleague definitely needs to be educated on the

difference between Customary Law which is informed by native mentality barriers and the Law or the Judiciary system which is backed by the State Constitution.

FAYA
The same Constitution recognizes the validity of Customary Law in its new policies to preserve the territorial patrimony of the Kibaakaba native inhabitants. Kibaaka Chiefdom is an ancestral territory of the Kibaaka people and the Fon is the traditional ruler of this communal land, following the lineage of the founder of that tribe. Fon Ghamogha who happens to be my client was recently co-opted into the administration by the Constitution as a special civil status registrar to ease the administration. Your Honour, wasn't that appointment a further recognition of the customs of the indigenous natives of Kibaaka?

BARRISTER JOHNSON
My Lord, I stand on legal grounds to insist that there is no legal basis for seizing landed property that the woman single-handedly acquired simply because the Constitution recognizes the place of the Traditional Ruler as the auxiliary of the administration!

JUDGE
Arguments from the Plaintiff's Counsel noted in evidence.

FAYA
Your Honour, I am not aware of any Law that says traditional customs should not be respected in the land where the customs originated.

BARRISTER JOHNSON
My Lord, Your Highness seized landed property belonging to my client simply because she is a woman and vulnerable. Your Honour, Your Highness abused my client by beating her in order to intimidate and dispossess her of the land which she owns by right of acquisition. Your Honour, the rights of my client are violated by the actions of Nwerong and Your Highness. Your Highness is guilty of complicity in land grabbing, threats to life, intimidation, domestic violence, and violation of the rights of the woman.

FAYA
Your Honour, there is no case against my client because Nwerong is the Kibaaka

Legislative Society and has ruled that land belongs to the man.

BARRISTER JOHNSON

We are here in court and the only code of trial that is used in Court is the Law, not ancestral customs which are discriminative, ego-oriented, gender insensitive, biased, and guided by native mentality barriers.

FAYA

The existence of the Law of the Judiciary does not in any way invalidate or annul the existence of traditional customs and folkways. Consequently, the land belongs to my client as Nwerong has rightly decreed.

BARRISTER JOHNSON

The laws of this nation are voted by the National Assembly and not by Nwerong. The Fon is arrogating ownership of land he wasn't wilfully given by his wife. He should be punished according to the Law of land grabbing, appropriation, and theft!

FAYA

Objection, My Lord; the Marriage Certificate turned in evidence earlier shows that bride price was paid on Mrs Ghamogha Manka by my client. With due respect to Kibaaka traditional marriage custom, a woman belongs to the man and his family when her bride price is paid. By interpretation, Your Honour, property does not own property.

JUDGE

Council for the Defendant, I will not tolerate offensive language in my Court!

FAYA

I'm sorry, Your Honour. *(The Fon yawns loudly).*

BARRISTER JOHNSON

My Lord, it is stated in the same Marriage Certificate my learned colleague cited that Fon Ghamogha married his wife, Mrs Ghamogha Manka, following the native laws and customs of the wife's tribe. We all know that Manka comes from Bafut. Nothing is said about Kibaaka native customs on Manka's Marriage Certificate. My Lord, when a custom originates from a particular tribe, its jurisdiction of influence and application is that tribe. Your Honour, in the case of whether the Marriage Certificate grants land ownership to my client or to her husband, it can be established from evidence presented here that the land in question belongs to Manka and not to her husband! This is because the Marriage Certificate is my evidence that the Fon knew about the customs of his wife's land at the time their marriage was solemnized. On the strength of that argument, My Lord, Your Highness is guilty of usurpation and land grabbing! *(The Fon yawns loudly and drops his head).*

FAYA
Your Honour, my client is feeling weak and can't endure the trial. I wish to apply for suspension of hearing until such a time as my client would be declared medically fit to appear in Court.

JUDGE
Motion of adjournment granted. This Court is adjourned. *(Bangs the table)* C-o-u-rt! *(Everybody rises and the judge walks out).*

(A Few Days Later)

(The Court Resumes)

BARRISTER JOHNSON
Your Honour, I have evidence that Barrister Faya knew very well that the land in question belongs to my client. He attempted to bribe me to accept money and convince my client to drop the charges against her husband.

JUDGE
Barrister Johnson, can I see your evidence?

BARRISTER JOHNSON
Yes, My Lord *(She steps forward, places a tape recorder on the table, before the Judge. The Judge presses a button on the recorder. Faya quickly drops his head, looking at his feet. As the Judge, together with the audience listen to recorded conversation, the Judge searches Faya's face for signs of guilt).*

JUDGE
The tape recorder is admitted in evidence.

FAYA
My Lord, someone who is good at imitating people's voices was definitely hired by Barrister Johnson and Manka to emulate my voice.

JUDGE
The Court will determine that.

BARRISTER JOHNSON
(Places another device before the Judge). My Lord, this is the footage of the CCT Camera which also recorded Barrister Faya the day he came to my office.

JUDGE
The CD is admitted in evidence. *(She touches a button and the image of Faya trying to convince Johnson to accept bribe pops up on the screen, attracting screams across the hall).*

VILLAGERS
Hooooooorrrrrr!

JUDGE
Order! Council for the Defendant, you just watched the video. How does it feel watching yourself trying to convince Barrister Johnson to accept money and persuade Mrs Ghamogha to withdraw the charges against her husband? Do you still hold that the land belongs to your client after watching this?

FAYA
Your Honour, give me just one day and I will go to the shop and get a mask, or order for one that looks like you.

JUDGE
It is the duty of the Court to determine that someone actually impersonated you. And that will be done very soon.

BARRISTER JOHNSON
Your Honour, Miss Regular is willing to testify that the Fon sent Ability to bribe Barrister Faya to help him win the land case *(the Fon, Ability, and Faya open their mouths wide).*

JUDGE
Regular may step forward, please. *(Regular steps forward)*. Regular, we will like to hear from you concerning the bribery issue.

REGULAR
Your Honour, Ability informed me that the Fon sent him to give money to Barrister Faya to help him win the case. I recorded what Ability told me. *(Regular turns in her telephone to the Judge in evidence)*.

JUDGE
Miss Regular, you may sit down. *(The Judge places a button and everybody listens to the recorded conversation between Regular and Ability during which Ability and the Fon stare fixedly at their feet)*. The telephone conversation is admitted in evidence.

BARRISTER JOHNSON
Your Honour, the bandage around my client's head is further evidence of attempts to dispossess her of her land through violence.

JUDGE
Mrs Ghamogha, can you explain to this Honourable Court how the wounds and scars on your face are related to the land dispute?

MANKA
Your Honour, I was beaten by my husband. He asked me to transfer ownership of my land to him and I refused. He argued that he would be dethroned and replaced and also deprived of royal privileges if he allows the land in my name. I was afraid that my children may grow up and find themselves fighting for ownership of the land I bought for them with the other children conceived on the leopard skin because the Fon is polygamous by nature. When I insisted that the Land Title must carry my name to avoid future problems of inheritance especially in polygamous homes, Your Highness became very angry and later accused me of sleeping with Honourable Shufai Wirkitum… *(There is a sudden roar across the hall meanwhile Barrister Johnson and her husband shrug, open-mouthed and wide-eyed)* …

JUDGE
(Bangs the table). Order! *(Turns to Manka)*. You may continue.

MANKA

That is why my husband beat me up.

JUDGE

Fon Ghamogha, your wife has just testified that you beat her up. Was it because she refused to give you the land or because she was allegedly sleeping with another man?

FON

Your Honour, Ability caught them hugging each other and informed me. *(Different emotions erupt across the hall meanwhile Manka, Johnson, and Honourable stare at Ability open-mouthed, wide-eyed).*

JUDGE

Order! You beat your wife because Ability said she was hugging and sleeping with another man, is that right?

FON

Yes, Your Honour.

JUDGE

Ability may step forward. *(Ability steps forward)*. Ability, do you have any proof that Honourable Wirkitum was intimate with Mrs Ghamogha?

ABILITY

Yes, My Lord. I am a man and I know when a man is in love. Honourable has feelings for Manka. They stood in close proximity, Honourable was touching Manka's cheeks. I saw it. He actually positioned himself where his eyes would easily locate Manka and gain direct access to her chest right down to her waist. *(The Judge rolls his eyes)*. Based on his actions, I knew that Wirkitum had hidden motives and intentions to invade the domestic territory of Your Highness.

JUDGE

(Shakes his head, smiling). And based on what you considered to be your understanding of intentions, motives, and feelings you concluded that Honourable Wirkitum was sleeping with Mrs Ghamogha and informed her husband? *(Ability nods approval)*. Ability, this Court determines that your allegation was partly responsible for the violence Mrs Ghamogha suffered from her husband.

(Ability drops his head).

BARRISTER JOHNSON

Ability, your allegation of a possible romantic relationship between Mrs. Ghamogha and Honourable Wirkitum is solely based on your understanding and interpretation of feelings, motives, and intensions, am I right?

ABILITY

Yes, Madame.

BARRISTER JOHNSON

To the best of my knowledge, when we talk about feelings, motives, and intentions, we are referring to mental and emotional states of a human being, and mental states are areas that the eyes cannot reach or see. Ability, my question to you is, how were you able to know what someone was thinking or feeling? Again, how was it possible to know what Honourable's motives and intentions were? Were you in his mind? Can one have visual access to areas of the human body such as motives, feelings, and intensions? *(Ability stares at his feet).* My Lord, Ability is manipulative. He is a chronic liar and should be charged with complicity in domestic violence and land-grabbing. His allegation of infidelity resulted in the beating of my client and caused her physical injuries and trauma. The fact that Ability's lies were masterminded to incite a harmful reaction against my client does not warrant any further investigation to determine ownership of the disputed land! Ability and the Fon are guilty of domestic violence!

FAYA

Your Honour, the adulterous activities of Manka robbed my client of the capacity for self-control. No man with balls will hear that his wife is sleeping with another man and hold back his fist. My client felt threatened and helpless with the lustful activities of Honourable Shufai Wirkitum around his wife. He was therefore under necessity to protect his domestic colony from encroachment and possible occupation. Your Honour, you will agree with me that no criminal offense can result from an action that was carried out in self-defence.

BARRISTER JOHNSON

Objection, Your Honour! No evidence of infidelity has so far been provided. Besides, Your Honour, no human being has the right to take the laws into his hands. On that note, My Lord, Your Highness remains guilty of violence, land-grabbing and threats to life. He committed domestic violence by beating his wife with the intention of compelling her to transfer ownership of her land to him.

JUDGE
Objection sustained.

FAYA
Your Honour, an item is considered stolen only when it is displaced from its original position without the consent of the owner. What happened is that Nwerong was negotiating for the ownership of the land to be transferred to my client. We cannot therefore charge my client with theft when the parcel of land under discussion has not moved from its original position.

BARRISTER JOHNSON
Would you say violence, bribery, intimidation, and threats to life are part of Nwerong's negotiation strategies?

FAYA
Your Honour, this land dispute is a purely domestic affair. We can't settle bedroom matters in court. I wish to request for out-of-court settlement.

JUDGE
Motion for out-of-court settlement denied!

BARRISTER JOHNSON
Thank you, Your Honour. My Lord, there is an injunction plant on my client's land placed there by Nwerong. In addition, my client told the Honourable Court that Nwerong judged the land dispute in favour of her husband and ordered her to pay fines and to transfer ownership of the said land to her husband or face banishment. I wish to remind the Court that the action of seizing my client's land and forbidding access to it is called deprivation. Your Honour, there is no denial that deprivation is an element of theft. My submission is that the Fon and Nwerong should surrender their baseless claims to ownership of land that belongs to my client in order to allow her and her group to continue with empowerment projects which are beneficial to everybody across Kibaaka.

FAYA
Your Honour, my learned colleague is aware that the Constitution recognizes the authority of the traditional rulers as the auxiliary of the administration. An obvious interpretation of the clause is that it acknowledges the preservation of culture and traditional customs which the Fon symbolizes. Your Honour, we cannot desecrate the culture we are fighting to preserve by giving land to a woman.

BARRISTER JOHNSON
Your Honour, recognizing the need to preserve traditional customs does not in any way promote exclusion and marginalization of women in matters relating to land ownership. Barrister Faya is twisting the law to suit his interests.

FAYA
My Lord, this trial is sensitive and must take into consideration the traditional customs of my client and his cultural mandate to preserve the ancestral customs of Kibaaka. We cannot force Kibaaka people to adopt and practice what does not make sense to them.

BARRISTER JOHNSON
My Lord, the need to respect and preserve traditional institutions and their customs is not a legal requirement for stepping outside the boundaries of the Law of Acquisition and Ownership.

FAYA
My Lord, we cannot impose a judicial code of law in a purely customary trial. The code of Law employed in the land dispute must be the law of tradition because it considers the native people and their customary practices.

BARRISTER JOHNSON
Your Honour, the Fon is guilty by legal standards…

FAYA
And exonerated if the code of law used in his trial is the law of tradition.

BARRISTER JOHNSON
My Lord, we are not here in the Customary Court. The action of the Fon and Nwerong violated the Law of Land Acquisition and Ownership.

FAYA

Your Honour, if the action and reactions of my client constitute a violation of the Law of Land Acquisition and Ownership, then it is society that should be held responsible for assigning unto their Fon the role of preserving tradition that violates legal ethics.

BARRISTER JOHNSON

Ignorance of the law is no excuse. Any traditional custom that directly or indirectly promotes discrimination and exclusion on grounds of gender and ethnic sentiments should be placed on the death row! That is all, My Lord.

JUDGE

I think I have had enough to take a decision on the land dispute. Let's do another case. Dzekewong may come forward. *(Dzekewong steps forward, shivering).* Dzekewong, tell this Honourable Court your involvement in the sexual assault of Bongkisheri women, and the people with whom you committed the act.

DZEKEWONG

Your Honour, *na* Tombir, Tomla, and Viban been beat and kick Mother of children, Mami Biy Wiiba and Binla, and open their legs and join. *(Tombir, Tomla, and Viban drop their heads, staring at their feet).* I did not join. When dem invite me to join, I deny and tell dem dat we work na to guard farm.

JUDGE

Mami Biy and Binla may step forward and join Mrs Ghamogha on stage. *(They step forward).* Dzekewong has just testified that it was Tombir, Tomla and Viban that assaulted and violated you, he says he didn't participate. Is that true.

WOMEN

Yes, Your Honour.

JUDGE

Biy and Binla, go back to your seats. I've had enough. The hearing is adjourned for a few minutes to allow us time for deliberations. You may leave the Courtroom now. *(Bangs the table)* Co-u-rt!

(The Magistrate and two Judges remain seated as the villagers walk out of the Courtroom).

(Thirty minutes later)

JUDGE

After listening to the Plaintiff, the Defendant, and the witnesses, and considering all other evidence presented in Court, this is my judgement. The women and Come-no-Gos are full citizens with rights to property ownership. Marriage is a family issue. Kibaaka people should learn to love, tolerate and live together with the Come-no-Gos. You have children through intermarriages. Your diversity should be your strength. Tomla, Viban, and Tombir, you are guilty of assault, violence and rape. You are each sentenced to fifty years in prison with hard labour and a fine of 500,000frs each. *(The villagers smile as the culprits bend their heads).* Dzekewong, you are hereby sentenced to six-months in prison for failing to report sexual assault. *(Dzekewong shrugs).* Barrister Faya, this Court finds you guilty of bribery, corruption, and lying under oath. You are also charged with conspiracy to facilitating land-grabbing and exploitation. You are hereby sentenced to five-months in prison with a fine of 150,000frs *(Faya shrugs shaking his head).* Ability, you are guilty of bribery and corruption; you are guilty of complicity and conspiracy in land grabbing; you are guilty of lying under oath, and also for bearing false witness in this Honourable Court. You are also charged with aiding and abetting domestic violence against women. You are hereby sentenced to four years in prison with hard labour and a fine of 300,000frs. *(Ability drops his head, meanwhile, Honourable Wirkitum stifles a smile).* In the case of the land ownership dispute between Fon Ghamogha and his wife, Mrs Ghamogha Manka to determine who owns the land, it has been established by this Honourable Court as follows: My judgement is for the Plaintiff, Mrs Ghamogha Manka. The piece of land in question is returned to Mrs Ghamogha. *(Manka and the women convulse with joy while Your Highness and some elders drop their heads in frustration).* Fon Ghamogha; you are guilty of land-grabbing, bribery and corruption, threats to life, intimidation, domestic violence, and complicity with Nwerong and Ability to deprive your wife of the parcel of land she owns by right of acquisition and possession. You are additionally guilty of using your position of authority as the Paramount head of the land and member of *Nwerong* to deny your wife her rights and also deny Bongkisheri their freedom of association. Your Highness, your threats and ban instilled fear in your wife and her group, frustrated and stalled the activities of the women's group. You are hereby sentenced to one year in prison with a fine of 200,000frs CFA...

(Different simultaneous reactions are manifested across the hall. Man-

ka lowers her buttocks to the floor, open-mouthed, wide-eyed. The men and women look at each other and then away, open-mouthed and wide-eyed, shaking their heads. Some could be heard groaning and screaming widely).

JUDGE
(Bangs the table). Order! I hereby order the Fon and Nwerong to desist from obstructing the activities of Bongkisheri and to allow Mrs Ghamogha to use her land freely. Elders of Kibaaka, we live in an evolving society and should be tolerant and receptive to change. Keep aside your differences and work together for the development and welfare of Kibaaka. Our differences should unite us more than they separate us. We have counselling services to help all of you. *(Turns and beckons the Police Officers and points to the indicted)*. Take them into custody.
C-o-urt!

(The Officers clamp heavy metal chains around the wrists of the Fon, Ability, Faya, Dzekewong, Tomla, Tombir, Viban, and guide them through a separate door. Meanwhile the Elders file out carrying hands on their heads with lips twisted; some keep shaking their heads and throwing hands apart. A similar reaction is observed as women walk out with their hands across their chests and across their heads. Biy Wiiba rushes forward, stares at Manka with hands crossed over her head, and smacks her hips).

(Outside the Courtroom)

(Regular and Binla hit the palms of their hands together, and repeatedly as they dance back and forth).

REGULAR
This is victory!

BINLA
The Court is our strength. Collective strength is victory!

BIY WIIBA
(Quickly holds and presses Regular's lips, saying in a muted voice). Where has that ever happened? I fear for Manka!

VILLAGERS
(Chanting) Bring back our Fon! Bring back our Fon…!

MANKA
(Muses). The battle is only complete if legal victory is accompanied by a complete change in cultural mentalities. What do I do now? *(Following Barrister Johnson toward her car, crying).* Barrister Johnson, I came here to say something was wrong. I didn't complain that my marriage was wrong. All I wanted was my land. My husband must not sleep behind bars, please. If you keep my husband behind bars, you have kept my marriage and tradition behind bars. No. I want my family together, please. I want to apply for bail. I need the Court to grant my husband bail. I need you to help me to process the bail application and to appeal the judgement. Barrister, please, help me to appeal the sentence. How will I even face the people of Kibaaka when the Fon is behind bars because of me? Where will I hide? I will never have peace if the Fon sleeps behind bars. What will I tell my children? That I kept their father behind bars? No, no… *(lowers her buttocks to the ground wiping tears flowing down her cheeks with the edge of her dress).* Please, liberate him or you lock me in too.

SHUFAI LAIKA
Barrister Johnson, the Fon sleeps only on the leopard skin. He cannot spend a night behind bars *(The Elders nod their heads in acceptance).* It has never happened. The people of Kibaaka will not go to bed until they see their Fon in the palace. Taa Gheeh, Medzefen and I have agreed to replace the Fon behind bars. Release the Fon and lock us up instead.

VILLAGERS
(The villagers nod their heads in acceptance).

BARRISTER JOHNSON
(Stares at the sobbing Manka, shaking her head. She hops into her car and drives off).

(Livinus, Savage, and Katika were later judged and remanded in custody. Alhadji Musa was later found guilty and imposed a heavy fine for allowing his cattle to destroy crops and plants).

The End

ABOUT THE AUTHOR

Photo credit: the author

Perpetua K. Nkamanyang Lola is a literary critic, poet, playwright, and novelist whose works have been published in national and international journals. Some of her highly acclaimed publications include *The Lock on My Lips*, *Rustles on Naked Trees*, *Healing Stings*, *Fictions of Memory: An Intercultural Studies*, and *Representing Fictional Minds* and *Consciousness: Analysis of some Cameroon (African) English Narratives*. Her research interests include narratology, gender/feminist studies, identity and memory cultures, postcolonial criticism, and intertextuality amidst dynamic interactive discourses and discussions with writers and experts on academic and creative fora. She has served in various capacities for over 23 years as Research and Documentation Officer at Giessen Graduate Centre for the Study of Culture hosted by Justus Liebig University, Germany; lecturer at the Universities of Douala and Bamenda, Head of Service for Extra-African Cooperation, University of Bamenda, First

Deputy Mayor of Mbiame Mbven Council. She is also an Associate Professor of English Literary and Cultural Studies, a Knight of the Cameroon Order of Merit, and a member of the Cameroon Anglophone Writers Association. Her drama, *The Lock on My Lips*, won the first Eko Prize for Emerging Anglophone Writers in 2015. She currently serves as the Cultural Attaché at the High Commission of Cameroon in Abuja, Nigeria. You may reach her by email at lolaperps@yahoo.com or telephone at (+234) 816 239 4648.

ABOUT THE PUBLISHER

Spears Books is an independent publisher dedicated to providing innovative publication strategies with emphasis on African/Africana stories and perspectives. As a platform for alternative voices, we prioritize the accessibility and affordability of our titles in order to ensure that relevant and often marginal voices are represented at the global marketplace of ideas. Our titles – poetry, fiction, narrative nonfiction, memoirs, reference, travel writing, African languages, and young people's literature – aim to bring African worldviews closer to diverse readers. Our titles are distributed in paperback and electronic formats globally by African Books Collective.

Connect with Us: Go to www.spearsbooks.org to learn about exclusive previews and read excerpts of new books, find detailed information on our titles, authors, subject area books, and special discounts.

Subscribe to our Free Newsletter: Be amongst the first to hear about our newest publications, special discount offers, news about bestsellers, author interviews, coupons and more! Subscribe to our newsletter by visiting www.spearsbooks.org

Quantity Discounts: Spears Books are available at quantity discounts for orders of ten or more copies. Contact Spears Books at orders@spearsmedia.com.

Host a Reading Group: Learn more about how to host a reading group on our website at www.spearsbooks.org

www.ingramcontent.com/pod-product-compliance
Lightning Source LLC
Chambersburg PA
CBHW021339230426
43666CB00006B/342